The Body Adorned

The Body Adorned

Dissolving Boundaries Between Sacred and Profane in India's Art

Vidya Dehejia

Columbia University Press / New York

Columbia University Press
Publishers Since 1893
New York   Chichester, West Sussex

Copyright © 2009 Columbia University Press
All rights reserved

Library of Congress Cataloging-in-Publication Data
Dehejia, Vidya.
  The body adorned : sacred and profane in Indian art / Vidya Dehejia.
      p. cm.
  Includes bibliographical references and index.
  ISBN 978-0-231-14028-7 (cloth : alk. paper)
  ISBN 978-0-231-51266-4 (e-book)
  1. Human figure in art. 2. Body, Human, in literature. 3. Beauty, Personal, in art.
  4. Beauty, Personal, in literature. 5. Arts, Indic. 6. Body, Human—Symbolic aspects.
  I. Title.
NX650.H74D45 2009
704.9'420954—dc22

                                    2008028861

Columbia University Press books are printed on permanent and durable acid-free paper.
Printed in Singapore
Designed by Revanta Sarabhai / Mapin Design Studio

c 10 9 8 7 6 5 4 3 2 1

Produced for Columbia University Press by
Mapin Publishing • www.mapinpub.com

CONTENTS

ILLUSTRATIONS

PREFACE AND ACKNOWLEDGMENTS

In *The Body Adorned*, I present a series of interrelated chapters on the primacy of the richly adorned human body in the artistic traditions of India, as also in the related traditions of courtly literature, inscriptional *prashastis* (dynastic eulogies), and the poetry of *bhakti* (devotion). I hope to demonstrate that across the Indian subcontinent there exists a near identity in sculptural and poetic representations of the idealized human body during the premodern period; I also suggest that we question the usage of the terms "sacred" and "profane" in the context of Indian sculpture and painting. Considering the extraordinary richness of the artistic material available from the subcontinent, it would be feasible to approach my subject in varying ways. It would certainly be worthwhile, for instance, to put together an extensive series of case studies of individual monuments or of groups of imagery belonging to specific time periods. I have chosen, however, to concentrate on a few select and intriguing issues that have continued to perplex scholars, students, and casual viewers alike, and I have attempted to account for them even while tracing their continuing significance across topographical, chronological, and religious boundaries. These issues frequently overlap and intersect, occasionally in a disconcerting manner; my hope, however, is that this approach may lead to a more richly hued discussion.

None of the source material as such is unknown to specialists. While many new translations of literary texts in Sanskrit, Prakrit, and a range of vernacular languages have been made in recent years, and more will become available through the expanding series of the Clay Sanskrit Library, scholars of literature have long been familiar with the texts themselves. The inscriptions likewise have been known to epigraphists and have been published in volumes such as *Epigraphia Indica*, and the Corpus Inscriptionum Indicarum, although frequently without translations. The poetry of *bhakti* has been the focus of some scholars of religion, while others have examined the role of images in temple rites and festivals. My own specialty, the artistic material, has been the subject of many studies by a range of scholars. My hope, however, in presenting these reflections on the human body in India's art is to provide a fresh approach to the material, bringing together diverse resources that, when seen in concert, enrich our appreciation of Indian art in its milieu. I hope also that the focus on artistic material will provide an added dimension to those whose prime interest may be in literature, religion, anthropology, or history.

Recent studies on the body, desire, and sexuality with varying geographical and cultural foci have informed my thinking, and I have felt free to draw on them to illuminate the Indian artistic material. My debt to my colleagues in the disciplines of Indian history, art history, literature, religious studies, and anthropology is immense; this book could not have been written without the groundwork they provided in their own publications. Although specific acknowledgments will be found in the notes, I would like to pay special tribute to Ananda Coomaraswamy, for whom my admiration has grown exponentially over the years; so often, when I imagine I have hit upon something significant, I have found an intuitive hint of the solution in one or another of his footnotes!

For intellectual discourse, I am indebted to colleagues who have commented on specific aspects of my manuscript, or have graciously read portions of it at various stages of its gestation. I would especially like to mention my gratitude to Daud Ali, Rick Asher, Milo Beach, Allison Busch, Richard Davis, Thomas Donaldson, Eberhard Fischer, Jack Hawley, Steven Hopkins, Dipti Khera, Jack Laughlin, Indira Peterson, Sheldon Pollock, David Rosand, Gregory Schopen, Rupert Snell, Doris Srinivasan, Job Thomas, Joanne Waghorne, Blake Wentworth, and Irene Winter. I am indebted to the anonymous readers of my manuscript for the probing questions they asked and the thorny issues they raised; their intervention was influential in helping me to make this a tighter and more forcefully argued manuscript. If, despite their urgings, I have failed to convey my thoughts adequately, the fault is entirely mine. Finally, I must mention students at Columbia University who have been subjected, from time to time, to my musings on the body; their pointed queries and suggestions have been invaluable in making me reevaluate my conclusions. For their help in securing photographic material from a range of institutions, museums, and individuals, I am grateful to Laura Weinsten and Yuthika Sharma; for the onerous task of tightening the Indic language transliterations (where I have chosen to avoid diacritical marks to create a more accessible text), I am indebted to Shreya Vora.

I would like to give special thanks to the Rockefeller Foundation for awarding me a residency at the Bellagio Study and Conference Center in Italy. It gave me the wonderful opportunity of a month of uninterrupted writing in the peace and luxury of its hilltop villa overlooking Lake Como; the company of fellow scholars working in a variety of fields provided remarkable stimulus to the production of this manuscript. For a subvention toward reproduction of the book's many plates, I am indebted to Columbia University's South Asia Institute. The finished book owes much to the professionalism of my editors, Lys Ann Weiss of Post Hoc Academic Publishing Services and Irene Pavitt of Columbia University Press, and designers Paulomi Shah and Revanta Sarabhai of Mapin Publishing; to all of them I express my deep gratitude.

The Body Adorned

1. THE BODY AS LEITMOTIF

Over the centuries, the sensuous bodily form, female and male, human and divine, has been a dominant feature in the vast and varied canvas of the Indian artistic tradition. The human figure—complete, elegant, adorned, and eye-catching—was, indeed, the leitmotif. An eleventh-century bronze image of the god Shiva from Tiruvenkadu in southern India, and a twelfth-century stone dancer from northern India, both displayed today in a museum context, illustrate this centrality. Shiva, a lithe, elegant figure with a slender torso, stands in gentle *contrapposto* known by the term *tri-bhanga* (triple-bend), with right leg gracefully crossed in front of the left (figure 1). One hand is held by his side in a gesture of ease, while the other is bent so as to rest his elbow against his now-missing bull mount. His face is exquisite and serene, with dreamy eyes that look into the distance, and his long, matted hair is wrapped around his head in turban-like fashion. Shiva wears

Figure 1. God Shiva, Chola bronze, Tiruvenkadu temple, Tamil Nadu, ca. 1011.

a short waist-cloth held in place by a jeweled hip-belt, and his rich adornment includes a forehead band, earrings, necklaces, a waist-band, sacred thread, armlets, bracelets, anklets, and rings on all ten fingers and toes. The god's identifying attributes include the vertical third eye on his forehead, the crescent moon crowning his locks, and the serpent that peeps out of his "turban." This most powerful of gods, the greatest of yogis, destroyer of demonic forces that threaten the world, is portrayed as the most beautiful of beings, a gorgeous figure, "the thief who stole my heart."[1] Equally seductive is the broken image of a dancer from a temple in northern India, perhaps Jamsot near Allahabad, who pirouettes in space so as to present the spectator with both a frontal view of her full breasts and a rear view of the curvature of her behind (figure 2). A long necklace swings away from her torso with her movement, while her translucent, scarf-like drapery blows away in the opposite direction. Necklaces, jeweled waist- and hip-bands, armlets, an elaborate hairstyle studded with decorative pins, a forehead band, and a tiara complete her rich ornamentation. Whether she is a celestial dancer or a human entertainer remains debatable, but either way her glamorous body holds center stage.

These exquisite images in bronze and stone, as also the painted manuscript pages we shall examine in chapter 5, were all created for the discerning viewer, the connoisseur, a man (occasionally a woman) who belonged to the realm of the cultivated social elite. The world of Indian imagery was intended for the viewing pleasure not of laborer or farmer, but of king, courtier, aristocrat, and *nagaraka* (refined man-about-town).[2] The world portrayed in Indian imagery too was not the everyday world of the peasant and worker, but the stately world of royalty and the divine courts of the gods. When the everyday world entered the artistic vocabulary, it was in the context of its interaction with monarchs and gods. It is true that stone statues adorned the walls of Hindu, Buddhist, and Jain temples, and bronze images were created to be honored within, suggesting that the images were available for viewing by all who chose to visit such shrines. But it is fair to assume that the subtleties of the sculptural program of the major temples were not created for the general viewer. We may have to rethink the idea of great temples—the Kailasanatha at Kanchipuram, the Kailasa at Ellora, the Rajarajeshvara at Tanjavur, the Lingaraja at Bhubaneshvar—as places of worship intended for the general public.[3] Most villagers worshipped, and still worship, in their own simple yet potent village shrines, generally containing nothing more elaborate than a rounded stone to represent the linga emblem of Shiva or a vermilion-daubed stone to suggest the presence of the goddess; grandeur and artistic merit were not their prime concern.[4] I do not believe I am overstating the case for elite involvement in the building of large stone temples that required a substantial influx of resources. It would be well to keep in mind that major royal temples, lavishly adorned with sculpted images, were frequently built to affirm and establish the conquest of a region by a new dynasty, and that successive monarchs also constructed similar grand temples to reaffirm their own overlordship.[5] The prime audience for such a

Figure 2. Dancer, stone, possibly Jamsot, Uttar Pradesh, twelfth century.

royal temple, and its exquisite sculptured decoration, comprised feudatory princes, officials at the court, and Brahmin priests, all of whom belonged to the elite of the kingdom. One may also assume that temples built by chieftains, court officials, wealthy ladies, or Brahmins were built to be admired and applauded by their own circle of aristocratic peers. They were intended to portray the realm of the gods and the world of royalty, not that of the ordinary citizen.

The discriminating audience that appreciated courtly literature in Sanskrit, as in Tamil and other vernacular languages, resembled the select circle of connoisseurs who recognized the aesthetic values of precisely modeled sculpture and finely crafted paintings. *Kavya*—the term given to Sanskrit poetry and drama, with their elaborate and sophisticated rules of vocabulary, figures of speech, and *shlesha* (double meaning)—largely focused on the divine world of the gods or of royalty on earth and was intended for recitation or performance at the court. A similarly elite performative venue is valid for much of the later vernacular literature, composed well into the eighteenth century, which included relatively erudite works calling for appreciation from connoisseurs who had the training necessary to appreciate their intricacies and overtones.

Equally restricted was the audience for the copper-plate and stone inscriptions, sometimes over a hundred verses long, issued by monarchs and highly placed officials. Copper-plate charters commence with verses invoking the deities, and devote the greater part of the inscription to the *prashasti* (praise of the dynastic line), which traces royal genealogy back to the sun or the moon; they conclude with a brief statement of the immediate reason for the proclamation. Southern Indian inscriptions, which commence in Sanskrit, generally change at this point to the vernacular to spell out the details of the gift of land, villages, or other property to a Brahmin or a temple.[6] These inscriptions served multiple purposes, not the least being that the *prashasti*, aptly termed "political poetry," was used to validate dynastic claims to the overlordship of a region.[7] The audience for these charters was, once again, the elite of the kingdom. Such documents were taken out to the site of the actual donation, where the proclamation was read aloud for all concerned to hear; the "luminous language," even if not comprehended by the population at large, represented "something sublime and exalted."[8] The Sanskrit part of these charters, which made up the greater part of the text, would have revealed its meaning only to learned court officials and Brahmins; the details of the gift, couched in the vernacular, had a somewhat wider audience that included local officials entrusted with the implementation of the terms of the gift. Inscriptions engraved on slabs of stone, to be placed in the temples or embedded into temple walls, were similar in their formulas and had an equally limited audience.

Estimates of the total number of inscribed records in India vary. Richard Salomon follows D. C. Sircar in quoting the figure of 90,000.[9] N. Karashima's estimate is somewhat lower, with inscriptions in Sanskrit and other northern languages numbering some 23,000, while those in Tamil are 30,000, and Kannada and Telugu inscriptions amount to 17,000 and 10,000, respectively.[10] Sheldon Pollock's more recent estimate of Kannada records as numbering 25,000 certainly makes Karnataka "one of the most densely inscribed pieces of real estate in the world."[11] The significance of these numbers remains to be assessed. The nature and length of the records in southern languages need to be determined before assuming that inscriptions were more popular in the south than in the north. Possibly too, as Karashima suggests, Sanskrit inscriptions from the north were lost when the area came under Muslim rule, or were minimally produced during that period. A recent study with a slightly different focus points out that scholars have recorded and studied inscriptions from temples to the detriment of records found in agricultural, village, and other contexts;[12] while the point is well taken, this factor does not affect the specific use of inscriptional material in this book.

My extensive use of literary sources to illuminate the sometimes more indeterminate world of sculpted and painted form is, I believe, appropriate because sculpture and painting, together with poetry, drama, and inscriptions, are part and parcel of the same refined and urbane world. It is relevant to remember that both the visual and literary worlds possess texts that treat aesthetic expression not as individual articulations, but as stylized and all-encompassing values. The poet is instructed into tropes like sandalwood hailing from the Malaya mountains, peacocks dancing in the rainy season, the moon in Shiva's locks as crescent-shaped; good poetic usage does not allow of sandalwood coming from anywhere other than the Malaya mountains.[13] Similarly, the artist is trained to portray eyes that resemble a carp or a lotus petal, to model the male torso on the frontal view of a bull's head, and to shape the female arm, especially in southern India, as the pliant green bamboo. Certainly, the rendering of eyes that resemble anything other than the carp or the lotus petal finds little favor in the Indian repertoire of artistic excellence. The sculpted images with which this chapter began are not an expression of an individual artist's idea of beauty; rather, the artist gave shape to a stylized concept, to a conventional and accepted ideal of beauty. These artistic conventions explain the striking similarity among the images adorning any one temple, whether at Khajuraho, Bhubaneshvar, Mount Abu, or Somnathpur, frequently making it impossible to distinguish the work of one artist from that of another belonging to the same workshop. An instructive case in point comes from the Hoysala temples, where artists frequently carved their names beneath the images they sculpted. A comparison of the work of sculptor Malitamma at Amritapura in his youth, at Harnahalli in his maturity, and at Somnathpur in his old age reveals no noticeable difference. Neither do we see any meaningful distinction between Malitamma's work at Somnathpur and that, say, of the sculptor Chaudaya.[14] Lee Siegel's comments regarding erotic poetry transfer exactly to the world of sculpture; like the poet, the artist "expresses collective emotions, institutionalized ideals, feelings which the aestheticians and rhetoricians had established as tasteful and true."[15] In this

how does aesthetic; rhetoric work together?

context, one cannot but recall Durkheim's concept of the collective mind of society as the cohesive bonds of the cultural imagination of a people. It is worth stressing that despite the apparent restrictions placed on artists and the specific formulas given to them, strict adherence to prescription alone does not lead to success; both excellent poets and mediocre ones referred to Malaya mountain sandalwood, just as hack artists as much as talented ones modeled eyes to resemble a carp.

The Body Envisioned: Inscriptions and Literary Sources

The emphasis on the centrality of the well-formed human body, so evident in the images we examined, is seen also in the creations of Indian poets and composers of inscriptional eulogies. It is intriguing to consider the manner in which the beauty of the physical human body was so often the touchstone against which poets compared the glories of nature, be they sky, earth, or gardens. Inanimate manmade objects, too, such as cities, temples, and wells, are frequently evoked in terms of a woman's body, and their "interaction" is compared to the coupling of human lovers. For instance, the sky and earth are described as lovers wrapping their thighs around each other; a water well, adorned with tufted plants, is compared to a woman adorned with jewels; a temple is said to be longing for the presence of the full-bosomed women who arrive for worship and linger. A few examples of these astonishing verbal comparisons will reinforce the centrality of the human form in the literary imagination of India.

A stone inscription of thirty Sanskrit verses composed in the late twelfth century speaks of the earth, the sky, and a temple in terms of human erotic love. The verses were composed by the donor, Devagana, to record his gift of a Shiva temple near Nagpur during the reign of the Chedi prince Prithvideva:

> First gratified, as it were, with the close embrace of the thighs
> of the earth, enjoyed by many princes, the surrounding sky,
> like a clever lover, accompanying his action with a smile of
> extreme love, eagerly, within sight of the damsels of heaven,
> kisses, as it were, the face of Fortune, this (temple) desirous
> of receiving on all sides the heavy embrace of bodies, trem-
> bling with the pangs of love, of the women of the regions.[16]

Waters joining the ocean, and women plunging in the waters of a well, are described in terms of human erotic union in a Sanskrit inscription of the year 467. Dattabhatta, commander of the forces of Prabhakara, a Gupta feudatory prince, made a gift of a well, a water-stall, a Buddhist stupa, and a garden to a Buddhist Lokottara monastery at Mandasore in central India:

> May this store of water (i.e., the well), that constantly enjoys
> the festivity of union with the bodies of many women (who
> go to bathe there), always be full[17] like the ocean that (also)
> enjoys the constant festivity of union with many rivers (who
> are, as it were) his wives.[18]

The stone slab inscription commences with a verse invoking the Buddha, but this in no way inhibits its use of erotic imagery.

Also from Mandasore is a record that commemorates the restoration of a brick temple to the sun god, originally built by a guild of silk weavers. The Sanskrit inscription compares the glories of the town to a beautiful, fully adorned woman:

> Just as a woman, though endowed with youth and beauty and
> adorned with the arrangement of golden necklaces and betel-
> leaves and flowers, does not go to meet her lover in a secret
> place until she has put on a pair of coloured silken cloths so
> the whole of this region of earth is adorned through them, as if
> with a silken garment, agreeable to the touch, variegated with
> divisions of different colours, and pleasing to the eye.

This inscription, incised in the year 529 during the reign of the Gupta king Kumaragupta, proceeds to compare the earth itself to the female form:

> While Kumaragupta was reigning over the whole earth,
> whose moving girdle is the verge of the four oceans, whose
> high breasts are the mountains, Sumeru and Kailasa, and
> whose smile are the blowing flowers showered forth from
> the borders of the woods.[19]

I will give one last example from the inscriptional corpus of this type of unique-ly body-centered verbal imagery. A Sanskrit record dated in the year 1227, during the rule of a Muslim Saka king, Nasaradin, from the town of Palam (today's Delhi), compares a well and its sustaining waters to a beautiful woman slaking the thirst of her lovers:

> May the well, like a lovely woman with rotund upheaving
> breasts, gorgeous with undulating necklaces, the assuager of
> the thirst of many a lovesick swain, decorated with the seried
> riches of flower-tufted plants, be for your gratification.[20]

It would appear that the human bodily form was hailed as the epitome of manifested perfection, and that all objects were seen to gain in meaning, and to be best understood, through comparisons with human beauty and human behavior, especially in the context of erotic love and union.

From the literary corpus, I will restrict myself to three examples that serve to further emphasize the extraordinary body-centered literary imagination, two taken from a Prakrit Apabhramsha text, and one from a Sanskrit *kavya*. The Apabhramsha *Pasanaha-chariu* (*Life of Parshvanatha*), which details the hagiography of the twenty-third Jina, Parshvanatha (Pasanaha), was composed by Shridhara in 1132. In its first book, Shridhara describes the glory of the city of Varanasi in terms of a lovely courtesan:

> The wide ramparts are like her bodice, highly valued by
> many types of paramours. It has rows of raised banners like
> her fingernails and temples erect like the nipples of her swol-
> len breasts. The city-gate, like her mouth, gives rise to pas-
> sion. The water-filled moat appears as the three folds [on her
> abdomen].[21]

In the same book, Shridhara visualizes the river Jamuna, too, as a beautiful courtesan:

> Her upper garment was the globules of foam and her glorious
> breasts the sporting rahanga birds. Her romavali, effective in
> distracting the minds of learned men, was the network of
> algae. Her beautiful ringlets of braided hair were the rows of
> bees, and her lengthy eyes, the petals of the blossomed lotus.
> Her navel, dispelling the heat of those with fever, was the
> whirlpool churned by the wind. . . . Her buttocks were the
> wide, glistening sand banks.[22]

Unique to the Sanskrit tradition is the idea of the *romavali* (a fine line of hair running upward from the navel and considered a mark of beauty); here it is compared to the ring of algae adorning a river.

The seventh-century Sanskrit poet Bharavi made use of comparable similes when he wrote of the *apsaras* in a riverine landscape that "the sandbanks could not equal / their full and heavy hips." Indira Peterson emphasizes that "convention governs every aspect of *kavya* composition, from the subject matter of poetry and the formal require-ments of the stanza and of figures of speech (*alankara*), to the objects with which a woman's face may be compared."[23] To demonstrate the deep-rooted nature and the per-sistence of these similes and metaphors as an indication of a body-centered imagination,

I shall cite yet another comparison of a woman and a river from one of the earliest Sanskrit *kavyas* that has come down to us, Ashvaghosha's first-century *Buddha-charita* (*Life of Buddha*). Here is his description of one of the women the Buddha views just before he leaves the palace in the episode known as The Great Departure:

> Another [woman], lying with her bamboo pipe in her hands
> and her white robe slipping off her breasts, resembled a riv-
> er with lotuses [hands] being enjoyed by a straight row of
> bees [flute] and with banks [breasts] laughing with the foam
> [white robe] of water.[24]

The overwhelming centrality of body-based imagery, in both inscriptional and literary texts, is striking and unmistakable.

We may note here what the reader has, no doubt, already intuited—that inscriptional poetry qualifies as "literature," even though it has been largely ignored by Sanskrit literary scholars and theoreticians, whether modern or historical.[25] Sheldon Pollock emphasizes "how closely intertwined were the histories of *prashasti* and *kavya*," and his work makes abundantly clear the necessity of studying both sources to explicate the circumstances surrounding the rise of the Sanskrit cosmopolis during the first millennium, as also the vernacularization of the early second millennium.[26] Inscriptions were composed by poets, some finer than others.[27] The poets generally state their names in the closing verse; frequently we find also the names of the scribe who copied the text on stone and of the artist who cut it into its final form. For instance, a Bengal stone inscription of Vijayasena dating from the late eleventh century, which we will encounter in chapter 4, was composed by the Sanskrit poet Umapatidhara, perhaps the very poet mentioned by Jayadeva of *Gita-govinda* fame.[28] It was engraved by Shulapani, who describes himself as the crest-jewel of the Varendra guild of artists.[29] More often, the poet of a eulogy is not known from other sources. Thus the Ratanpur stone inscription from 1163/1164, which we will also encounter in chapter 4,[30] was composed in Sanskrit by Tribhuvanapala, written (on the stone) by Kumarapala, and incised by the *shilpis* (artists) Dhanapati and Ishvara.[31] The Kalinjar Sanskrit stone inscription in the Nilakantha temple, dated to 1201, was composed by the patron himself, the Chandela monarch Paramarddi, and was both written on stone and incised by *shilpi* Padma.[32] Such *prashasti* poets not infrequently referred to their works as *kavya*, and indeed both types of literary works were produced at and for the court.[33] Yet, as Pollock points out, a clear hierarchy emerges in which the *prashasti* writers were held in lesser regard than those who wrote *kavya*.[34]

Additionally, at least one quotation from a Sanskrit *kavya*—the introductory verse of seventh-century poet Bana's *Harsha-charita* (*Life of Emperor Harsha*)[35]—was used repeatedly as the first verse of a wide range of inscriptions from the southern part of the subcontinent:[36]

> *Namas tunga-shiras-chumbi-chandra-chamara-charave*
> *Trailokya-nagara-arambha-mula-sthambhaya-shambhave*

> Praise be to Shambhu, beautified
> by the chowrie moon touching his lofty head,
> like to a foundation pillar of the city
> that is the universe.[37]

This eulogy prefaces numerous copper-plate and stone inscriptions, from Hampi in the northern Deccan to Tanjavur in the south, and across the various districts of Karnataka. The records range in date from the tenth to the fifteenth century, the period of "vernacularization," and include those of the later Chalukyas, Yadavas, Shilaharas, and Kalachuris; the Vijayanagar emperors; the Tanjavur Nayaks; and a range of feudatory princes. Several of these records are in Kannada, making it relevant to refer to a Kannada text on aesthetics, the *Kavi-raja-margam* (*Path of Master Poets*), written at the very end of the ninth century. Introducing this text, Pollock points out that it "announced the new vernacular aesthetics," and that it salutes Bana in its prologue before praising Kannada prose writers.[38] It seems possible that the high esteem in which Bana was held in the Kannada-language region may have been responsible for the frequent use of Bana's Sanskrit stanza as the initial invocation in so many Kannada *prashastis*.[39] Another such verse dedicated to Vishnu as Varaha, whose source I have been unable to trace, occurs in inscriptions between the seventh and thirteenth centuries; it is most often seen on its own, although occasionally it follows Bana's verse in praise of Shiva.[40]

The Body: Beauty, *Rasa*, the Auspicious

Sculpted images in the medium of stone and bronze, wood and clay decorated the walls of temples and palaces or were the object of *puja* and adoration by devotees. The creation of such images and their reception will be addressed in parallel as we consider varying aspects of the body in this study. I shall make use of neglected inscriptional material, and highlight passages from known literary texts, in order to better understand and appreciate ancient works of sculpture and to establish contextualization that enables an awareness of the original viewers' responses to such imagery. Both traditional literary texts and inscriptional eulogies shed light on the manner in which Indians of bygone days, of the "there and then," viewed and responded to the beautiful, well-adorned body. Word and image appear as twins so that it is difficult to say which was rendered into the other.

Were the tropes of Sanskrit *kavya*, Prakrit literature, or Tamil poetry in the minds of artists creating images, or were sculpted images the inspiration for the poets' productions? It appears that these interchangeable alternatives must both have come into play at one time or another. The danger of speaking wrongly for the silent other, of "well-intentioned ventriloquism," is indeed an issue.[41] Equally vital, however, is the need to "recognize the unspoken" in textual sources and to keep in mind the authors' possible agendas and audiences.[42] The use of literary material to illuminate sculptural and pictorial imagery appears to put us on a less dangerous if still slippery path, one that we should tread with a degree of awareness. In addition, we should keep in mind the admittedly partial and incomplete nature of the artistic remains that have come down to us. We have to agree with Nanette Salomon on the "profound impossibility of retrieving an accurate and objective account of the past," although at the same time there appears to be definite value in allowing ourselves to be "seduced by the fragments to try to do so."[43]

It may appear trite in certain contexts to emphasize that the gendered body of an artistic tradition is a social construct.[44] Still, it is useful to repeat this in the context of the South Asian artistic tradition, and to stress that the body of the visual arts is best understood when evaluated within its correct social milieu. Another truism worth repeating is that the works of art that constitute our focus spoke differently to different people in differing eras. Viewers of the eleventh and twelfth centuries surely reacted differently to the two images we have already discussed than did those of the mid-twentieth century when the bronze was unearthed and placed in a local museum for safekeeping, and the stone statue traveled to the United States to enter a museum collection.[45] So, too, the indigenous temple-goers' reaction—awe, wonder, devotion—was at odds with the negative critical response of the British officials entrusted with the preservation of an ancient heritage. Thomas Biggs, a nineteenth-century officer of the Bombay Artillery entrusted with recording temple sculptures through the new medium of photography, lamented the "indecent sculptures" that proved, for him, "the early date at which the morals of India assume such a headlong and downward decay."[46]

Recent years have witnessed some discussion on the question of whether cross-cultural universals exist in the field of aesthetics, or whether one should emphasize cultural specificity. The arena of anthropology has been the prime venue for these discussions, although more recently art historians, too, have entered the debate.[47] The balance of opinion is in favor of specificity, reinforcing the age-old adage that beauty lies in the eyes of the beholder—a beholder attuned to a particular ethos, its cultural mores, its ideals, and its aspirations. Most of these discussions and reflections, it should be noted, have taken place among scholars who study cultures that lack extensive literary records, such as those of Africa or parts of the ancient Near Eastern world. For instance, Irene Winter has demonstrated that ancient Mesopotamians had no term that corresponds to the word "beauty"; instead, their inscriptions speak of "luster," "radiance," and a "well-formed body" as desirable or enviable qualities of an excellent physique.[48]

India possesses an extensive corpus of works on ancient art and aesthetics; the Sanskrit term for "art" is *shilpa*, artists are *shilpis*, and art texts are *shilpa shastras*. Sanskrit has over a hundred words and phrases to describe beauty, loveliness, and attraction, a large proportion of which are connected with the concept of amorous play. In an insightful article published more than forty years ago, Daniel Ingalls highlighted this plethora of choices and spoke of some of the reasons for it.[49] One explanation is that beauty, in India, is frequently expressed in subjective terms, as it affects the senses of the viewer. The eyes are specially favored with a range of phrases that include "a drink for one's eyes alone" (*netraika-peya*), "a festival for one's eyes" (*netrotsava*), and "a resting place for one's eyes" (*netra-vishrama-patra*). The heart and mind are captivated by beauty that "captures the heart" (*harati-hridaya*) or "steals the heart" (*hridaya chaura*). Another explanation for the vastly expanded vocabulary for beauty is that Sanskrit has a complete set of words to describe beauty in motion as against beauty at rest. The verb *lasati*, for example, is used to suggest grace in repose that arouses desire; with a prefix, *vilasati* indicates coquettish beauty expressed through movement.

The basic Sanskrit word for "beauty," *saundarya*, to which are related *sundara* (beautiful) and *sundari* (beautiful woman), is rarely used in poetry, perhaps because it was considered general, colorless, or nondescriptive. More popular is *lavanya* for "beauty," "loveliness," or "charm." The word *rupa*, which merely means "form," generally implies a beautiful or handsome form, beauty, elegance, or grace. Feminine nouns used in the context of beauty include *taruni* (literally, "creeper"), for a slender young woman; *divya* (a heavenly woman); *kanta* (a lovely woman or beloved); and *kamini* (a woman desirous of love). Masculine nouns for "beloved" include *kanta* and *vallabha*. Verbs used in the context of love include *rama* (to play or have sexual intercourse) and *hara* (to attract, captivate, or capture). Also popular are adjectives like *nandana* (gladdening) or the slightly stronger *ranjana* (exciting passion). The prefix *su* (good or beautiful) is frequently used to transform words, as in *sutanu* (beautiful body), *subhru* (beautiful eyebrows), *sukantha* (beautiful neck), and the like. *Charu* refers to something precious and hence loved. Several of these words—including *sundara*, *kanta*, *charu*, *rupa*, and words with the prefix *su*—are equally appropriate to describe male or female beauty.[50] Additionally, as in other languages, there are words that introduce the idea of radiance through light, including *shobha* (splendor), *ruchi* (luster), and *kanti* (brilliance). The sheer number of words, with their subtle overtones and nuances of meaning, used to describe the infinite variety of the human figure and its effect on the viewer could in itself be indicative of the primacy accorded to the excellence of the body beautified.

Rasa

India's theory of aesthetics, known by the term *rasa* (largely restricted to the Sanskrit tradition), likewise laid emphasis on the variety of thought, feeling, and emotion experienced by human beings. Enunciated by the famous writer Bharata, perhaps in the fourth century, in a work titled *Natya-shashtra* (*Treatise on Drama*), the *rasa* theory is undoubtedly of earlier origin, since Bharata himself speaks of his debt to earlier masters. Literally, *rasa* is the juice or extract of a fruit or vegetable, its finest and subtlest part. In the context of aesthetics, *rasa* is the heightened sense of awareness evoked by any of the fine arts, be it dance, drama, poetry, music, painting, or sculpture. The ability of the artist to communicate the varying emotions (*bhavas*), and of the viewer to experience them as the corresponding aesthetic sensation, constitute the basis of the *rasa* theory. The *rasas* were originally eight in number: the erotic (*shringara*), comic (*hasya*), pathetic (*karuna*), furious (*raudra*), heroic (*virya*), terrible (*bhayanaka*), odious (*bibhatsa*), and wondrous (*adbhuta*). Each is created by the artist's ability to evoke its concomitant *bhava*: love (*rati*), mirth (*hasa*), sorrow (*shoka*), anger (*krodha*), energy (*utsaha*), fear (*bhaya*), disgust (*jugupsa*), and astonishment (*vismaya*). At a somewhat later date, a ninth *rasa*—the quiescent (*shanta*), together with its corresponding *bhava* of equanimity (*shama*)—was introduced. *8 Rasas*

The unique and well-enunciated *rasa* theory appears to center on viewer response. According to most aestheticians, *rasa* is created by the artist—actor, dancer, painter, sculptor—but is experienced solely by the discerning, cultivated viewer, known as a *rasika* (connoisseur). However, others argue that *rasa* must be felt by the actors in order to communicate it adequately to their viewers. While *rasa* is most easily experienced in dance and drama, texts on painting also include a discussion of this concept. Thus the *Chitra-sutra* (*Painting Text*), which makes up a section of the well-known *Vishnu-dharmottara-purana*, a work that may date to the sixth century, specifies that works of art intended for display in public spaces may exhibit any of the nine *rasas*, but that those intended to decorate private homes should be restricted to three: the erotic, the comic, and the quiescent![51] The erotic *rasa* of *shringara* is described as the king of *rasas* and has high visibility in the visual and literary material that is our concern. Many writers treated all *rasas* but *shringara* in a perfunctory manner, while the great king and theoretician, Bhoja of Dhara, wrote a major treatise, *Shringara-prakasha* (*Light on the Erotic [rasa]*), on this most excellent and primary of *rasas*.

Another concept that plays a central role in this book is "the auspicious," a word that undoubtedly seems "a little strange and old-fashioned in modern English."[52] Still, it is a term whose importance cannot be overstated. Two decades ago, scholars lamented how the concept of purity had overshadowed auspiciousness as a category in understanding the cultural context of premodern India.[53] But in recent years, this situation has been largely rectified. An anthropological study first highlighted the category of "the auspicious," and its antonym "the inauspicious," as a central node of interpretation, and pointed out that its resonance is also seen in texts of the premodern period. Gloria Raheja's research demonstrates that the basic function of *dana* (gifting) in the northern Indian village she studied is to promote the auspiciousness and well-being of an entire village or community by transferring inauspiciousness to the recipients of the gift, generally Brahmins, who are willing to accept such offerings.[54] I believe the auspicious is a factor of crucial significance in understanding both the subject matter of the artistic tradition of premodern India and its social context.

The most commonly used words for the auspicious appear to be *mangala*, *shubha*, and *kalyana*, all of which imply welfare, good fortune, happiness, and prosperity. These words, especially *shubha*, are routinely used as a prefix for a variety of events—*shubha-kala* (time), *shubha-masa* (month), *shubha-muhurta* (astrological conjunction), *shubha-yatra* (journey), and the like—and are thus used as attributes of objects.[55] Major events such as childbirth, puberty, and marriage are as obviously associated with the auspicious as death is with the inauspicious. One may also view certain places, objects, and persons as embodying the auspicious, such as a pilgrimage spot (*tirtha-sthana*) or a pot of overflowing foliage (*purna-kalasha*). To go a step further, by embodying auspiciousness, the fertile woman (*kanya*, *nari*) and the monarch (*raja*, *chakravartin*) become in themselves emblems of the auspicious; they provide instances in which the "transferred epithet" has warranted validity.[56] Further, as Frédérique Marglin has pointed out in her study of Puri temple dancers, the union of male and female invariably signifies the "stable state of auspiciousness."[57] I would suggest that this applies not only to societal life and to literature, but also to the visual arts of sculpture and painting.

Sanskrit words for the auspicious further include *shiva*, *shreyas*, *bhadra*, *dhanya*, *ishta*, and *svasti*, all of which carry the implied meanings of "agreeable, propitious, favorable, desirable, beautiful, radiant, beneficial," or in other words, bringing fortune.[58] In the various inscriptions on which I have drawn liberally throughout this book, groups of words, clustered in various formations, appear as opening prayers for the bestowal of auspiciousness. *Om svasti* is one such; others include *siddham astu*, *shubham astu*, and *om svasti shri*. Verses or phrases of *mangala* (auspiciousness) in literary texts are also spoken of as *ashish*, from which comes *ashirvada* (literally, "words of auspiciousness," or simply an approval, a sanction, a blessing). *Om* itself, or the more appropriate term of *pranava*, is also a blessing, a benediction, and its very sound is considered a means of conferring auspiciousness; it is the totally appropriate manner of commencing any and all inscriptions, social and sacred rituals, and a range of other undertakings. One cannot overstate the all-encompassing and pervasive nature of the concept of auspiciousness in the Indian context; it is an underlying perception that permeates everyday life, infusing it with marked significance.

The Body and Woman: Sanskrit and Tamil Poetry

In the course of this book, I shall use extracts drawn primarily from Sanskrit and Tamil poetry, both traditions with an ancient history, and later from Hindi, to make a variety of points about beauty, love, auspiciousness, and the centrality of the body. There are commonalities, but also differences, between the literary traditions, a subject on which Martha Selby has written eloquently.[59] Sanskrit poetics is perhaps best understood in terms of the *rasas* and their corresponding "permanent feelings" or human emotions, the *sthayi-bhavas*. We have seen the connection between *rasa* and *bhava* and, for instance, that the *rasa* of the erotic (*shringara*) is the result of the underlying emotion of passion (*rati*), while the *raudra-rasa* (furious) is the result of the emotion of *krodha* (anger). In the tradition of Sanskrit love poetry, more often than not woman is confined to a variety of interior spaces that represent the apartments of the palace or mansion that she inhabits, together with its terraces, pavilions, and courtyards.[60] Poets created extensive classifications of the *nayika* (heroine) with her friend and confidante (*sakhi*), devoting somewhat briefer sections to the *nayaka* (hero) and his companion (*sakha*). In Selby's words, "[I]n this sequestered world, the woman is treated as something to be classified, typified, measured, and endlessly described."[61] Elaborate systems of classification of women are seen in the *nayika-bheda* (classifications of heroines) systems of the later Sanskritic and Hindi traditions; Sheldon Pollock's translation of the Sanskrit *Rasa-manjari* (*Bouquet of Delights*) of around 1500 indicates that the text's various permutations and combinations yield as many as 384 types.[62] These descriptive systems, which Selby terms "biologic," will enter our discussion in the final chapter.

In Tamil poetry, woman appears to move more freely through space, and the entire landscape emotes with her. It is best read according to a convention exemplified by A. K. Ramanujan's use of the title *The Interior Landscape* for his translations of early Tamil poetry.[63] These poems are of two categories—either the *akam* love genre or the *puram* war genre. Central to the *akam* corpus is the concept of five *tinais* (contexts) that have geographical, spatial, temporal, and emotional connotations. *Kurinchi*, the fertile hilly tract that signifies lovers' union, has at its opposite extreme the *palai* (desert wasteland), which connotes separation. In between are varying love experiences with the *mullai* (forest region), which suggests uncomplaining anticipation of the lover's return; the salty, sandy *neytal*, which indicates lamenting the lover's absence; and the *marutam* (fertile plains), which signals jealous quarreling. The mention of the seashore, as in a verse that commences "That man from the shores / with their spreading waters," immediately signals to the knowledgeable reader/listener that the poem will be about irrevocable separation.[64] A similar mood is indicated by the opening phrase "Like that nectar from the sea / with its rows of waves."[65] These works of Sangam poetry, substantially composed perhaps between 200 B.C.E. and 200 C.E., form the foundation for the verses of the later poet-saints, both Shaiva and Vaishnava, which we shall encounter in chapter 4. The Tamil tradition is less taxonomic than that of northern India, as we will see in chapter 2. Nevertheless, it categorizes women into seven different groups on the basis of age and sexual experience, ranging from the innocent *petai* (girl of five to seven years old) to the mature, experienced *perilampen* (thirty-two to forty years old).

Common to both northern and southern traditions is the convention of describing the human form from head to toe, whether male or female, human or divine. The trope is known by the term *nakh-sikh* (toenail to crest) in Sanskrit and Hindi, *sarapa* (head to foot) in Urdu, and *padadi-kesha* (foot-first to hair) in Sanskrit and Sanskritic Tamil. A distinction is often drawn in texts between the description of a god or goddess, in which the viewers' eyes and that of the poet should rest first on the divine feet and only then move upward, and that of a human, which may commence with the face and proceed downward. Any single head-to-toe description may range from a dozen lines of prose to over a hundred verses of poetry.

The Sacred and the Profane

In the mid-twentieth century, Mircea Eliade spoke of "the abyss that divides the two modalities of experience—sacred and profane."[66] He described the sacred as "*the opposite of the profane*," proclaiming that his aim was "to illustrate and define this opposition between sacred and profane."[67] He spoke of "the experience of profane space which is in direct contrast to the experience of sacred space."[68] While an Eliade-style analysis is outdated in writings that deal with India, it is interesting to note that his pronouncement on the dichotomy of sacred and profane coincided with the perceptive observation of Stella Kramrisch, pioneering scholar and interpreter of Indian art: "The art of India is neither religious nor secular, for the consistent fabric of Indian life was never rent by the western dichotomy of religious belief and worldly practice."[69] Her statement, contained in a thought-provoking essay that accompanied a rich selection of photographs of the sculpture, painting, and architecture of India, has rarely been quoted since; nor have the reasons for this lack of dichotomy been the subject of further exploration. I interpret her words to mean that she saw no sharp line between the sacred and the secular (or profane), and that the boundaries, if they existed, often blend and blur.

Current scholarship rightly questions the very use of the terms "religious" and "secular" as applied to the architectural spaces of India.[70] Places of worship, whether dedicated to the Buddhist, Hindu, or Jain faith, did not pertain exclusively to the gods, and they do not do so today. Rather, they serve a variety of other functions, including community gatherings of a more mundane character. For example, associated with the great Chola temples of the eleventh and twelfth centuries, and funded and sponsored by them, were a whole nexus of administrative units, banking institutions, hospitals, schools, jewelry workshops, and dance, drama, and music companies. Indeed, the same applies to the celebrated Buddhist monastic universities, such as Nalanda and Vikramashila, or the impressive mountaintop Jain pilgrimage centers, such as Shatrunjaya and Girnar. At the other end of the spectrum, every palace, whether at Amber or Udaipur in Rajasthan or at Shri-ranga-patnam or Padmanabha-puram in the south, invariably included within its premises a temple shrine, even two, as indeed did the *haveli* or *tinnai* courtyard houses of India.

That we might be surprised at the possibility of the coexistence of the sacred with the secular, the profane, or the sensuous discloses our Western mind-set. In order to adopt a postcolonial approach to the visual material, however, it is necessary to examine deep-rooted misconceptions before dismissing them as inapplicable to India. Let us take a look at words used in a precolonial context that seem to designate comparable differences. There is the worldly and the other-worldly (*laukika* and *alaukika*), the worldly and the sacred-textual (*laukika* and *agamika*), or the revealed and the unrevealed (*drishtartha* and *adrishtartha*).[71] These pairs, however, do not denote an easy binary opposition between the spiritual and the material. As Jitendra Mohanty emphasizes, in a consideration of any system of thought, it is important that we do not import into our thinking distinctions that do not apply to that system.[72] However, the weight of a hundred years of scholarship that has assumed the overall applicability of a dichotomous way of thinking requires a fully argued, richly documented interpretation to convincingly demonstrate that while the words "sacred" and "profane" might be meaningfully juxtaposed in the Western context, such a binary distinction has limited resonance on the Indian scene.

In this study, whose chapters are in the nature of reflections on the artistic treatment of the human body, I propose to explore the intermingling of the sacred with the sensuous, the profane, and the secular—which, in the context of Indian art, adds to the negation of Eliade's perceived dichotomy. Since several of the words I will be using are likely to resonate differently for each reader, it will be useful to clarify my usage. I use the term "profane," as did Eliade, in its original meaning of "nonsacred," or "outside the temple precincts," from the Latin *pro* (before) and *fanum* (temple). My occasional use of the word "secular," as a substitute for "profane," is intended to be understood in its dictionary meaning of "not religious or spiritual"; it carries none of the nuances derived from its present-day political associations in the context of the Indian subcontinent. By "sensuous," I refer to those images that display the human form in all its bodily glory— smoothly slender, curvaceous, and somewhat provocative—and that occasionally evoke a reaction of some discomfiture in the modern viewer. Sensuous imagery frequently has overtones of the erotic, a word somewhat more difficult to define; basically, I use "erotic" for sexually suggestive imagery, visual and verbal, but not for actual sexual acts. I shall not deal here with the overtly sexual art of India, which features coupling figures and a range of other sexual activities; that is a vast subject in itself, which has received considerable, if uneven, treatment.[73] Some readers may find this omission surprising, but my intention is not to deliberate on phenomena that are somewhat localized in space and time. My focus is the central position accorded, down the ages and across the length and breadth of the country, to the human form, a body that is exceptionally sensuous in its portrayal; since we are dealing with the artistically perfect human body, overtones of the erotic are bound to arise. This chapter, in particular, is devoted to highlighting the centrality of the body in the artistic and literary imagination of India and, indeed, in its religious ritual practices.

The Body in Life and Ritual

While this book focuses on the proliferation of art in stone and bronze during the post-Vedic period, and on the accompanying post-Vedic literature, I shall begin with a brief consideration of the Rigvedic *Purusha-sukta* hymn, which speaks of the universe as originating from the sacrificial body of the divine Purusha. Vedic ritual centered on the brick sacrificial altar where offerings were made to the gods; no images were created of these deities, although they were already visualized verbally in bodily form. The artistic innovation of divine form arose only in the post-Vedic period, when images of Brahmanic deities, as indeed of the Buddha and Jina, were fashioned in human form. Yet even the Vedas chose to depict the absolute, the supreme Purusha, in anthropomorphic form as a glorious all-embracing body. The *Purusha-sukta* pictures every manifestation of power in creation as having emerged from a specific part of his body.[74] The moon emerged from his mind, the sun from his eye, fire from his mouth, wind from his breath, space from his navel, the world of gods from his head, and the earth from his feet. In this manner, even Vedic imagination appears to have visualized a perfect bodily form as the source of all beauty and power.

We might commence our study of the post-Vedic dominance of the body by examining one obvious explanation for the lack of dichotomy between worldly and otherworldly imagery. The Indian, largely the Hindu, pictured the ideal life in the world as a journey with four connected, graded, and successive paths, the goals of each facilitating entry into the next. Stella Kramrisch referred to this briefly when she categorized release (*moksha*) as the ultimate aim of life in India, and spoke of India's "entire social structure, with its *Dharma* or laws of human righteousness and cosmic order, its *Artha* or accumulated wealth, and *Kama*, the fountain springs of love and passion."[75] This concept is further elaborated by the formulation of the four successive *ashramas* (stages) of life: the student stage (*brahma-charin*), the married state (*griha-stha*), the phase of the recluse who withdraws from active participation in worldly affairs to a life of study and contemplation (*vanaprastha*), and finally the life of the renunciant whose withdrawal from the world becomes complete and total (*sannyasin*). Needless to say, the four goals and the four *ashramas* were ideals and not necessarily exemplars of practice. Patrick Olivelle points out that in their origin, the four *ashramas* were permanent life choices and not temporary phases of life.[76] However, as he himself notes, by the fifth century, as evidenced by Kalidasa's works and inscriptions of the period, the system had transformed itself so that "the four *ashramas* form a ladder of four rungs."[77]

The four goals of life commence with the accent on *dharma*, a word with subtle overtones and one that is difficult to translate since it not only includes ideas of virtue, righteousness, morality, ethical conduct, and duty, but also can vary with people and situations.[78] Thus, as the god Krishna explains to the warrior-hero Arjuna on the battlefield, for a warrior *dharma* entails engaging in battle even if it involves killing his own kith and kin. *Dharma* is basic and placed first because its special values for the individual should permeate the pursuit of the following two goals of acquiring material wealth (*artha*) and seeking love and pleasure (*kama*). *Moksha* (liberation), which signifies release from the cycle of rebirth, is the final, supreme goal. The graded structure of the four *ashramas* may have arisen to enable individuals to follow the fourfold path according to individual capacity and fitness. All four goals and each of the four stages of life were considered to have their rightful place in every individual's life. *Kama* (love), sought through a married life, need not be bypassed in favor of *moksha*; in fact, the married state of *grihastha* was extolled as the stage that allowed the greatest scope for individuals to cultivate the qualities necessary not only to make a success of the pleasures of love (*kama*) and material wealth (*artha*), lived by the rules of virtue and righteousness (*dharma*), but also to achieve eligibility for the final stage of *moksha*. Writing in Tamil toward the end of the seventh century, the child saint (*nayanar*)[79] Sambandar laid stress on this very aspect when he sang, lauding the example of the god Shiva himself and his beloved consort, Uma:

> Here, on this good earth, you may lead a life of joy
> living each day in fullness—
> indeed this hinders not the goal of liberation.
> In the green and plenteous plains of Sirkali
> thus too did the lord [Shiva] dwell,
> beside him, the fairest of women.[80]

This holistic attitude toward life naturally had an impact on both art and literature. Sculpted imagery pertaining to the four goals found a place in both sacred and worldly contexts, being evident on the walls of sacred as well as secular structures. Hindu, Buddhist, or Jain shrines may have been intended primarily to instill awareness of the final goal of salvation, but their intention was not thereby to inculcate total renunciation of the other goals. It was considered appropriate that a sacred structure carry images pertaining to rituals and righteous conduct (*dharma*), depicting the earning and use of wealth in a dharmic way (the pursuit of *artha*), and portraying marriage and sexual love (*kama*), in addition to those laying emphasis on the necessity and glory of the final goal of liberation (*moksha*). In this context, it becomes apparent, as Kramrisch remarked, that in India the realm of religious belief and that of worldly practice are far from incompatible—a dharmic way of life in the world would lead gradually, in the fullness of time, to the final goal of liberation. Such a worldview is as distinctive and unique to India as is the plurality of its vision of manifested divinity compared with the monotheistic view of the Judeo-Christian-Islamic world. If it appears that I have given short shrift in this book to renunciation and liberation—both concepts of vital importance to Indian religious thought—it is largely because the visual material, the starting point of my inquiry, does not emphasize these directly. Similarly, the reason for the minimal discussion of the repulsive or ugly in the artistic corpus is that, with the exception of the goddess Kali-Chamunda, ugly or deformed figures occur only in marginal areas of sculpted panels or painted murals.

It is of crucial relevance to note that the centrality of the human body is emphasized also in the externalized rituals of the Hindus. All ceremonial ritual in India, which seeks to establish contact with the spirit or the powers of the spirit, invariably begins by rendering the body pure, fit, and appropriately prepared for such contact. Yoga postures (*asanas*) and systematic breathing (*pranayama*) represent the preparation of the body for the further six stages of yogic practice that leads to liberation, the first two being the cultivation of moral and virtuous conduct (*shama dama*). In addition, by a range of symbolic actions and chants, the body is temporarily made into a fitting vehicle for the descent of cosmic forces. A major preparatory rite known as *nyasa* (literally, "putting down or placing") involves touching various parts of the body with one's fingers, and it constitutes an essential precursor to the ritual of *mantra-japa*, which is mainly a mental repetition or chant of a special prayer or verse for a required number of times. Specific parts of the body, regarded as the resting place of individual deities or forces that may both purify and empower, are made fit to undertake sacred ritual and later to receive the infusion of power. For instance, when Sarasvati, goddess of learning and knowledge, is visualized as a deity pervading the entire body, each letter of the Sanskrit alphabet, which represents her "sound" form, is visualized as residing at a specific spot on the body, and is indicated and enlivened by touching the spot concerned while enunciating the letter of the alphabet. The body is central to ritual religious practice and thus to climbing the rungs toward *moksha*; it is initially purified and perfected, and is rarely viewed as an obstacle to be surmounted.

The pure, well-formed human body without defect, honed perhaps through the practice of yoga *asana*, was considered the perfect receptacle within which the spiritually advanced could aspire to greater stature and the average devotee could experience the joy of closeness to the divine.[81] One might note here the well-documented fact that several of the sacred and philosophic treatises of India, attempting to convey to their audiences some concept of a state of emancipated bliss, of ecstatic spiritual joy, resorted to imagery borrowed from the erotic bliss of the bodily union of man and woman as providing the closest external parallel. Sexuality was neither forbidden nor unmentionable. Rather, erotic imagery, with all its nuances, was often used to describe the total surrender of the individual soul, and its oneness with the divine, whether in the context of the divine manifested god Krishna and the cowherd *gopi* girls, or in the abstract and formless Upanishadic concept that tells of the embodied individual soul (*atman*) and the eternal spirit (Brahman) as being one in essence. In the Western imaginary, by contrast, the sensuous and erotic is generally considered totally unsuited to religious imagery, one contributing factor being, no doubt, the association of original sin with the body and specifically the body of Eve. While the Hebrew Bible's famous erotic love poem, Song of Songs, is interpreted as God's relationship with Israel or, in the Christian understanding, as God's relationship with the Church, it is an exception, not the rule.[82] In India, by contrast, poets and writers found no comparison to spiritual bliss so close and so easily understood as human sexual union, and apparently one that was permissible in the prevailing cultural context, even in a sacred philosophic text.

We must recognize, too, the central role of the anthropomorphic body of god in ritual temple worship. Diana Eck's work has been crucial in emphasizing that devotees go to a temple for *darshana*, a purposeful act of seeing the divine image, and receiving in turn a transfer of grace.[83] Such *darshana* occurs after the sanctum image, generally of stone, has received *puja*, a series of rites whereby the image is honored as one might honor a highly esteemed guest. *Puja* involves ritual bathing of the divine body in a series of powders and liquids, dressing the image in silks, adorning it with jewels and flowers, offering food and water, ringing bells, and waving lamps.[84] As we shall see in detail in chapter 4, *puja* harnesses all the senses, directing them toward the glory of the body of god; the divine image in bodily form is critical and essential to Hindu worship.

Emphasis on the body in ritual is not restricted to the Hindus; with a somewhat different point of reference, *puja* is extended to the body of the Jina among the Murti-pujak Jains of western India. John Cort has detailed the nine-limbed *puja* in which the Jain worshipper applies sandalwood paste to thirteen spots on nine limbs of the body of the Jina image—two toes, two knees, two wrists, two shoulders, the head, forehead, throat, heart, and navel.[85] It will be noticed that in a manner resembling the sacred sequence in Hindu worship, the Jain devotee commences with the feet of the divine being and proceeds upward, but he then concludes with the central navel.

Exploring the Body: Human and Divine

Having briefly highlighted the centrality of the body in the Indian milieu, I turn in chapter 2 to explore the characterization, in both artistic and literary expression, of the ideal bodily form, female and male, and its adornment (*alankara*), as it pertains to the urban realm of the elite and to royalty itself. I emphasize that the sensuous body of the Indian sculpted tradition is never a nude body; it is always the body adorned. In the Indian imagination, *alankara* always gave the final touches to the perfection of the body in both life and art, just as it is fundamental and crucial in poetic expression and architectural decoration.

Chapter 3 examines the apparently comfortable juxtaposition and coexistence of what are normally considered divergent concepts—the sensuous and the sacred—within a range of "sacred spaces." That such juxtaposition was totally acceptable in Buddhist, Jain, and Hindu sacred precincts indicates a worldview at variance with the one to which we are today accustomed, especially in the West; it raises the need to question terms like "sacred" and "secular" when discussing architectural spaces in India. Chapter 4 considers the extraordinary level of comfort, in the Indian context, with the concept of a sensuous divine form, and examines the artistic depictions of deities in the context of the passionate poetry addressed to gods and goddesses by their closest devotees, the saints and *acharyas*. It highlights the fact that one significant, easy, and totally appropriate mode of approaching the divine, through the love and devotion of the path of *bhakti*, involves focusing on the beauty and adornment of the divine body and reveling in its bodily perfection. Many saints have been primarily *bhaktas*.

The final chapter turns to post–sixteenth-century secular painting in the Rajput courts of northern India, and explores the easy insertion of the gods into the world of men in a genre of painted manuscripts devoid of direct sacred intent. Both painters and poets freely transposed sacred images, largely of the god Krishna, into the worldly realm of the classification of heroines and heroes of the *nayika-bheda* texts, once again demonstrating the fluidity of borders between the sacred and the profane in premodern times. It is my hope that these initial reflections, which bring together visual and verbal material in an attempt to create a more complete picture of the premodern milieu in which the art was created, will spur further studies into the many "whys" and "wherefores" that still exist in this and other Indian art-historical material.

India's artistic, literary, and inscriptional traditions considered in the course of this study indicate that a worldview that sees no dichotomy between a religious or spiritual way of life leading to emancipation and a joyous ethical life lived in the midst of the world prevailed from at least the second century B.C.E. to around the eighteenth century C.E. or later. That such a worldview was able to thrive uninterrupted in many parts of India for some two thousand years contributes to the picture drawn by current scholarship that emphasizes a lack of rupture with the inception of Muslim rule.[86] The intermingling and overlapping of the sacred with the sensuous in monuments across the length and breadth of the country, in the *kavyas* of Indian literature, and in commemorative inscriptions—whether in Sanskrit, Tamil, Kannada, or Telugu—clearly indicates that this was the prevailing and accepted outlook. The problems involved in handling this material are those of current reception; they arise because our vision, which is based on the "here and now" in place and time, is at variance with the "there and then." Today's readers and viewers, both Indian and Western, may theoretically accept the concept of a lack of dichotomy between worldly and other-worldly. Not too many, however, are really comfortable with the overtly sensuous nature of India's artistic tradition and its high visibility in the mode of sculpture and painting. A partial explanation in the case of Indian viewers lies in their recent historical experience of two centuries of British colonialism. A culture that emphasized the distinction between the worldly and the other-worldly, as indeed did Islam, was superimposed on some two thousand years of a lack of such a dichotomy. I am not suggesting that the British made a conscious attempt to change the prevailing worldview. Rather, the indigenous cultural aura changed gradually by the very fact of being surrounded by a completely different worldview and its contrasting lifestyle. The result is the mind-set of the majority of today's Indians. They have learned to accept, or explain away and be comfortable with, the contradictions and inconsistencies of the original faiths that gave rise to sensuous verbal and visual imagery. But many are still uncomfortable with the imagery itself and find it as difficult to accept as to explain. The case of Western viewers varies, depending on whether they are scholars or casual viewers; those familiar with the culture express little discomfort, while those unfamiliar with it are totally bemused.

The chapters in this book largely adopt the voice of the "there and then," and are an attempt to demonstrate that the sensuous character of India's artistic and literary tradition was totally acceptable and customary within the societies in which they flourished and which were responsible for their creation. Recognizing that neither the creation of the art nor its reception was ever a problem in its original milieu will, I hope, create a better understanding for those of us in the "here and now," both Indian and Western, who find this earlier tradition perplexing or calling for explanation. While bodily beauty and sexual love are part of human life, their celebration in the artistic medium demands a contextual exploration. Premodern India's attitude of acceptance—indeed, celebration—of the sensuous bodily form, both sacred and profane, is unparalleled.

2. THE IDEALIZED BODY AND ORNAMENT

An initial encounter with the vibrant figure sculptures of India—associated with temples, monastic centers, and other structures like stepwells—has occasionally led viewers to the unwarranted assumption that the sensuous stone and bronze images are naked.[1] With the exception of certain manuscripts dealing with erotica, the human body of the Indian artistic tradition is neither naked nor nude; it is invariably the body adorned.[2] *Alankara* (ornament) always includes clothing, as indeed does *shringara*, a word that means "adornment" in addition to being the term for the erotic *rasa*. The perfectly formed body of the Indian tradition, whether male or female, is decorated with fine fabrics, jeweled ornaments, and flowers. It is further adorned with an entire range of conventions that may be subsumed under the term "body culture," coined by Daud Ali.[3] Body culture includes elaborate hairstyling; the heightening of the body's beauty by anointing it with oils, pastes, cosmetics, and fragrances; and a range of other refinements, such as elegance of gait, gesture, and posture.

During the twentieth century, specially in the West, the word "ornamentation" had negative overtones when applied, for instance, to architecture, in which smooth, unadorned planes were considered eminently desirable. In like manner, with the female body, the ruffled and crinolined dresses of the past yielded place to the elegant lines of a black sheath. But the situation in the premodern context was quite different. As early as 1939, in response to criticism that regarded ornament as excess, A. K. Coomaraswamy explored the etymology of both Sanskrit and Latin words for ornament, and pointed out that decoration was considered an essential ingredient for a good work of art.[4] The Sanskrit term *alankara* derives from the literal meaning "to make sufficient or strengthen, to make adequate," and suggests enhancement in the efficacy of the thing or person thus adorned. So, too, the primary meaning of the Latin word *ornare* is "to fit out, furnish, provide with necessaries," and only secondarily "to embellish."[5] Ornament was thus viewed as a prerequisite that added to the body's elegance and gave it the final touches that were considered indispensable.[6] Coomaraswamy critiqued, as a later denigration of meaning, the modern tendency to consider ornament as a superfluous addition.

Yet another Sanskrit word for ornament, *abharanam*, is etymologically revealing since it means "to bring near, or attract (through magical power)," and suggests the potency of ornament.[7] While Coomaraswamy emphasized that ornamentation of Indian women was "not a matter of mere vanity, but rather one of propriety," it is, in actuality, much more.[8] Ornament is auspicious; ornament is protective; ornament makes the body complete, whole, beautiful, and desirable. To be without ornament is to provoke the forces of inauspiciousness, to expose oneself to danger, even to court danger. I give here just one preliminary example. When innocent, young Shakuntala, untutored in the ways of the world, prepares to leave the forest hermitage to join her husband, Dushyanta, playwright Kalidasa (ca. 400) has her companions adorn their pregnant friend with auspicious unguents (Prakrit, *mangala-samalahan*) in an attempt to provide her with protection.[9] In the context of India, the significance of ornament cannot be overstated.

This chapter is devoted to the characterization of the idealized human body and the importance of *alankara* to complete, beautify, and protect the body, as expressed in both the visual and the literary traditions. I focus first on the female body and then on the male, and within each gender category, I also highlight the special importance given to the royal body. I conclude with a study of the king and queen as a beautiful, devoted, and amorous couple and the significance of such an ideal for their citizens. As a coda, I briefly discuss the significance of *alankara* in architecture and poetry.

The Female Form

The Idealized Body

One of the earliest and most sensational stone sculptures in India is a life-size image of a woman, carved from sandstone and polished to a glossy tan finish (figure 3). She stands in perfect poise, a voluptuous figure with sloping shoulders, substantial breasts, a narrow waist, a rounded stomach with lightly incised folds, wide hips, and strong tapering thighs. Viewed from the rear, her erect stance is even more striking, revealing the spinal column held inward and shoulder blades lowered (figure 4). She wears a long skirt, held by a jeweled hip-belt (*mekhala*), and its inner folds fall in a series of looped folds between her legs, while the heavily pleated outer end drapes across her back and over her right arm, from which it hangs all the way to the ground. The artist has carved this sari-like drapery to bypass the figure's torso and allow a clear view of her breasts. She is adorned with a jeweled tiara, gem-set hair ornaments, heavy earrings, a choker, a long necklace that meets to slither between her breasts only to open out below with a dangling pendant, rows of bangles, armlets, and heavy, chunky anklets. The 5 foot, 2¼–inch scale of the image suggests her importance.

Who is this strong, erect woman who holds herself so proudly and gazes directly at the viewer? She provides a total contrast, for instance, to the roughly contemporaneous and celebrated images of Greek Aphrodite, whose slight stoop and inwardly curved body suggests vulnerability, who avoids eye contact with the viewer, and who uses her hands to cover her genitals and breasts.[10] Like the Greek deity, this figure is the product of a strongly patriarchal society; yet she seems neither humble nor humiliated by her sexuality, which she proudly exhibits. She was found accidentally in 1917 along the banks of the Ganges in the Bihar village of Didarganj adjoining Patna, the capital city of

Figure 3. *Chowri*-bearer (*front view*), sandstone, Didarganj, ca. second century.

Figure 4. *Chowri*-bearer (*rear view*), sandstone, Didarganj, ca. second century.

the ancient Mauryan monarchs (320–180 B.C.E.).[11] The stunning Didarganj image has been assigned to the third century B.C.E., partly on the basis of her find-spot and partly because of the so-called Mauryan polish she shares with a range of columns erected by Emperor Ashoka and his predecessors. Her original context is unknown, and we have no clues as to whether she once stood in a palace complex, a Buddhist or Jain establishment, or a Hindu sacred space. One thing is certain: despite the scale of the sculpture, she is no divinity, since she holds an attendant's fly whisk (*chowri*) in one hand and could never have occupied the central place in any conceivable tableau. Additionally, since the Indian system of artistic proportions dictates that a female figure, whether attendant or consort, be of significantly lesser height than the central image, the group of which she was once part must have been of truly monumental proportions. Could she be one of two flanking royal attendants, such as we encounter in later groupings? If indeed she stood alone, she must have held a very special status within the courtly milieu to have merited so major an individual "portrait." The possibility must be raised that she was a *ganika*, a highly placed royal courtesan of great talent and enviable accomplishments, whose prerogative it was to stand by the monarch at court and hold the fly whisk.[12] Kautilya's *Artha-shastra*, a text on government, speaks of the *ganika* as being assigned this precise privileged role.[13]

A substantial body of evidence suggests that the Didarganj *chowri*-bearer may have been dated too early and that she may have to be relocated to the second century C.E.[14] In whatever manner this evidence may ultimately play out, she is certainly the largest and most significant stone image, male or female, from early India. Her sensuous monumentality is not only breathtaking, but also a sure indication of the importance assigned to the body adorned—in this instance, the female body adorned—in the artistic milieu of ancient India.

The Didarganj image makes it evident that the sculpted human form owes little to the artist's observation of life and reality. Veracity was never the aim of the sculptor who, instead, produced an idealized form that incorporated the very specific concept of beauty prevalent in premodern India. Every feature of the body was visualized as perfect, and a favorite poetic mode of describing woman was to compare each feature of her physical makeup to an element of the natural world. Poets likened her face to the moon or lotus flower, eyes to the lotus petal or a carp and their pupils to bees, ears to tender furled leaves, breasts to mountain peaks or golden pots of holy water, arms to the pliant vine or bamboo, waist to a creeper, thighs to the smooth swelling stem of plantain trees or the elephant's trunk, and the mound of Venus to the soft, curved, spreading hood of the cobra. And yet, in poetry, everything in nature had to bow to a superior double in the feminine form. In his Sanskrit poem *Naishadhiya-charita* (*Life of Nala of Nishadha*), written toward the end of the twelfth century, the poet Shriharsha devotes over a hundred verses to the mental picture that Prince Nala conjures up of his beloved Damayanti, in the head-to-toe fashion mentioned in chapter 1. Here I give the briefest extracts that will illustrate how the human form is envisioned in terms of the beauties of nature (which it often surpasses):

> the lock of her hair that surpasses the peacock's train . . .

> It is the darkness in the front and on either side, dispelled
>   by the moon of her face, that is tied behind her in the
>   guise of her clearly undulating hair.

> did the gazelles ever borrow from her the beauty of her eyes . . .
> the outline of her lower lip . . . resembling the bandhuka
>   flower by the beauty of its crimson hue . . .

... her face excelling the moon ...

"The making of lotus blossoms is my sketching practice for
    the making of thy hand"—did the Creator announce to
    the deer-eyed damsel ...

are these creeper-like arms lotus-stalks visible on both sides ...

the palm fruit would be able to imitate her breasts, happy in
    their ascent, if it did not at times fall to the ground ...

the two stems of the damsel's thighs surpassed the
    elephant's trunk[15]

Women in Indic poetry, as in sculpture and painting, are invariably young and beautiful. "Not to be both is impossible, inconceivable," David Smith says of the women in Ratnakara's Sanskrit epic, the *Hara-vijaya* (*Victory of Hara* [*Shiva*]), which belongs around the year 1000. "They are a good thing; indeed they are a good thing, and one cannot have too much of them," he remarks of the women who, with the exception of the heroine and her immediate companions, have so little individuality that the text does not even give them names.[16] The very same could be said of the majority of women in sculpture and painting who are treated alike as generic entities. The numerous figures of women carved on the walls of any one of the temples at Khajuraho in central India, for instance, demonstrate clearly that female visual imagery, like the verbal, is generically idealized, stereotyped, predictable, and repetitive. And so it is with the female forms adorning the walls of a range of other monuments, from the richly sculpted "queen's stepwell" at Patan in Gujarat, to the Lingaraj temple in eastern Orissa, and the Hoysala temples of southern Karnataka. Poetry read aloud in courts, dramas performed for select audiences, and art admired by an elite audience all transported one into an idealized world where women and men, queens and kings, goddesses and gods were all beautiful, young, and nubile. Youth, beauty, and the ability to attract others translated into power and authority, whether in the earthly or the divine sphere.

India possesses a range of *silpa shastras* (art texts) that are often phrased to read as instructions for sculptors, painters, and architects; among the earliest extant is the "Chitra-sutra" section of the sixth-century *Vishnu-dharmottara-purana*. It is certainly a matter for debate whether the texts or the art came first; quite likely the texts drew on the artistic corpus. Yet some of them must have served as artists' manuals, particularly in the hereditary guild and workshop tradition in which craftsmen took up sculpture or painting, not because they had a particular talent in that direction, but because it was the traditional family profession. The art texts seemingly parallel the poetic tropes in proposing models for sculptors to follow in their creation of the human physique. One model for woman's torso was the *damaru* drum (Tamil, *tuti*), which is held at its waist and flares out above and below. That this continued to be the literary trope into the eighteenth century is seen from Indira Peterson's translation of the Tamil *Kuttralak Kuravanji* (*The Fortune-teller Play of Kuttralam*):

> One hand could encircle
> her waist, tapered like the tuti drum[17]

A second model for the female torso is the *vajra* (double-headed thunderbolt), which is likewise held at its center.[18] Either model automatically results in the traditional, although currently unfashionable, hourglass figure evident in the Didarganj image.[19]

The Indian artistic tradition laid considerable emphasis on ample breasts. As is evident from the Didarganj figure, artists sculpted women with full breasts placed high and touching each other, forcing the long necklaces they wore to snake their way between. This was a concept matched by the poet's fancy, and he repeatedly used the favorite trope of the difficulty of extricating one's gaze from the tight space between a woman's breasts:

> A young man, seeing the breasts of a pretty girl,
> shakes his head.
> Is it admiration,
> or is it to extricate his glance from the narrow interval?[20]

Sanskrit verses describing the breasts of the goddess or of a beautiful woman extol their weight, which causes her to bend forward; the embarrassed laugh evoked in contemporary society by such a description confirms the cultural and time-bound specificity of concepts of beauty and their expression in art and literature. The rounded figure of woman, not one overly slender, was most admired, as seen in this lover's description of his beloved, which cannot but remind us again of the Didarganj image:

> My eyes with difficulty pass her thighs
> to wander long in the land about her hips,
> then at her waist, uneven with triple fold,
> become quite powerless to move.
> But now at last, like travelers parched by thirst
> they've climbed the mountains of her breasts
> and see at last what they had hoped,
> their counterparts, her eyes, that flow with tears.[21]

Indian v. western female images

The well-turned ankle, much admired in the Western world, has never appealed to India's imagination, literary or artistic. By contrast, the smooth shoulder and slender arm received much attention, and routine comparisons for a woman's gracefully elongated arms were the vine-like creeper or, in southern India, the pliant green bamboo shoot. The almond eyes of Western imagination are replaced in India by eyes shaped like a lotus petal or a fish, considered the height of beauty. To have eyes like the fish referred also to the darting quality of the eyes, likened to a darting silvery fish.[22] One of India's most renowned forms of the goddess Parvati, as she abides in the temple at Madurai, is hailed as Minakshi (fish-eyed one). Concepts of beauty are indeed specific to both place and time. As John Hay points out, for instance, the very same Chinese pictures of the human body that appear to Western eyes as "meager, schematic and inadequate" evoked from Chinese authors the most erotic of literary passages.[23] The unique idealized concept of the body in premodern India, so evident in its poetry, finds its corresponding echo in stone and paint.

A ninth-century Tamil poem, the *Tirukkailaya-nana-ula* (*Procession of the Lord of Kailasa*), recently translated by Blake Wentworth, provides this description of a beautiful mature woman known as the *perilampen*. Like his Sanskrit counterpart, the Tamil poet provides an entire list of comparisons with nature—mound of Venus like a snake's hood, waist like rattan, arms like bamboo, hands like the lily, eyes like the carp:

> Her soft fingers have fine burnished nails
>> shining like mirrored spheres,
> her pubic delta flares like the hood of a frightened serpent
> her slight waist trembles like choice rattan,
> like two auspicious water pots made of everlasting gold
>> crowned with gems, verdant, uplifted, proportioned,
> spread with pale streaks and beauty marks,
> arising as the ambrosia which torments all who see,
> her breasts rub against each other in rhythm.
> She is the best of women
>> a beauty without peer among beauties;
> her lissome arms are like young bamboo
> with her lovely hands she shames the family of the glory lily
> she is the passion of Kamavel
> her breast shines like sandalwood.
> Sumptuous, balanced, rounded and full,
> both corners upturned, glossy, trembling, red as coral,
> bearing honey and glittering pearls,

her crimson mouth demands tribute even from the
    thoughts of hermits.
Streaked with even lines, accented with kohl,
shaped like gems at their center,
the semblance of the cool fringed carp and the mythic
    conch,
her piercing eyes are like the gleaming sea.[24]

As late as the eighteenth century, in a Tamil play written for a Maravar chieftain in the Tirunelveli region of Tamil Nadu, the same principles governed poetic expression. Peterson's translation of the *Kuttralak Kuravanji*, already encountered, indicates that the beauty of the young heroine, Vasantavalli, continues to be compared to elements of nature:

Her lips are the delicate buds of the murukku flower,
Her forehead is a bent bow, the crescent moon.
Her eyebrows surpass the rainbow's curve . . .
The beauty of the moon finds
its permanent home in her face.
Adorned by bright jewels, her neck
surpasses the beauty of the areca tree
entwined by betel vines . . .
Her thighs are banana-trees
planted at the gate of the rogue love-god's palace[25]

Unique to the visual artist was the problem of how to capture the rhythmic and graceful movement of the body—the elegant bearing, stride, posture, and carriage and the sense of playfulness that were considered signs of tasteful refinement.[26] Poets spoke often of beauty of movement: a graceful young male is described as "a moving *tamala* tree in the mountains";[27] a heroine's "gait is more graceful than the walk of the wild goose";[28] a prince has "this stance erect and motionless / left arm akimbo";[29] and the goddess's "flawless gait / mocks the peacock's grace."[30] The sculptor opted to freeze the moving body in the *tri-bhanga* (triple-bent) posture, which captures the essence of movement. Both male and female figures are portrayed with the head, and the limbs below the hips, poised at the same angle, while the torso in between moves in the opposite direction. It is indeed a stylized pose, but the sculptors were pleased with it, and it became the standard way to express poise and grace of movement. A few deities, primarily Vishnu and the Jinas, are portrayed in the erect standing posture of *sama-bhanga*; in the case of the Jinas, the posture additionally includes downward-stretched arms and makes reference to the *kayotsarga* pose of penance.

Systems of bodily proportion seem to have varied across time and in differing regions and political units of India. This becomes evident by merely comparing two sets of roughly contemporaneous images from adjoining areas of southern India: late Chola and Hoysala images, the first tall and slender, and the second shorter and sturdier.[31] One system found in southern India and compiled by Ganapati Sthapati for use by today's traditional artists is based on the *tala* (span), measured either as the reach from the tip of the thumb to the tip of the little finger or, alternately, as the upward-pointing hand in the gesture of protection, from wrist joint to tip of middle finger.[32] Either way, the result is roughly a 9-inch unit. Each *tala* is further subdivided into the *uttama* (highest order), the *madhyama* (middle order), and the *adhama* (lower order). The entire world is then calibrated according to the *tala*. Thus, for instance, the height of a major god must be 10 *talas* of the highest order inclusive of his crown; major goddesses, 10 *talas* of the middle order; and lesser gods and saints, 10 *talas* of the lower order. The size of 9 *talas* is reserved for a variety of semidivine beings, with 8 and 7 *talas* being the height for humans. The classification continues all the way down to 5 *talas* for Ganesha and the child Krishna, and 1 *tala* for the tortoise and fish avatar of Vishnu. Additionally, detailed measurements for the width of various parts of the body are provided down a central plumb line so that newly apprenticed sculptors may more easily learn their craft. However, the comparison makes it clear that this is only one of several systems used by the sculptors; while Chola sculptors appear to have subscribed to its use, their Hoysala counterparts apparently followed a different scheme. Recent scholarly attempts to come up with, say, a Gupta system of proportions, after a detailed and painstaking exercise of measuring a large corpus of images, have failed to yield definitive results.[33] Computer simulation, thus far attempted only with bronze images, may yield more rapid results, but this too appears to have been abandoned for now. A quick solution does not seem to be on the horizon, and the art historian's eye remains the best gauge.

Although idealized, the sculpted Indian physique incorporated the essential elements of the yogic body. The rear view of sculpted images, both male and female, reveals a spine held noticeably inward, with the shoulder blades drawn back and down. The abdominal muscles are released rather than being held in or tightened, so that one may visualize breath flowing through the body. In addition, many of the pirouetting bodies seen on temples should be reassessed in terms of yogic postures that feature bodily twists. It might be well to remember the artists' familiarity with yogic *asanas* in the Indian milieu in which the human body in a variety of yogic poses would have been readily visible.[34]

Alankara of the Female Form

Drapery is an integral part of *alankara* (ornament), and the female body, whether sculpt-ed or painted, is invariably a body adorned with fine, often translucent clothing. Indeed, what makes Indian sculpted imagery so very sensuous is the tantalizing reference to clothing; as Anne Hollander remarks in her study of the subject, an erotic awareness of the body invariably contains an awareness of clothing.[35] Sculptors in India depicted their figures seemingly bare, but a close observation will reveal—at ankles, waist, neck, and arms—hints of the delicate folds of fine drapery. Long skirts, consisting of a few yards of unsewn fabric, were pleated into folds at both ends and knotted together to create a va-riety of elaborate looped arrangements. Sculptors depicted these skirt folds quite promi-nently and with considerable attention, but they rarely allowed the folds to obstruct the view of the limbs, placing them so that they swing away from the body. Frequently, the lower limbs are so clearly visible that viewers assume they are unclothed; but once the eye is trained to notice the skirt folds, they seem to appear everywhere, so that one won-ders how they could possibly have been missed. No doubt, the adroit positioning of the fabric pleats indicates the artists' intention to emphasize the sensuous bodies of the figures unencumbered by details of drapery. This same desire on the part of the artists explains why sculpted women appear so uniformly bare-breasted. A close scrutiny of these figures will generally reveal traces of a scarf-like garment (*dupatta, odhni, davani*) intended to cover the breasts, but sculptors took the artistic liberty of moving the fabric aside in one manner or another. The fine, pleated scarf of the dancer from Jamsot (see figure 2), for instance, is displaced by her pirouetting movement and swings out behind her; the sari of the Didarganj *ganika* (see figures 3 and 4), which should indeed have cov-ered her torso completely, is treated as a heavy, pleated swath of fabric that has slipped off to rest in the crook of her arm; the pleated translucency of the fine, scarf-like wraps of the women on the walls of the Vamana temple in Khajuraho (figure 5), seen clearly in rear view, do little to cover their torsos, sliding down instead to afford a view of their breasts. With the warm Indian climate encouraging fine muslin clothing, the artists' re-sponse was invariably to resort to translucent drapery. On occasion, the artist dispensed with the pretense altogether, portraying his women freely without need for the artifice of clothing that has slipped to reveal their breasts.

It is important that we do not assume that the sculpted and painted images are an accurate reflection of prevalent practices and thence proceed to infer that partial nudity was the accepted norm in the ancient Indian milieu. Indeed, it has been stressed in a va-riety of artistic contexts that "what images tell us is how rarely they directly reflect institu-tions and behavior."[36] As scholars around the world agree, the human body of any tradition of sculpture and painting—be it Greek, Roman, or Renaissance—is a social construct and not a reflection of life as it was actually lived. Greek sculpture and vase paintings depict

Figure 5. Women, sandstone, Vamana temple, Khajuraho, Madhya Pradesh, ca. 1000.

nude males, tall and muscular, fighting, competing in sports, and taking part in city processions. But as Andrew Stewart points out, "Not only did Greeks not fight or go about the city naked, they did not look like their marbles and bronzes either."[37]

Confirmation of the use of drapery in India, often fine and diaphanous drapery, may be found in a wide range of literary sources. The first-century poet Ashvaghosha, author of the *Buddha-charita*, a Sanskrit poem on the life of the Buddha that we encountered briefly in chapter 1, often makes passing reference to women's clothing. One such passage occurs when King Suddhodana, realizing that his son Siddhartha is bent on leaving the palace in search of enlightenment, sends a messenger to the women of the palace urging them to use their utmost powers of seduction to lure the prince back to a life of pleasure: "Exert yourselves boldly, so that the good fortune of the king's family may not turn away from here."[38] The poet's many verses on the responses of the women include the following two:

> Another repeatedly let her blue garments slip down under
> the pretext of intoxication, and with her girdle partly seen
> she seemed like the night with the lightning flashing.

> Some walked up and down so as to make their golden zones tin-
> kle and displayed to him their hips veiled by diaphanous robes.[39]

The plays of Kalidasa contain frequent allusions to women's clothing. Shakun-tala, who lives in a forest hermitage, wears a bark dress that quite clearly covers her body from the breasts down. When she complains that her friend has fastened the garment too tightly, it is loosened, and she is teased and told that her swelling breasts, not her friend, are to blame.[40] In another play by Kalidasa, King Agnimitra describes Malavika as wearing "dazzling silks that drape discreetly."[41] And in the poem *Kumara-sambhava* (*Birth of Kumara*), Kalidasa describes Parvati, while tending to the god Shiva's needs, as wearing a dress "the color of the young sun," which she abandons for rough bark garments when she resorts to penance to win the god as husband.[42] When Parvati succeeds in her mission, the poet speaks of the dress she wears to take a premarital oil bath, followed by the white silks she dons for the wedding ceremony itself. In the poem *Megha-duta* (*Cloud Messenger*), Kalidasa describes the pleasures of Alaka, the city of the *yakshas*:

> Where the linen garments of women with lips like bimba fruit are loosened by the unbinding of the cloth ties of their undergarments which are removed by lovers with hands emboldened by lust.[43]

The Tamil poetry of southern India, too, clarifies that drapery is an integral part of *alankara*. For instance, we read of the young woman whose "swaying loins are draped in brightly dyed cloth";[44] a second who "puts on shimmering garments to enhance her radiance";[45] a third who "wrapped herself in an elegant gown";[46] and a fourth who "clothes herself in silk / crimson like the shining red water lily."[47] Certainly the word "naked" should have no place in the Indian artistic vocabulary, although one may indeed speak of the seemingly nude figures adorning the monuments of India.

Apart from silks and translucent fabrics, *alankara* implied the expected elements of abundant jewelry, blossoms wreathed into plaited braids, an elaborate system of hairstyling, and flower garlands. But it included much more in the form of cosmetics and unguents, including kohl, sandal-paste, perfumes, fragrant oils, and body paint or tattoos, as seen on the cheeks of the moon *yakshi* carved on a railing pillar surrounding the Buddhist stupa at Bharhut (figure 6). Hennaed designs on hands and feet still survive in India, but other types of body paint, clearly attested in both visual and literary texts, seem to have been abandoned, unless we view the modern *bindi* on women's foreheads as a surviving relic. When the *Gita-govinda*'s Radha, triumphant in her control over Krishna, commands him, "Paint a leaf design here with deer musk on Love's ritual vessel!" this was no mere poet's fancy, but a reflection of the reality of body paint.[48] Daud Ali points out that the seventh-century poet Bana describes in his *Kadambari* how Queen Vilasavati refrains from adornment in her grief over her failure to bear King Tarapida a child. The king questions

[handwritten marginal note: other adornment]

Figure 6. Chanda *yakshi*, sandstone, Bharhut stupa, Uttar Pradesh, ca. 100 B.C.E.

her thus: "Why haven't you put *alaktaka* dye on your feet . . . why is the ornamental design . . . not painted on your expansive breasts . . . why have the line decorations on your cheeks been washed off by your tears . . . why is your forehead without a *tilaka* mark . . . and your hair unbound?[49]

The *Tirukkailaya-nana-ula* gives us an interesting glimpse into the way that women of seven different age groups (a trope unique to Tamil poetics) dress and adorn themselves preparatory to encountering public gaze. Among them are the *petumpai* (a young girl eight to eleven years of age), the *mankai* (a nubile girl twelve to thirteen years old), the *matantai* (an ingénue fourteen to nineteen years of age), and the *arivai* (a lovely woman twenty to twenty-four years old).

The *petumpai*:

> She puts on a necklace of impeccable jewels
> and places rings on her delicate fingers
> while jeweled armlets glitter on her arms.[50]

The *mankai*:

> Beautified by the chain around her neck
> she puts on a lush garland teeming with lively bees;
> hoops decorate her ears

a sumptuous girdle enhances her

and the exquisite designs traced on her body gleam.[51]

The *matantai*:

A necklace of burnished pearls adorns her neck

and myriad gems crowd together

ringing out in clamor.

She deftly scents herself with flower essences, musk and salves

to achieve perfection within and without,

she puts on shimmering garments to increase her radiance

and places a circlet set with a crest jewel upon her forehead;

Taking up cooling sandalwood

she spreads it on her arms,

the bright sandal lending her its color.[52]

The *arivai*:

She adorns her feet with a pair of anklets

and stacks her wrists with heavy bangles

thick with encrusted gems.

She decks her hair with an impeccable garland

strung with a golden thread

and enlivens her shapely neck with jewels,

she is a match for Shri herself.[53]

In India, and especially in a public milieu, the body elegantly adorned is both appropriate and aesthetically appealing, while the unornamented form is unworthy of attention. In his *Kavi-priya* (*Poets' Delight*) of 1601, written in Braj, the major northern dialect of literary, precolonial India, the poet Keshavdas makes this quite clear:

A woman may be noble, she may have good features. She may have a nice complexion, be filled with love, be shapely. But without ornaments, my friend, she is not beautiful. The same goes for poetry.[54]

To be unornamented implies grief, and to this day, in the more traditional segments of society, the absence of ornament implies mourning and a death in the family. An inscription of a Shilahara king (other examples abound) testifies to the women of his defeated rival abandoning adornment:

(He) caused the ladies in the harems of his enemies, slain by his sharp sword drawn out (of its scabbard), to have

dangling (unbraided) hair, to discard necklaces from their
pitcher-like breasts, and to have eyes without collyrium.[55]

Belief in the necessity of ornamentation is the one aspect of Indian culture that many in the diaspora have the greatest difficulty setting aside in order to fit into the social pattern, the environment, in which they have chosen to live. To this day, Indian women of a certain generation, whether in India or overseas, wear a necklace, bangles, and earrings into a swimming pool or on a beach. The roots of such a practice date back over a thousand years. As David Smith points out in his study of the tenth-century *Hara-vijaya*, women take off their clothes to bathe but retain their ornaments, a practice that has nothing to do with worry about the safety of the jewels.[56] In a similar vein, a magnificent illustrated *Amaru-shataka* (*Hundred Verses on Amaru*) palm-leaf manuscript from Orissa, perhaps of the seventeenth century, depicts couples making love, having discarded their clothes but retained all their jeweled ornaments.[57]

An important function of ornament, explicitly affirmed by the *Tirukkailaya-nana-ula*, is to protect and safeguard its wearer—in this case, the women of the poem. Its phraseology is noteworthy: metaphorically speaking, the sound of her anklets keeps undesirables away, her bodice locks away her breast, armlets protect her arms, necklaces screen her neck, and earrings shelter her ears. Here is the poem's description of the *terivai* (a woman twenty-five to thirty years of age), as she adorns herself:

> Anklets are like drums, proclaiming
> "refined men may stay, but those who aren't must go!"
> knowing this, she puts them on her splendid feet.
> Knowing that there must be no unguarded movements to her loins
> she girds them with a fine dress and girdle,
> knowing that her charming breasts bewitch young men
> she quickly locks them away in an elegant bodice.
> With golden armlets she protects her bamboo-like arms,
> she screens her lovely neck with a fine necklace
> and gleaming earrings shelter her ears,
> as though cooling the passion of her lily-dark eyes
> she quells them with highlights of kohl.
> Her beauty torments everyone
> she bears the hallmarks of the goose's stride and the cuckoo's call.
> Carefully tied, raven hued,
> a crore of flowers worked into the plaits,
> no longer veiled within her dress
> falling low, free to cast its scent

her black braid exudes its misted nectars
She clothes herself in silk
crimson like the shining red waterlily
and paints a beautiful lily of saffron on her brow.[58]

Blake Wentworth suggests that apart from making a woman more attractive and providing her with protection, ornament contains, limits, and perhaps restricts the awesome power of women's fertility and eroticism, rendering those around them safe.[59] In the *Maha-bharata* story of Draupadi's vow to avenge her humiliation at the hands of the Kauravas, it is made clear that when a woman, here Draupadi, no longer oils and braids her hair, ornamenting it with blossoms, but instead chooses to let it loose and unadorned, she becomes dangerous.[60] The multiple ways in which ornament worked—its role in enhancing beauty, ensuring protection, and providing containment—are all brought home graphically by this ninth-century Tamil poem. It is in this context that we must consider the extravagantly adorned images featured on the walls of Indian monuments. To ornament or not to ornament was not the sculptor's option; it was mandated by its underlying significance. It may be useful, too, to note the dangerous ornaments, such as garlands of skulls and earrings of human corpses, worn by fearsome, powerful, yet dangerous goddesses like Kali.

Appropriate "ornament" went beyond what has been discussed thus far; it involved a range of courtly conventions that included gait and posture, graceful sitting, appropriate gestures, and a general protocol of body language. A woman's walk and stance was as much feted in literature, and translated into sculpture and painting, as her eyes and eyebrows. Ideas of ornament were also extended to relations between people so that, as Ali succinctly phrases it in his study of courtly culture, ornamentation is "a cultural figuration of practices and ideas so vast and significant as to subsume within it both anatomical and gestural beauty."[61]

Queens and Princesses

What applies to elite town and city women applies doubly to the beauty, charms, and accomplishments of women at the court, whether the queen herself or the wife of a general or chief minister. Standing in dignified elegance in a niche on the southern wall of the Nageshvara temple in Kumbakonam is the gorgeous figure of an unidentified queen, perhaps a member of the Chola royal family, which seems to have been responsible for building the temple (figure 7). Exceedingly slender, with a small, narrow waist and luscious breasts, she is carved so deeply that she seems about to step out of her niche. One hand rests by her side, while the other holds up a lotus bud. Her long skirt, slung way below her navel and held in place by hip-bands, clings to her limbs in gentle folds with

Figure 7. Queen, granite, Nageshvara temple, Kumbakonam, Tamil Nadu, ninth century.

its pleated ends rippling downward. She has an exquisite oval face with full lips, delicate nose, and elongated eyes that glance downward. Her hair is styled in an amazing, blossom-studded arrangement on the top of her head, and completing her adornment are a forehead band, large earrings, necklaces, wide armlets, a stack of bangles, and rings on all ten fingers. It has been suggested by one scholar that she might represent Queen Kaushalya, mother of Rama.[62] Whether she represents a mythical queen or a queen contemporary with the temple's construction around the end of the ninth century, she presents a sensuous portrait of royalty that was clearly in the approved mode.

It is rare to find portrait sculptures of specific queens. An inscription speaks of a bronze image of the Chola queen Sembiyan Mahadevi, installed in the Kailasanatha Shiva temple in the town of Sembiyan Mahadevi (named after the queen). The record makes monetary provisions to ensure that on the queen's birthday, the image would be taken on a processional tour of the town and that Brahmins and townsfolk would be invited to a lavish celebratory feast. In premodern times, royal portraiture was invariably stylized, usually modeled to closely resemble divine figures, and it incorporated little in the way of specificity or verisimilitude. Devotees would likely have "recognized" the bronze as Sembiyan Mahadevi only because it was brought out in procession on the specific occasion of the queen's birthday honors. We know from inscriptions that Rajaraja's great temple at Tanjavur contained bronze "portraits" of Rajaraja himself and his chief queen, Lokamahadevi, as well as of his parents, King Sundara Chola and Queen Vanavan Mahadevi. Unfortunately, none of these images appears to have survived.[63]

I have suggested elsewhere the possibility that a bronze image in the Freer Gallery of Art, Washington, D.C., that has generally been taken to represent the goddess Uma may in fact be a "portrait" of Queen Sembiyan Mahadevi.[64] The argument on the interchangeable nature of divine and royal portraiture gains strength from Bhasa's fifth-century(?) drama *Pratima-lakshana* (*Cognizances of an Image*).[65] The story narrates that Prince Bharata, of *Ramayana* fame, returned to Ayodhya, unaware that his father had died in the interim. He enters a newly built pavilion containing four beautiful sculpted images, ponders their identity, and, concluding that they must represent the gods, prepares to worship them. At that moment, the keeper of the pavilion arrives, recognizes Prince Bharata, and identifies the first three images as those of Bharata's great-great-grandfather Dilipa, great-grandfather Raghu, and grandfather Aja. Bharata, inferring that the fourth image could only be that of his own father, who must hence be dead, breaks down and weeps. If the audience watching the drama did not find anything strange in Bharata failing to recognize his own father, it could only be because the stylization of royal portraits, modeled on divine images, was an accepted norm. We shall see later that only inscribed labels, or prior knowledge that a structure was a dynastic shrine, would yield clues to the identity of royal portraits.

Imagery chosen for Maya—a very special queen, wife of the chieftain Suddhodhana and mother of Siddhartha, who later became the Buddha—reveals the same persisting characteristic of idealized representation. Painted in a mural on the walls of the rock-cut Buddhist monastery of Ajanta is a slender, curvaceous figure, adorned with exquisite jewels and clad in an apparently translucent garment (figure 8). Standing in a pillared pavilion, leaning languorously against one of its columns as though pondering some deep secret, she looks like any gorgeous princess or queen. In the mode typical of continuous narrative, we see her a second time, to the left of the first scene, seated with Suddhodhana as they confer with courtiers. Few viewers unfamiliar with the art of India would visualize this gorgeous female as having any connection with the sacred. But she has, for she is Maya, the lovely young mother of

Figure 8. Queen Maya, painted mural, Vihara 2, Ajanta caves, Maharashtra, fifth century.

the Buddha. Standing Maya is seen in a reverie, obviously pondering the meaning of her dream of the night before, in which she saw a white elephant entering her womb. To the left, soothsayers at the court interpret her dream, telling her that she will give birth to a son who will be a universal conqueror. But they added a caveat. Either he would conquer the territories of this earth, or he would conquer the minds of men; if the latter, he would do so after renouncing the world. This painted mural, which emphasizes the aspect of Maya as the sensuously beautiful queen and downplays her role as the "sacred" mother of the Buddha-to-be, adorns the walls of a monastic residential *vihara* at Ajanta. The fifth-century artist of this mural saw nothing incongruous in his depiction of Maya as a sensuous beauty; neither did the monks who prayed and meditated within the painted *vihara*. Both artists and monks were part and parcel of a cultural milieu, to be explored more fully in chapter 4, in which bodily beauty was viewed as inseparable from innate spiritual beauty. In the context of sacred imagery, we shall see, the two were intertwined and inextricably linked.

When we turn to the literary material contained in inscriptions, we find a resounding reinforcement of the idea that the queen or elite female patron is always a woman of enthralling beauty. To demonstrate how female physical allure is applauded as publicly as female piety, I shall present three examples: one from a Jain dedication, the second from a Buddhist donor, and the third from a Hindu milieu. Two of the inscriptions are in Kannada, and the third is in Sanskrit.

During the twelfth century, Mailama, wife of Prince Beta, who was a feudatory of the Chalukyan monarch Vikramaditya VI, built a temple for the Jain goddess Kadalalaya at Hanumkonda near Warangal in southern Karnataka. The Kannada inscription that records her construction of the temple and her gift of land to provide for sustained worship dates to the reign of her son, and is inscribed on a granite pillar that stands in front of the temple. In applauding her gift, the epigraph praises the beauty of her body as fully as her devotion to the Jain faith:

> Mailama, whose face was (as pleasant as) the moon (and) whose lips were (red like) the bimba (fruit), the colour of whose body was praised as being fair and her full breasts as being golden pots, (who was) the veritable lady Bharati, a Sasanadevi (par excellence) acceptable to the doctrines of the Jain religion (and) decidedly (the goddess) Lakshmi (but) without (the latter's) fickleness.
>
> (verse 6)

> Who, who in this world does not extol Mailama saying: "The lotus-born (Brahma) having produced, out of the five gems (such) as best suited the portion of the body (under creation), the (several) limbs with (their) adjuncts from the feet right up to those tremulous curls, (and) having filled (them) with happiness, grace, joy (and) beauty (which he) culled from among the celestial nymphs—(he) loved (to see) this gem of womankind (—his own creation)."
>
> (verse 7)

> The whole, whole world praise deservedly the wife of the minister Beta saying: "She possesses praiseworthy beauty; she is full of luster; (she) is a Rati in dalliance; (she) is the lady Sri (Lakshmi); (she) is the lady Ghantaki [a Jain reference]; (she) is the lady Vani (Sarasvati)."[66]
>
> (verse 8)

In similar vein, when Kumaradevi, wife of King Govindachandra of Kanauj, gifted a Buddhist *vihara* at Sarnath, both her physical beauty and her devotion to the Buddha were acclaimed in a set of Sanskrit verses of the twelfth century inscribed on a stone slab. The poet uses the idea that Brahma was filled with wonder at the excellence of his own creation, a conceit frequently encountered in Indian literature:

> After having created her, Brahma was filled with pride at his
> own cleverness in applying his art; excelled by her face the
> moon, being ashamed, remains in the air, rises at night, be-
> comes impure and subsequently full of spots; how can this,
> her marvelous beauty, be described by people like us?[67]

The verse that follows elaborates on her beauty, which, according to the poet, outdoes
that of the goddess Parvati, and he then devotes the next verse to her devotion to the
Buddha: "Her mind was set on religion [*dharma*] alone; her desire was bent on virtues
[*guna*]; she had undertaken to lay in a store of merit [*punya*]; she found a noble satis-
faction in bestowing gifts [*dana*]." But the poet is unable to get away from her physical
beauty. He continues: "[H]er gait was that of an elephant [a reference to a woman's full
hips, which slow her down];[68] her appearance charming to the eye."

The Hindu context is no different. The Kadamba queen Mailaladevi donated a
town and garden as an endowment to support a Shiva temple near Dharwar in the year
1125, and a Kannada inscription records her beauty in fulsome terms as being greater
than that of Rambha and Tilottama (celestial nymphs of ravishing beauty):

> The beauty of this Mailaladevi surpasses (that of) Ramb-
> ha and Tilottama, much more so (that of) mortal women;
> it is charming, look you, verily a hundred times.
>
> (verse 31)

> "This is a sea of the nectar of loveliness that has been be-
> held; this grace is the play of the Moon's brows; a regular
> expansion of beauty . . . verily, look you, a wealth of jas-
> mine; this is Sarasvati's natal place": in these words people
> (extol) the abundance of the greatness of Mailaladevi's
> beauty that has arisen in this world.[69]

The inscription moves into the mode of high hyperbole (Sanskrit, *atishayokti*), an approved mode of poetic embellishment, in specifying that the queen's grace is twice that
of Parvati and her virtue twelve times that of Sita!

These three examples from an entire range of similarly constructed public poems, composed as official poetry to applaud the patron who constructed a temple or *vihara* or who made a generous donation to an already existing shrine, are instructive. Some
of the donations were made by queen mothers during the reign of their sons; while they
were certainly not in their prime, it is clear that physical beauty was an expected adjunct
to piety. The multiple instances that one might cite of the use of similar tropes indicate

this to be the official stance! In addition, as we shall see shortly, queens were supposed to be well versed in the ways of sexual pleasure, and numerous epigraphs evoke Rati, the celebrated consort of Kama, god of love, applauding queens as "a Rati in dalliance."[70]

Each of these women was, of course, a mother whose womb had borne a princely hero, and an allusion to this role frequently follows the fulsome description of her beauty. The following verse from a lengthy Sanskrit stone inscription at Khajuraho describes the glory of the Chandella queen Kanchuka, wife of King Dhanga and mother of King Yashovarman, who built the Lakshmana temple:

> As her complexion was of golden hue, the pair of eyes like
> sapphire and the moonstone, her hands and feet having the
> luster of ruby, the lips like coral and the mind pure like the
> pearl just released from its parent shell, this lady of unique
> constancy became a jewel among women and a matchless
> ornament of the world.
> From her was born his son Yasovarmadeva[71]

We may note here that the queen herself is seen as an ornament for this world, and we shall see that the monarch, too, was often extolled with similar phraseology. We cannot help but note the linkage of beauty with fertility, as well as virtue, and perhaps even with eugenics in producing a perfect heir to the kingdom.

The Male Form

The Idealized Body and *Alankara*

The male figure portrayed on the temples, stupas, and caves of India is smooth, slender, and pliant, with body hair noticeably absent, and displays an idealized gender portrayal characteristic of the Indian tradition. It is a far cry from the musculature of Greek and Roman statues poised in action and, in this respect, bears a closer resemblance to the traditions of China, Korea, and Japan. The term "beautiful" may be applied to the portrayal in art of the Indian male physique, with its gentle oval face, elongated eyes, and full lips, set off by long hair pulled back into an elegant knot. It bears repetition here that the literature of India employed equally for men and women many of the words that connote beauty, such as *sundara*, *charu*, and *kanta* as well as terms with the prefix *su*. Men frequently shared with women a set of established poetic tropes, such as faces that put the moon to shame, eyes that outdo the lotus, arched eyebrows, feet and hands like lotuses, full red lips, and gleaming toenails.[72] Like women, men adorned themselves with appropriate ornament (*alankara*). In this context, we may recall the legendary ease with

Figure 9. Future Buddha Maitreya, copper alloy with gilding and color,
Nepal, ninth to tenth century.

which Krishna, on many an occasion, disguised himself as a woman to get access to his beloved Radha. Seventeenth- and eighteenth-century painted manuscripts all emphasize this artistic ideal, whether they portray Krishna in the guise of a female bangle-seller, as a participant in the all-women's Holi celebrations, or as a beautiful male figure bathing with the *gopis* in the waters of the Jamuna.

It is perhaps not really surprising that nine out of ten people unfamiliar with South Asian art are likely to use the pronoun "she" when exclaiming over the beauty of a sensuous Nepalese image of the future Buddha Maitreya (figure 9). Wearing a patterned dhoti with a slanting hip-band, Maitreya is depicted as a beautiful figure, swaying gently as he stands, with a slender torso; sloping shoulders; long, pliant arms of which one holds his attribute, the water vessel; smooth, tapering thighs; and neat ankles. His exquisite face has perfectly arched eyebrows, elongated eyes, full lips, and hair piled up in elaborate curled locks. A range of jewelry adorns him, from his crown, necklace, sacred thread, and ear-rings, to armlets, bracelets, and anklets. With the exception of images of the renunciant

Figure 10. *Dvarapala*, sandstone, north gateway,
Sanchi stupa, Madhya Pradesh, first century B.C.E.

Jinas, artists generally avoided the issue of the portrayal of the male sexual organs by the strategic placement of the hip-belt or the drapery folds. However, rare instances do occur in which an artist created a molded curve. The portrayal of the outline of the scrotum occurs, for instance, on the slender, sensuous figure of a *dvarapala* (guardian warrior), clad in a transparent dhoti, carved against a pillar of the northern gateway of the Buddhist stupa at Sanchi during the first century B.C.E. (figure 10).[73] The artists of the *dvarapalas* on the other three gateways avoided this issue by resorting to the central placement of the dhoti folds.

Gender similarity is further encountered in the elaborately styled, long hair that male figures sported in premodern times, as well as the rich jewelry they wore. Embracing couples on the walls of the Khajuraho temples of central India have in common long hair, often pulled back into similarly elaborate knots; jeweled forehead bands; and large earrings (figure 11). The abundant jewelry worn by the men includes rows of necklaces short and long, armlets, bangles, anklets, and rings; male beauty, too, was considered enhanced by rich and varied jewelry. And like the women, the men are clad in fine, translucent drapery. It is worth noting the emphasis placed on adornment in Vatsyayana's *Kama-sutra* (*Text on Erotic Love*), a text that probably dates to the third century. In its list of the sixty-four arts that every cultivated man-about-town (*nagaraka*) should master, as many as fifteen relate to adornment: nine deal with the ornamentation of the body, and six concern the adornment of one's surroundings.[74]

Figure 11. Embracing couple, sandstone, Lakshmana temple, Khajuraho, Madhya Pradesh, ca. 954.

Kings and Princes

The importance accorded in eulogistic inscriptions and literary texts to the monarch's valor in battle, his piety and righteousness, and his *dakshinya* (gracious courtesy and gentility) is always accompanied by an emphasis on his physical beauty, sexual attraction, and mastery of the erotic arts. The art-historical material, however, is regrettably meager, and the few stone images of kings and monarchs that survive are badly damaged. The earliest known set of royal portraits is sculpted in bas-relief into the rock face of a cave at Naneghat, cut into the walls of a mountain pass on a trade route that led through the Western Ghats to ports along the west coast of India. These images are totally destroyed, leaving intact only their inscribed labels. Carved at the behest of Queen Nayanika, the images commence with the founder of the Satavahana dynasty, followed by Queen Nayanika herself and her husband, Satakarni (the third dynastic monarch), three princes, and a general. While the destruction of what seem to be the earliest full-size Indian royal portraits—they may date to around 70 b.c.e.—is deeply regrettable, it is almost certain that the figures were stylized images, identifiable by their labels rather than by physical resemblance. We have seen from Bhasa's *Pratima-lakshana* that verisimilitude was never the favored ideal. Additionally, Bhavabhuti's eighth-century play *Uttara-rama-charita* (*Rama's Last Act*), which commences with Rama, Sita, and Lakshmana viewing a set of painted murals of their life, depicts them recognizing episodes due to the unique setting, with nothing to suggest recognition of their own "portraits" because of any actual resemblance.[75]

The Kushan rulers of the first century c.e. erected royal shrines, one of which was located at Mat, just outside the town of Mathura. Remains of only three royal images survive, one sitting and two standing, all unfortunately damaged and lacking their heads, but identified by inscriptions along the body of each image itself. Emperor Kanishka is portrayed as an imperious figure, wearing a heavy woolen military mantle and padded boots and leaning lightly on his sword, which rests within its scabbard. His body beneath is totally concealed, and the emphasis is on the hierarchic authority conveyed by the silhouette of the cloak. The official Kushan costume of the Central Asian steppes could hardly have been worn on a regular basis in the heat of the plains of Mathura. It was chosen for the portraits in the royal shrine presumably because, as "foreigners" ruling India, the Kushans sought to convey authority and assert their legitimate right to rule. Kushan coins likewise portray hierarchic images of royalty, clad in the official military-style mantle, boots, and tall conical headdress, all of which speak emphatically of authority and power.

By contrast, Gupta gold coins portray sinuous images of the monarchs, tall and slender, and swaying gently as they stand, all with haloes to emphasize their royal status. Although the coins are worn out through circulation, one can decipher sufficient details on them to permit the use of the term "royal portraiture" (figure 12). On one coin, Samudragupta (r. ca. 335–376) stands frontally, although with his face in profile, wearing a short tunic over a short dhoti and holding the typical, double-curved Indian bow in his left hand. Beside him is a pedestal topped with an owl, and beneath the upraised arm that holds the bow are the three letters *sa mu dra*, clearly engraved from top to bottom. That valor was a vital quality of a monarch is seen in a coin on which the ruler is portrayed as the beautiful hero battling a lion

Figure 12. Portrait coins of Samudragupta, gold, ca. 355–376.

that rears at him from the left edge of the coin. The broad-chested, narrow-waisted monarch with muscular thighs stands with his right foot planted on the ground and his left foot raised on a rock or mound. With his left hand, he reaches into the quiver slung on his back to pull out an arrow, while his outstretched right hand holds the bow. The range of coin imagery makes it evident that there is more to monarchy than battle-worthiness; mastery of the sixty-four arts was an expected accomplishment. One coin portrays Samudragupta as a musician playing the lyre, seated elegantly on a low couch with his right leg bent and placed on the seat and his left leg resting on the ground. Yet another gold coin depicts him as the beautiful monarch accompanied by his beloved queen. Wearing a tunic over a long dhoti, Samudragupta holds a staff in his left hand and with his right hand he raises the queen's chin in an intimate gesture of love. The queen is portrayed with voluptuous breasts, a slender waist, long limbs, and translucent, flowing drapery that reveals her limbs. Only gold coins have been considered here because they were not part of everyday exchange, and as a result their imagery is better preserved than that on the copper coins of daily use, which are badly abraded. It should not surprise us to find sensuous imagery on Gupta coinage. After all, the poet Kalidasa, probably writing at a Gupta court soon after these coins were minted, laid great emphasis on the beauty of the monarch. In his *Raghu-vamsha* (*Family of Raghu*), he describes Dilipa, founder of the Raghu dynasty, as "a king refreshing, cool and like the moon, the purest of great Manu's line . . . broad-chested, tall, with shoulders like the bull's, with rounded arms and body strong befitting well his royal duties high."[76]

At the Pallava port town of Mamallapuram, the Adi-varaha cave of the seventh century, dedicated to Vishnu in his avatar of the great boar Varaha, carries two royal portrait groups along the side walls where they meet the rear wall. The right wall features a monarch, with broad shoulders and exceedingly narrow torso, standing in frontal view but pointing with his right hand toward the shrine at the center of the rear wall. With his left hand, he grasps the wrist of his chief queen, who stands demurely behind him, followed by a second queen. Both queens are strikingly sensuous figures with high, rounded breasts, tiny waists, and limbs revealed by translucent drapery. The inscribed label above the panel reads "Pallava king Mahendra." The opposite wall features a seated monarch with similar broad shoulders and narrow torso, with his left leg folded on the seat and his right leg pendant. He is flanked by standing queens of the same sensuous characterization as those just encountered. The label above reads "Pallava king Simhavishnu." It is most likely that the seated monarch is Simhavishnu (r. ca. 555–590) and the standing figure is his son and successor, Mahendra I (r. ca. 590–630).[77] Without the labels, however, it would have been impossible to identify the monarchs, both of whom are generic in portrayal, with bare torso and a long lower garment.

Analogous in their nonspecific portrayal of the Pallava monarchs are the bas-reliefs that lay out the genealogy of the Pallavas along the walls of the pillared cloister enclosing the Vaikuntha Perumal temple in Kanchipuram.[78] Built in the eighth century by the later Pallava king, Nandivarman Pallavamalla, the reliefs are carved in two horizontal levels, separated by a narrow band intended to carry inscriptions; however, it is only in the final third of the reliefs, devoted to Pallavamalla himself, that these inscriptions have been added. Identification of the earlier monarchs remains sheer guesswork, since all are similarly portrayed, wearing identical garments and crowns, with generalized, nonspecific faces. Such tentative identifications as are possible are largely the result of moving from one coronation lustration scene to the next and generally working backward from Pallavamalla. And even then, the coronation of Simhavishnu looks exactly like the coronation of Pallavamalla.[79]

Among the few identifiable royal portraits from premodern India are images of King Narasimhadeva of the Ganga dynasty (r. 1238–1264), who was responsible for the construction of the imposing sun temple at Konarak. A set of four damaged panels, cut in deep relief in a fine-grained chlorite, depict the king, accompanied by members of his court, engaging in a series of activities that may perhaps be read to indicate his observance of the four goals of life. This must remain a mere suggestion, since we cannot be sure if other panels, lost today, once existed. A panel portraying the seated monarch holding a manuscript in one hand and perhaps dispensing justice and attending to affairs of the court could be read as representing *dharma*. *Artha* is perhaps suggested by his portrayal as an archer, a professional status for some. *Kama* is indicated by Narasimhadeva sitting on a swing in the women's quarters with queens and female attendants. *Moksha* may be implied by the portrayal of the king receiving blessings from his guru in front of three images: a Shiva linga, the Jagannatha image of Vishnu, and Devi killing the buffalo-demon. These panels once adorned the 6-foot-high pedestal of the monumental image of the Sun God enshrined within the Konarak sanctum.

Narasimhadeva is portrayed from one panel to the next as a mustached male, wearing a tiara on his long hair, which is pulled to the right side of his face to form a magnificent chignon studded with jewels. His face is moon-shaped, with strongly arched eyebrows, elongated eyes, a sharp nose, and a pert chin. His vigorous body displays broad shoulders, a full chest, a narrow waist, and sturdy thighs and calves. He wears a short dhoti with an elaborately worked border that is held in place by a jeweled belt; the edge of his dhoti spreads out, fan-shaped, in pleated folds, and his upper cloth is seen behind him as a scarf-like throw. Elaborate earrings, rows of necklaces, a sacred thread, rich armlets, anklets, and rings on all his toes complete his adornment. In the archery panel, he stands poised for action, with feet planted widely apart; attendants stand behind him, and a series of onlookers face him with hands in the *anjali* gesture of adoration. Today, both the bow and the arrow are broken away (figure 13). When Narasimhadeva sits on the swing, a wooden plank suspended by chains, his left leg is bent on the seat and his right is pendant. Apart from two small males depicted behind him (perhaps the eunuchs who guard

Figure 13. King Narasimhadeva as an archer, chlorite, Konarak temple, Orissa.

Figure 14. King Narasimhadeva on a swing, chlorite, Konarak temple, Orissa.

the women's quarters of a palace), all the other figures, whether standing beside the swing or sitting at his feet, are female and hold either fly whisks or musical instruments (figure 14). Although his body and its ornament follow established poetic and artistic tropes, Narasimhadeva is recognizable from one portrait to the next by his mustached visage. Yet, as a precautionary note, we must keep in mind that he is the only Ganga ruler of whom we have a portrait. Perhaps if similarly stylized images of his various predecessors had survived, we would have complained of the difficulty of distinguishing one ruler from the next.

As we turn from the visual to the verbal, a point to be emphasized is the homology, even identity, that Hindu monarchs claimed with the god Vishnu, together with his consorts Lakshmi (Shri), goddess of fortune, and Bhu, earth goddess. The rescue of Bhu by Vishnu's Varaha avatar lent itself perfectly to an aspiring *chakravartin's* territorial claims. Monarch after monarch claimed Vishnu-like status by proclaiming that they, too, had rescued the earth (*bhu*) and that they, too, were the abode of the goddess of fortune (*shri*). In fact, one scholar has pointed to the need to reexamine the very large number of imposing sculptures of Vishnu Varaha—both in anthropomorphic form with a boar head and in purely theriomorphic form as a giant boar, holding up the earth goddess, whom he has rescued from the cosmic waters—that exist at sites of the Gupta period.[80] This homology was proudly adopted even by those monarchs who were staunch Shaivites, as seen in the invariable preamble to all inscriptions of Rajaraja Chola (r. 985–1014). To identify a record as belonging to Rajaraja I, all we need is its opening: "one who took as wife the goddess earth just as he had already taken the goddess of wealth."[81] When the seventh-century Chalukyan monarch Pulakesin II wished to make this homology evident, his inscription states that the sandal oil smeared on his body "is rubbed off by [the clinging of] the bulky breasts of the goddess of fortune who practices [toward him] the vow of treating a husband like a god."[82] The similarity of phraseology between this record and one we shall encounter in chapter 4 that speaks of the lines of color being rubbed off Lakshmi's breasts and onto Vishnu's chest is striking confirmation of the intention.[83] One further example serves to make the point: concerning the Paramara prince Madanadeva, a Sanskrit inscription of the year 1080 states, with considerable audacity, that the goddess Sri (Lakshmi) was more attracted to the prince than to Vishnu himself: "Finding him arisen in his career, broad of breast, charming, Sri, as I imagine, held no [more] amorous commerce with her ancient husband [Vishnu]."[84]

Both literary texts and eulogistic inscriptions present a similar, repeated emphasis on the monarch's physical attractiveness and beauty, which are accorded importance as indispensable attributes, side by side with his valor, gentility, and piety. On earth, the king was the supreme ruler who ensured the felicity of his subjects. Beauty was listed among the *gunas* (virtues), and the beautiful monarch's power to captivate the hearts of his subjects and, in particular, the magnetic power of his personality over the hearts of women were hailed as vital royal attributes.[85] His physical beauty, enhanced with scintillating ornament, and his consequent splendor were given a status equal to the excellence of his attainments, character, integrity, and munificence. In the seventh-century prose biography of the historical king Harsha of Kanauj, the beauty of the king's body, appropriately adorned, is described in great detail by his court poet Bana:

> His two thighs were like ruby pillars . . . like two sandal
>   trees . . . like two streams from the ocean of beauty . . .
>   like two huge tusks . . .

> He shone with his broad chest . . .

> His neck was encircled by a necklace of pearls . . .

> His breast was wrapped in a fold of rays from the pearls in
>   his necklace . . .

> . . . the redness of his lip . . .

> . . . the gleaming flashes of his teeth . . .

... the perfume of his breath ...

... the brightness of his milk-white eye

... broad forehead

... his locks encircled by a wreath of white jasmine flowers
...

> He was consecrated by the light of the pearls in his top-knot
> and the dark rays of emeralds, as they crossed in their
> intermingling, as if the braid-like streams of the united
> Yamuna and Ganges had come of their own accord from
> Prayaga.[86]

The panegyric inscriptions of the various monarchs of India, irrespective of chronology or topography, sound remarkably similar. The monarch Sundara Chola (r. 957–969) was one "who quite surpassed Cupid in beauty,"[87] while the Chola emperor Rajaraja I (r. 985–1014) "had a body as beautiful as Cupid, and handsome lotus eyes."[88] Chalukya king Pulakesin II (r. 610–642) was "the sole aim of the arrows which are the eyes of nice young women,"[89] and Chalukya Vikramaditya's son was one "who to woman-kind was like the god of love."[90] A Rashtrakuta copper-plate inscription of the year 915, whose specific purpose was to record the gift of certain villages, describes King Jagattunga as one "who surpassed the beauty of Madana" and was "the ravisher of the hearts of beautiful women [sundari-chitta-hari]";[91] his son Indraraja (r. 915–927) "dwelt in the hearts of beautiful women";[92] and Rashtrakuta Krishna III's (r. 939–966) body "had a dark glossy colour, long arms, and a broad massive chest."[93] An inscription of the twelfth century from Huli in the Belgaum district, written in old Kannada, speaks thus of the chieftain Malapayya: "The souls of choice damsels became a place for the shafts of the god of the flower arrows . . . through the lord Malapayya, by reason of the perfection of his grace of form."[94] Being an adept in the art of love was another trait that was much hailed; accordingly, the Chandella king Paramarddi (r. 1166–1202) is described as "a guide in the mysteries of amorous and heroic senti-ments [shringara-vira-vratacharya]."[95] These concepts of male physical beauty and sexual attractiveness, considered in their entirety, are like a resounding echo of the point made by Irene Winter in the context of ancient Mesopotamia: that sexuality was linked to potency, in turn to male vigor, in turn to authority and dominance, and hence to the right to rule.[96]

The symbolism attached to the human body in Hindu ritual, mentioned in chapter 1, is emphasized and intensified in the royal *abhisheka* (bathing ceremonial of *[one of the Vedic rituals?]* coronation), which invests the king with extraordinary powers. As Ronald Inden has pointed out, such bathing was no mere purification but an act by which the king's body was imbued with divine energy. Inden maintains that an elaborate bathing ceremony was part of every major ritual connected with the establishment or reaffirmation of kingship and authority.[97] One especially relevant part of the coronation bathing ceremony involved daubing the different parts of the king's body with soil brought from various parts of the kingdom to symbolize "a kind of extraordinary marriage of the king and the earth, his bride"—a clear reference to his dominion over the earth conferred through symbolic ritual.[98] Its importance in this context is its emphasis on the centrality of the human body, here that of the monarch. Royal power and the authority to rule were vested in the dynamic and beautiful body of the king.

The comparison of a monarch's territorial conquests to his conquest over the body of a woman is an accepted trope in the Indian poetic tradition.[99] Ronald Davidson has pointed to another well-attested phenomenon in which "war became depicted as a facet of the erotic play of the king," suggesting that "the eroticization of warfare served the purpose of belligerence."[100] Allison Busch draws attention to an example of such eroticization, through an unusual use of the *nakh-sikh* (toenail-to-head) convention of beauty, contained in the Braj poet Keshavdas's 1607 poem on his patron, Bir Singh Deo of Orchha. He constructs the army contingents of the enemy in terms of a sexualized woman whom Bir Singh confronts as bridegroom. The following two verses give an idea of such a construct:

> 18. The Kanaujiyas were her beautiful bodice; think of the Karachulis as her firm breasts. The supremely clever Pavaiyas were her hands; the lion-like kings her freshly manicured fingernails.

> 19. The Kosala kings were her waist; the Yadavas her two thighs. The Kaikeyas were said to be her shoot-like feet. The Tomars were love, and the Pariharas her heart. The Rathores were her garment, and the Pamars her beauty.[101]

Equally remarkable is the manner in which the Rashtrakuta king Dantidurga's many territorial conquests are described in the specific terms of human lovemaking. The inscription seems to suggest that the authority to rule and the manner of a monarch's dominance lie in his ability to conquer territories, not by wresting them violently and making them submit by force, but by tactfully coaxing them into a willing surrender. His strategy of territorial conquest, juxtaposed with love-play with his beloved, is brought out in graphic detail:

> The hand [that is, prowess] of this (prince) matchless in bat-
> tle, having (first) established itself on the beautiful lowermost
> region of the earth, and having again overcome in a gentle
> manner at its own will the central region (Madhyadesha),
> again established itself in the province of Kanchi, just as the
> hand (of a lover), after (first) establishing itself on the hips of
> a woman, attractive to the heart [*hridaya hari*], and pressing
> again gently at her will (her) waist, again establishes itself on
> the region (below the waist) where the girdle (is worn).[102]

Kanchi, in this inscription, is a word with *shlesha* (double meaning); it makes reference
both to the town of Kanchipuram, over which the monarch has triumphed, and to the
hip-girdle (*kanchi*) on the body of a woman whom he has similarly conquered.

The importance of ornament for a *kshatriya* monarch or chieftain is emphasized in a number of textual sources, including the Jain *Kalpa-sutra*, which narrates the
lives of the Jain liberators, the Jinas. The adornment of *kshatriya* Siddhartha, whose wife
Trishala was chosen to bear in her womb the Jina Mahavira, is described in extraordinary detail:

> He dressed in precious and best of robes,
> had his body rubbed with soft and scented *gosirsa* and
>   sandal pastes,
> after this were celebrated and performed hundreds of after-
>   bath pleasant, blissful and blest ceremonies,
> then were placed on him a wreath of flowers purified by the
>   spray of sandal paste and a gold necklace set with pearls,
> a three-fold necklace of pearls, with a pearl pendant dang-
>   ling therefrom,
> a golden zone at the waist, a collar round his neck, rings on
>   his tender fingers, bangles and bracelets adorning the
>   arms, ear-rings brightening the face, and a shining
>   crown
> —all these imparting extra grace to his charming person
> . . . well-dressed and well-decorated, he looked like the
>   *kalpa* tree, the leader of men.[103]

Bodily beauty and adornment of a monarch were considered important, regardless of
his connection with a faith that stressed the primacy of renunciation and penance in the
context of advanced spirituality.

The *Ula* (processional) genre of Tamil poetry, encountered earlier with the god as the protagonist, was utilized equally to celebrate the earthly monarch. Ottukutar, court poet to two successive Chola monarchs—Kulottunga I (r. 1070–1125) and Vikrama Chola (r. ca. 1120–1135)—wrote *Ula* poems that focused on them. He describes the *alankara* of the monarchs, indicating its crucial importance to kingship and state welfare. *Alankara* increased the beauty of the king, and the monarch's attractiveness was one vital feature in ensuring the prosperity, fame, and welfare of the kingdom. The excerpt that follows is from Daud Ali's translation of the *Vikrama-chola-ula* (*Procession of Vikrama Chola*):

> On his face, which was like a bloomed flower around which
> bees thronged, where the Goddess of Eloquence resided,
> Sarasvati, glittered makara earrings.
> On his shoulders, where the broad-breasted Goddess of the
> Earth, stayed, were epaulets brilliant with gems.
> On his hand, where the unsteady Goddess of Fame was
> fixed, sparkled a bracelet of gems.
> On his chest, where the Goddess of Fortune lovingly em-
> braced him, shone with increasing splendour a jewel
> from the sea.
> On his hip, where the beautiful Goddess of Victory, free of
> distress, resided, was a beautiful sword.
> Having put on numerous rare ornaments of suitably lofty
> beauty, he obtained matchless elegance and grace such
> that it seemed as if Siva had bestowed on him, while he
> was bowing with the crest of his crown, the beauty he
> had once attained as "respect" from Kama's bow.
> The king then departed from the palace . . .[104]

Several scholars have made the point that in these *Ula* poems, the king (or the god) remains distant and detached and apparently oblivious to the impassioned responses of the women of various ages who "swoon, collectively and individually, at this unbearably alluring vision."[105] Yet this display of the king's beauty, virility, and power, with its accompanying display of passion by the lovesick, distraught women, was considered necessary for the self-construction of monarchy. Through this ritual, the king "symbolizes and focuses the fertile and auspicious forces necessary for the kingdom's growth."[106] The king displayed publicly his handsome, virile, sexually attractive, and sumptuously adorned person, giving *darshana* (transferring grace to the viewer) similar to that of the temple deity, and thereby bestowing fortune on his audience. *Darshana* of the king was auspicious.

Alankara of the monarch, and the ritual display of his person in processions and at court *darbars*, retained its importance throughout India's history. Joanne Waghorne's study of the Pudukkottai rajas during the period of British rule brings this home in many ways. Her pithy observation that "the act of getting dressed and of dressing others was the primary ritual act at court in Pudukkottai" is deeply insightful and certainly parallels the situation highlighted in Ali's study of premodern India.[107] The raja displayed himself in *darbar* (in all his ornamented glory), and Waghorne points out that "the word used for the king seated in state, *samalankara*, quite literally means fully ornamented."[108] The "dressing others" refers largely, although not exclusively, to the raja's bestowing forms of clothing and ornaments as honors upon his officers; this was a custom initiated by monarchs from very early times, and continued throughout Mughal and Rajput rule into the British period. We may note, too, that the famed maharajas of the colonial period often commissioned the most dramatic and extravagant jewelry for themselves, the monarchs, and not for their wives or daughters. It was the royal body for which such sumptuous display was deemed necessary. A case in point is the maharaja of Patiala's magnificent diamond, emerald, and pearl necklace, which covered his chest from neck to navel and which he commissioned in 1928 from Cartier in Paris. With its centerpiece a pale yellow diamond, the size of a golf ball and weighing 234 carats, the extraordinary necklace, strung on five rows of platinum chains, contained 2,930 diamonds weighing just under 1,000 carats. After the necklace was rediscovered in 1998, damaged and missing its major gemstones, Cartier repaired and re-created the piece and placed it on display in 2002 in the firm's New York showroom, where it stunned viewers.[109]

Chakravartin Buddha

The images of Siddhartha, who became the Buddha, constitute a unique instance of a being born into a royal lineage but later considered divine. Siddhartha is said to have exhibited all thirty-two signs of a *chakravartin* (universal emperor). During the second and first centuries B.C.E., when the story of the Buddha first began to be told in art, only signs were used to indicate his presence, perhaps because the artists found it an impossible task to express in bodily form the grandeur of one who had escaped the cycle of rebirth after some five hundred births on earth.[110] The very first anthropomorphic images of the Buddha, produced around the turn of the current era, appear to display characteristics of royal imagery, making it appropriate to consider them in the context of this chapter.

From an early date, and certainly from the time of the composition of the *Ashokavadana* (*Legend of Ashoka*) in the second century, emphasis was laid on the bodily appearance of the Buddha.[111] As John Strong points out in his analysis of the text, while Emperor Ashoka makes a pilgrimage to the various sites associated with events in the life of the Buddha, it is a description of the Buddha himself that interests him. At Lumbini, where the Buddha was born, Ashoka speaks to a tree spirit of the body of the Master:

> You witnessed his birth and saw
> his body adorned with the marks!
> You gazed upon his large lotus-like eyes![112]

Seeking out the *naga* king Kalika, who saw the Buddha before his enlightenment, Ashoka asks him to recount the glory of the Buddha's body:

> You saw my peerless Master
> his complexion like blazing gold
> and his face like the autumn moon.
> Recount for me some of the Buddha's qualities;
> tell me what it was like—
> the splendor of the Sugata.[113]

Early literary texts also stress the physical beauty of Suddhodhana, father of Siddhartha, the Buddha-to-be. In his *Buddha-charita*, the poet Ashvagosha says of the Buddha's father: "By his beauty he attracted, like the moon, the gaze of his subjects." Siddhartha, too, was "radiant with wondrous beauty." Once he leaves the palace in his quest of enlightenment, young Siddhartha (not yet the enlightened Buddha) is lamented thus:

> Have those hairs of his which are worthy of being encircled
> by a royal diadem, been cast to the ground, hairs which were
> soft, black and glossy, in great locks and curling upwards
> with each hair growing separately from its own orifice?
>
> His arms are long, his gait that of the king of beasts, his
> eyes like a mighty bull's, his chest broad, his voice like the
> drum of the gods, and he shines with the brilliance of gold.
> Ought such a one to live in a hermitage?
>
> His feet are soft with a beautiful network spread over the
> toes, tender as the fibre of a lotus or a flower, with the ankle-
> bones concealed and wheels in the middle of the soles. Shall
> they tread on the hard ground of the jungle?
>
> He is ennobled by race [*kula*], goodness, strength, beauty,
> learning, majesty and youth, and so fitted to give, not to ask.
> Is he to practice begging alms from others?[114]

The mood and mode of the lament are very likely modeled on the parallel lament in the *Ramayana* over Prince Rama, accustomed to palace luxury, being forced to live in forest exile.[115] It is also analogous to the lament over the exile of the Pandava princes, whether detailed in the *Maha-bharata* epic itself or in *kavyas* like Bharavi's seventh-century *Kiratarjuniya* (*The Hunter and Arjuna*).[116]

The thirty-two marks (*lakshanas*) of the Buddha's superhuman perfection listed in the *Digha Nikaya*, a Pali text translated into English under the title *Dialogues of the Buddha*, constitute, in fact, the thirty-two marks of a *chakravartin* (literally, "wheel-turning monarch").[117] Although the *Digha Nikaya* text was committed to writing only during the third or fourth century, a widely known oral version must have existed at a much earlier date, since the *Buddha-charita* of the first century c.e. displays knowledge of these thirty-two signs. In the verses that lament the departure of Siddhartha, the description of the Buddha is not mere poetic fancy, but deliberately includes either the exact *lakshanas* attributed to the Buddha as *chakravartin* or closely parallel *lakshana*s. His hair grows from separate pores (*lakshana* 13) and is black and curly (*lakshana* 14), his complexion is the color of gold (*lakshana* 11), his gait is that of a lion (*lakshana* 17), his arms are long (*lakshana* 4), his voice is that of the drum of the gods (*lakshana* 29: voice is of a *karavika* bird), and his eyes are like those of a bull (*lakshana* 29: eyes are intensely blue). The description of his feet incorporates a further four *lakshana*s: they are soft and tender (*lakshana* 5), with ankles like rounded shells (*lakshana* 3), with wheels on his soles (*lakshana* 2), and with toes joined by a network (*lakshana* 6). This last mentioned *lakshana* extends also to the fingers of the Buddha's hand, which are said to be webbed or joined by a network. These *lakshana*s, so closely linked with the Buddha through Buddhistic studies of the twentieth century, were associated in ancient times with all royal *chakravartins*. This is clearly evident from the reference to the webbed hand in Kalidasa's drama *Shakuntala*. When King Dushyanta unknowingly encounters his own son in Maricha's hermitage and sees him reach out to grab a tiger cub, he is deeply attracted to the child and ponders:

> Why does he bear the mark of a king who turns the
>   wheel of empire?
> A hand with fine ribs connecting the fingers
> opens as he reaches for the object greedily,
> like a single lotus with faint open petals
> spread open in the red glow of early dawn.[118]

Images of the Buddha were modeled so as to display the thirty-two *lakshana*s, or at any rate those that are clearly recognizable, such as the webbed hand, the *ushnisha* (interpreted by artists as a cranial protuberance disguised with his hair), and the *urna*

Figure 15. Future Buddha Maitreya, sandstone,
Ahicchattra, Uttar Pradesh, first century.

dot between the eyebrows, to constitute what one scholar has described as "canonical adornment."[119]

It is intriguing to note that when the Buddha began to be sculpted in bodily form in the region of Mathura during the first century C.E., his sexual virility was emphasized.[120] This emphasis on sexuality is shared by a group of more-than-life-size standing images created at the behest of prominent monks and nuns. These comprise a 10-foot-high Buddha image at Sarnath and an 11-foot-high image at Sravasti, both commissioned by monk Bala; an equally monumental image at Kaushambi donated by nun Buddhamitra; and a somewhat smaller, uninscribed image of the future Buddha Maitreya from Ahicchattra, now in the National Museum in New Delhi (figure 15). The artist portraying Maitreya with his typical attribute, the water vessel, gave him a sturdy bare torso, massive shoulders, and strong chest. He clad him in a transparent dhoti whose knot is moved to one side to delineate the prominent curve of his barely concealed male sexual organs. His upper wrap hangs down his left shoulder, crosses his back, and emerges to be held in front across his left arm.

The original Pali phrase (*kosohita-vattha-guhyo*)[121] that refers to the Buddha's sexuality is open to varying interpretations.[122] One possible translation reads: "[H]is male organs are concealed in a sheath."[123] The early artists of the Mathura region may have understood the phrase to mean that the sexual organs of the virile *chakravartin*-Buddha were to be depicted as though covered by a codpiece. Artists of later images, which emphasize the Buddha's divinity and show not a trace of his sexuality, may have interpreted the phrase to suggest that the sheathed sexual organs were subsumed, at will, into his body. One may recall that it was predicted that the Buddha would definitely be a *chakravartin*; the only open question was whether he would conquer the territories of the earth, or renounce the world to conquer the minds of men. Either way, evidence of his virility and sexuality—essential qualities in any monarch, and even more so in a *chakravartin*—seems to have been considered important enough in the first and second centuries to be specifically portrayed. While the Buddha had renounced the world, he remained a *chakravartin*, a wheel-turner of the Buddhist doctrine, whose virility and potency had been transmuted into spiritual power over the minds of men. The depiction of the Buddha's sexuality in sculptural imagery seems to have been one way of stressing his imperial identity; in those very early days, his *chakravartin* qualities may even have helped the Buddhist undertaking to sway the minds of men to the path the Buddha had founded.[124] One point may be stated with some certainty: this early portrayal of the Buddha's sexuality was considered entirely appropriate by the monks and nuns who commissioned these monumental images for prominent display in their monasteries.[125]

In his article on the origin of the Buddha image, A. K. Coomaraswamy indicated that the visual prototype used to create the first anthropomorphic Buddha images in the region of Mathura was in all likelihood the semidivine *yaksha* or *deva* (god).[126] He also pointed to the Pali *Nidana Katha* (*Story of the Recent Epoch*) for textual confirmation that during his lifetime the Buddha had been mistaken for a *yaksha-deva*. The text speaks of a woman named Sujata from the town of Uruvela who had vowed to make an offering of milk-rice to the *deva* of the *nigrodha* (ficus) tree; accordingly, she sent her maid Punna to keep watch by the tree: "And Punna coming there saw the Bodhisat sitting at the foot of the tree and lighting up all the region of the East; and she saw the whole tree in colour like gold from the rays issuing from his body. And she thought: 'Today our deva, descending from the tree, is seated to receive our offering in his own hand.'"[127] The earliest *deva* or *yaksha* figures, from Patna, Parkham, and Vidisha, were powerfully modeled with broad shoulders, an ample torso, and sturdy thighs and legs, but with sexual organs hidden beneath the knotted folds of their dhotis. Contrasting with them are the first Buddha images, in which a clear protrusion of the sexual organs is depicted to emphasize, we suggest, his innate royal status as a *chakravartin*. However, the emphasis on the male virility of the Buddha/*chakravartin* was soon abandoned, being replaced by the smooth, uninterrupted flow of the monastic robe; thenceforth, the spiritual and divine status of the Buddha was to dominate his visual portrayal.[128]

Bodily Beauty and Moral Perfections

The link between beauty, on the one hand, and morality or the perfection of character induced by a totally dharmic way of life, on the other, is perhaps most clearly spelled out in the Buddhist *Lakkhana-suttanta* (*Text on Perfections*).[129] The word *lakkhana* (Sanskrit, *lakshana*) is used in the text to describe the bodily marks of perfection that distinguish a great soul (*maha-purusha*) who has only two avenues open to him: that of a *chakravartin* or of a fully enlightened Buddha who has sway over the minds of men. Later, *lakshana* came to be used as a synonym for "beauty" and, in fact, continues to be used to speak of a person with a well-proportioned body that is also well clothed and well adorned. The *Lakkhana-suttanta* makes it clear that each of the thirty-two bodily marks and perfections is the outcome of moral actions, the result of "performing that *kamma*, heaping it up, lavishly and abundantly"; the *lakkhana*s are thus signs of moral worth.[130] The text specifies that each bodily mark is the outcome of a particular good action in a previous birth and is accompanied by specific enjoyments in this life. Thus the webbed hand of *lakkhana* 6 is attributed to a constantly giving nature and helpfulness:

> Through giving, and through helpful acts,
> Pleasing speech and evenness
> of mind, of benefit to all[131]

Lakkhana 17 specifies that a leonine gait is due to constant wishes for the goodness and prosperity of others:

> Faith, morality, learning, wisdom,
> Restraint and justice, much good else,
> Wealth, possessions, wives and sons,
> Flocks, kin, friends, colleagues,
> Strength, good looks and happiness:
> These things he wished for others
> That they might keep and never lose[132]

The text also makes it clear that the thirty-two *lakkhana*s were signs of beauty. In its verses devoted to the various *lakkhana*s, the phrases used to describe the *maha-purusha*'s body include "fair to see, and shapely-limbed / his fingers tender, soft and long"; "well-formed above, and beautiful"; "graceful and fair his limbs will be"; and "like fine-wrought gold / his body is, more fair than all / the gods he seems, great Indra's like."[133] A well-formed and healthy body, adorned with a variety of pastes, unguents, and colors, and ornamented with silks, jewels, and flowers, is both a sign of moral perfection and a result of moral perfection. Although the text that spells this out is Buddhist, the *lakshana*s are associated with *chakravartins*, Buddhist, Hindu, or Jain; clearly, the linkage between beauty and morality is one that cuts across religious boundaries. It is perhaps in this context that we should try to assess and review the closely similar tropes of adornment used to describe evolved humans as well as divinities—the simple Shakuntala reared by *maha-rishi* Kanva as well as the supreme goddess Uma.

The linkage among beauty, health, adornment, and morality allows for a considerable degree of variation, however. For instance, a later Buddhist text, the Sanskrit *Lalita-vistara*, tells us that the Buddha's body is so resplendent from the light of his accumulated merit that he has no need of gemstones for further adornment; indeed, next to his radiance, gold appears like ink.[134] We are here presented with a critique of external ornament as against internal moral adornment. A variation on this is seen in the poetic statement that gemstones longed to be placed on the god Vishnu's body in order to enhance their own luster.[135]

The Aristocratic and Royal Couple

The married couple as the ideal initiators of religious and social rites is a long-standing convention in India—so much so that a widower may often hand over the rituals of a daughter's marriage to a younger brother and his wife. The same ideal apparently existed in the case of donors commissioning sacred works; when artists created donor portraits, they most often portrayed husband and wife together, as is clearly evident in the few donor portraits, mostly Jain, so identified by inscription. The value accorded to an idealized and sensuous form of physical beauty, and its accompanying ornamentation, is seen in a deeply cut relief slab featuring Minister Tejahpala and his wife, Anupamadevi, carved from marble and placed within their commission, the Luna Vasahi temple at Dilwara on Mount Abu (figure 16).[136] Another such slab of a similarly portrayed aristocratic donor couple, cemented today into the premises of the same temple, follows these accepted conventions; their well-formed, sensuous bodies, richly ornamented and clad in translucent clothing that reveals the form beneath, embody the overall aesthetic norms prevalent at the time.[137]

When we turn to the king and queen, it appears that throughout history their mutual love and total absorption in each other was among the factors considered to be of critical significance for the stability, prosperity, and ongoing success of a kingdom. The coin struck by Samudragupta in which he is portrayed as the beloved monarch who turns his queen's face toward him (see figure 12d) is a proclamation of this ethos. In Kalidasa's *Raghu-vamsha*, the beauty of King Dilipa, considered earlier, is closely followed by a verse extolling the intimacy of the love between him and his queen. The couple is compared to the legendary *chakravaka* birds, which were unable to live without each other:

Figure 16. Donor couple (probably minister Tejahpala and his wife), marble, Luna Vasahi temple, Mount Abu, thirteenth century.

Like *chakravaka* birds united close
the royal couple linked in heart by love
and mutual charm released a part of love
for their dear child, an only son, but yet
they found their love not diminished, but yet
enhanced[138]

One of the few surviving portrait sculptures of a king and queen, clearly identified by inscription, comes from the collection of the National Museum in New Delhi and portrays King Prithivideva and Queen Kelachchadevi, of the Gahadvala dynasty, carved in deep relief so as to stand out from the background of the marble stele to which they are attached.[139] The inscription provides a date (1183) and speaks of the queen being widowed, persuaded not to perform *sati*, and instead constructing a Shiva temple and commissioning the portrait image, which is like a vehicle that will

Figure 17. King Prithivideva and Queen Kelachchadevi, marble, Rajasthan, 1183.

provide him/them with the divine nectar of immortality (*devamrita-syandinim*).[140] In his study of portraiture in western India, Jack Laughlin emphasizes the merit-making potential of the portrait.[141] Of relevance here is the bodily beauty and intimacy of the couple (figure 17). The beautiful, bearded king is broad-shouldered and smooth-bodied; he wears a lower garment and ample jewels, and holds a lotus flower in one hand. The queen, poised to stand close to her husband so that her right breast brushes his arm, is an exquisite figure with a lovely face, high breasts, a narrow waist, and slender limbs and torso; richly adorned and wearing a skirt, she holds a water vessel in one hand. Considering that the queen commissioned the portraits after the death of her husband, we may indeed assume that the sensuous bodies with which the couple have been endowed reflect an accepted ideal. A rayed halo is intended for both figures, and a male and a female attendant are carved along the stele's lower portion.

The world of Rajput miniature painting took pride in lauding the role of the monarch as lover. Mewar Rana Ari Singh (r. 1761–1773), for instance, seems to have relished himself in this role, commissioning many portraits of himself holding his beloved, a queen or perhaps a favorite concubine (*paswan*), in his lap.[142] Portrayed in a golden pavilion on a terrace, or within idyllic garden surroundings, the monarch as lover holds center stage with female attendants arrayed on either side. Other Rajput monarchs had themselves similarly portrayed.

Inscriptions, too, take delight in declaring, in no uncertain terms, the conjugal intimacy of king and queen. I shall provide examples from varying regions of India in an attempt to demonstrate the overall applicability of this unusual, but clearly significant, concept. The pleasure that the Chalukya queen Lakshmadevi and king Vikramaditya VI took in each other, apparently regarded as an asset by their subjects, is candidly detailed in a Kannada inscription of the year 1084 in the southern state of Karnataka. Carved on a gateway in the town of Sudi, the inscription records the queen's gift of the village of Pongari to a certain Someshvara *pandit* for sustained worship at the Amareshvara Shiva temple at Sudi:

> She who is his soul's darling [*tan-mano-vallabhe*] hail!—who shares in the enjoyment of the fruits of thousands of issues of unceasing supreme felicity; who revels [*bhogini*] in possession of fortune's choicest in mortal life; a manifest Lakshmi resting on the broad bosom of that Narayana among kings; a goddess of spring in the gladdening park of youth [*yauvana-nandana-vana*]; she who sports in mastery over the series of all the arts; a mistress of the arts of pleasure [*vilasa- vidyadhare*]; delighting king Vikramaditya's soul [*vikramaditya-deva-mano- ranjani*].[143]

From northeastern India, a Sanskrit copper-plate inscription of the year 1185 likewise celebrates the loving relationship of Queen Ahiavadevi and King Nihshankasimha. The inscription, from the site of Tezpur in Assam, belongs to the reign of their son Vallabhadeva, and records a gift of a major almshouse and seven villages for its support:

> King Nihshankasimha had a queen, dear to him as life, who bore the name Ahiavadevi.
>
> A swan in that Manasa lake which was the heart of king Nihshankasimha; for every kind of amorous dalliance [*shringara-keli*] what the moon in loveliness is to the waterlily, glorious as the lotus in that lake which is the quintessence of mundane existence [*samsara-sara-sarasi-sarasiruha*], she stood manifested as the one dwelling-place of exquisite beauty[144]

From Bhubaneshvar in eastern India, a Sanskrit inscription speaks of the beauty of the Eastern Ganga princess Chandradevi and records her marriage to the Haihaiya prince Paramarddi. It continues:

> After he had practiced with this wife diverse kinds of pleasures, in which delight was attendant upon amorous passions, the valiant Paramardi-deva went [into battle].[145]

The purpose of this Sanskrit epigraph is to record the queen's construction of a Vishnu temple at Bhubaneshvar.

From Dewal in the North-West Provinces comes a Sanskrit inscription that speaks of a chieftain Lalla and his wife whose "pleasing mutual affection is even as high grown as that of Hara [Shiva] and the Daughter of the Mountain [Parvati]."[146] And from the Tirunelveli district of Tamil Nadu, a Sanskrit inscription dated to 1634 describes Queen Bangaramamba as one whose "heavenly form [*divya-murti*] is the abode of the kingdom of love [*shringara-rajya*]."[147]

The affluence and welfare of a kingdom depended, of course, on a variety of practical factors, such as possessing a strong army, providing irrigation to ensure good harvests, and maintaining a strong trading network. However, this brief selection of verses from across India that celebrate royal intimacy indicates that in the milieu of premodern India, in addition to practical matters, one significant factor contributing to the ruler's authority was the personality of a handsome monarch and his beautiful queen, as well as their conjugal felicity and erotic enjoyment. The frank expression of this idea is yet another example of cultural specificity.[148] In chapter 4, we shall encounter this same, much-celebrated attribute of beauty and mutual attraction applied in equal measure to the supreme divine couples: Shiva and Parvati, and Vishnu and Lakshmi. Their divine love was ecstatically extolled in an even more heroic manner in art, literature, and inscriptions.

Alankara in Architecture, *Kavya*, and the Body

Ornament (*alankara*) that plays so crucial a role in the adornment of women and men is critical also for the beautification, completion, and protection of architecture, whether temple or palace. The adornment of temples with miniature architectural forms is not random additional ornament. Adam Hardy's writings have clearly illustrated that what might appear to be superficial external decoration actually represents the surfaces of aedicular structures that are conceived as embedded shrines.[149] Such architectural units are part of the structural formulation of a temple and not mere excess.

Whether a structure was sacred or mundane, the quality of excellence of its elegant pinnacles, towers, and gateways had to be enhanced by the addition to the monument of scintillating shapes and arrangements. Doubtless, Heinrich Zimmer was partially correct when he remarked, in *The Art of Indian Asia*, that "the Indian ideal is that only things covered with ornaments are beautiful."[150] Temples are indeed covered with profuse ornamentation that is largely figural and in which images of the deities and figures of women and couples predominate; in addition, an almost equal amount of vegetal and foliate motifs occupies the multiple vertical and horizontal bands that crisscross the walls (figure 18). Frequently, barely an inch of plain space remains visible, so that this tendency toward overflowing ornamentation has been termed "horror vacui." But the underlying idea is not so simplistic: *alankara* is much more than a mere dislike or abhorrence of plain surfaces. The ornamentation of buildings in premodern India is not "mere" ornament; *alankara* had a symbolic content of auspiciousness, protection, and apotropaism. For instance, images of happy couples, symbolizing marital bliss, had a connotation of stability and long-lasting prosperity in the context of both town and court, of commoners and kings. India is not isolated in assigning symbolic meaning to ornament; Irene Winter stresses the need to view the repetitive vegetal ornament in Assyrian palace decoration as a reiterated symbol of the ruler's promise of agrarian abundance.[151]

The term *alankara* is frequently used in inscriptions on temples and monasteries. Varahadeva, minister to the Vakataka king Harisena and patron of the richly sculpted and lavishly painted Buddhist *vihara* 16 at Ajanta, speaks proudly in his donatory inscription of the magnificence of the cave, "adorned [*alankrita*] with windows, doors, beautiful picture-galleries, ledges, statues of the nymphs of Indra, and the like, which is ornamented [*bhushita*] with beautiful pillars and stairs and has a temple of the Buddha inside."[152] The impulse to adorn was certainly no mere whim of the architects of India. In addition to enhancing and affording auspiciousness and protection to both sacred and secular spaces, *alankara* held the deeper artistic significance of captivating the viewer's mind and creating a heightened awareness, while fulfilling a sacred purpose. Thus the *shilpa-shastras*, texts that often provide

71

Figure 18. Wall of Lingaraja temple, sandstone, Bhubaneshvar, Orissa, eleventh century.

instructions for architects and sculptors, contain entire chapters dealing in minute and specific detail with the ornamentation of architectural structures. The Orissan *Shilpa-prakasha* (*Light on Art*) specifies:

> Without making ornamental work [*alankara*] the temple
> will remain mediocre [*madhyama*].
>   That temple, in which every part is covered with decorations [*bhushana*], is always called the highest [*uttama*] type.

> The temple shorn of any decorations [*bhushana*] is definitely
> the lowest [*adhama*] type.[153]

It is true that temples in certain parts of India, such as the Hemadpanti temples of the Yadavas of the western Deccan or some of the temples in Himachal Pradesh, place less emphasis on abundant *alankara*.[154] To eyes used to the richness of ornament on the temples of Orissa, Khajuraho, and Mount Abu and in Hoysala territory, the temples at Jageshvar in the Kumaon hills may have a relatively lesser impact. However, even here, architectural units themselves are finished with crisply delineated, horizontal *pidha* levels of the superstructure and well-outlined decorative arches above doorways and deity-niches. *Alankara* is present but not in the abundance seen elsewhere.

Ornament is, of course, an essential and exuberant feature of Sanskrit poetry, the very heart and soul of its vitality; in fact, as Jan Gonda emphasizes, poetic *alankara* is "an ornamentation of the sense or the sound."[155] He points to a commentary on Visvanatha's *Sahitya-darpana* (*Mirror on Literature*) that specifies: "[A]s bracelets and the like resound to the man's advantage by adding to his beauty, so alliteration, simile, and so on, by promoting the beauty of word and sense and the *rasa*, etc, are (called) *alankara*."[156] *Alankara* constitutes an entire section of poetics, where it refers, as indicated, to such elements as figures of speech, double meaning (*shlesha*), similes, metaphors, puns, and the like that adorn verse and prose. *Alankara-shastra* is the general term applied to the science of poetics. If poetry may be thought of as verbal sound, expressiveness, and beauty that serves to induce a state of heightened awareness, *alankara* adds significance to the description of the human form by importing similes and metaphors from nature, with the spontaneity of its flowing beauty, movement, and vibrancy. Ornament is as essential to *kavya* as *alankara* is to the female form or to the walls of temples and monasteries. The seventh-century court poet Bana, writing his *Harsha-charita*, compared the appropriate presentation of plays (he refers to his predecessor Bhasa) to the construction of a temple, richly and appropriately ornamented:

> Bhasa gained as much splendour by his plays with introductions spoken by the manager, full of various characters, and furnished with startling episodes, as he would have done by the erection of temples, created by architects, adorned with several stories, and decorated with banners.[157]

Such comparisons between artfully constructed plays and poems, on the one hand, and finely constructed temples, on the other, are fairly widespread. Equally pertinent is the comparison made by Bhoja, an eleventh-century monarch of literary renown, between poetic ornamentation and bodily adornment—a comparison that is repeated by several other writers. Sheldon Pollock draws attention to Bhoja's text on literary aesthetics, the *Sarasvati-kanthabharana* (*Adornment of Sarasvati's Neck*), which postulates the threefold nature of poetic ornamentation as external, internal, and external-internal.[158] With analogies to bodily ornament, Bhoja specifies external *alankara* as both poetic ornamentation and its equivalent in clothing and jewelry; internal as literary description and exemplification corresponding to perfect teeth or manicured nails; and external-internal *alankara* as similes and *shlesha* comparable to perfumes and creams.

In the Indian context, an appreciation of ornament, or *alankara*, is never complete without this symbolic content as its recurring melodic theme. The deep-rooted "impulse to adorn" has a richer significance, an undertone deeper than sheer love of decoration.[159] Its unseen presence in the portrayal of the bodies of man and woman, king and queen, god and goddess is equally important whether the context is human or divine. Yes, adornment enhances, completes, delights; but it also makes the wearer invincible, courts the favors of fortune, and so becomes auspicious. *Alankara* is a vital component of the visual and verbal arts of India.[160]

3. THE SENSUOUS
WITHIN SACRED BOUNDARIES

I invite my readers to accompany me, in this chapter, on an exploratory journey to a few sacred sites in India, commencing with Buddhist monastic establishments and moving on through time to Hindu and Jain temple complexes. The aim is to investigate what seems a paradox to modern viewers—that sensuous figures of women and men are carved in prominent positions on what are classified as sacred structures, sometimes serving as arresting accents on pillars and walls, and at other times punctuating sacred biographies or mythological narratives. Such sensuous imagery at sacred sites represented much more than merely eye-catching or attention-grabbing motifs; rather, these images were imbued with auspicious ideas and were thus considered both noteworthy and indispensable. And while Hindu and Jain temples, as well as Buddhist monastic establishments, were certainly places of worship, they also served a multitude of other functions not directly connected with devotional activities. Temples and monasteries almost always served as spaces where people of similar bent might congregate to discuss matters of worldly interest, while frequently schools, dance and music institutions, and hospitals were attached to them as adjuncts. This exploration raises the issue of whether it is useful, or indeed meaningful, to speak of spaces as being either "sacred" or "secular."

Buddhist Monastic Establishments

The stupa, which serves as a Buddhist shrine, came into existence as a dome-shaped funerary mound that enclosed a relic casket generally holding a portion of the cremated relics of the Buddha (figure 19).[1] Inscriptions reveal that the enshrined relics were believed to be imbued with the living presence of the Buddha, so that Buddhists visited stupas primarily to experience the power of the Buddha's presence.[2] A wide range of residential and assembly halls developed around the stupa, resulting in the typical Buddhist monastic establishments of India.

The second and first centuries B.C.E. witnessed, for the first time, the widespread use of stone as a medium of sculpture and architecture. We can discover no clear-cut reasons why this innovation, which followed centuries of construction and decoration in the medium of brick and wood, occurred almost exclusively in the context of Buddhism.[3] Existing brick-faced stupas were now faced with stone, and the earlier wooden railings and gateways were replaced with richly carved stone structures.

One of the earliest surviving stupas, from the site of Bharhut near Allahabad, now partially reconstructed and displayed in the Indian Museum in Kolkata, carries inscrip-

Figure 19. Buddhist stupa, Sanchi, Madhya Pradesh, first century B.C.E.

tions on its gateways (it has been possible to restore only one) that associate its construction with the period of the Sungas, a dynasty whose rule ended around 80 B.C.E. The stupa was surrounded by a tall railing composed of richly sculpted pillars, nearly 7 feet tall, connected by three crossbars and crowned with lengths of coping stone so as to enclose a path for ritual circumambulation (*pradakshina*). The railing is carved on both faces, carrying simpler decorative motifs on the outer face and the more important Buddhist imagery on the inner face. The majority of the railing pillars are carved with a central medallion and half-medallions above and below, while the pillars at the four entranceways are divided into rectangular panels that narrate Buddhist legend. Our focus here will be the third pillar type, which gave pride of place to the human body, male and female. Carved against the entire length of such image-pillars are sensuous standing images of semidivine beings who have little direct connection with Buddhist concepts: female *yakshis* and *devatas*, male *yakshas* and *nagarajas*, as well as the occasional human devotee or warrior.

Figure 20. "First pillar," sandstone, Bharhut stupa, Madhya Pradesh, ca. 100 B.C.E.

Figure 21. Chanda *yakshi*, sandstone, Bharhut stupa, Madhya Pradesh, ca. 100 B.C.E.

At the eastern entrance to the stupa enclosure is the railing's first pillar, labeled as such in its Prakrit inscription (*pathamo thabho*), which records that it was the gift of a woman named Chapadevi, wife of Revatimita from the town of Vidisha. The entering visitor sees an aristocratic male figure riding an elephant and holding a large round, lidded relic casket that rests on the elephant's head (figure 20). Two flanking elephants follow him, while along the inner face of the pillar is carved a horse-rider holding aloft a standard, the entire scene being suggestive of a procession, perhaps the very procession once held to honor the relics enshrined in the stupa's interior.

The pillar directly across this eastern entranceway portrays a sensuous female with her left leg and arm wrapped around the trunk of a tree, her right hip thrust outward, and her right arm drawing one of its leafy branches down toward her (figure 21; see also figure 6). A skirt slung low on her hips below her navel is held in place with a jeweled hip-belt (*mekhala*), and its pleated end is arranged in precise folds between her legs. Her left hand, held at the level of her pudenda, holds a flowering stem from the tree beneath which she stands, and may perhaps be intended to draw attention to the parallel fertility of trees and women, a concept we shall soon consider. A transparent scarf draped across her torso reveals her well-formed breasts. As one might expect, she is richly ornamented. Woven fabric bands wrap around her head and are plaited into her long braid, which is further adorned with blossoms, while her forehead is decorated by a pendant along the line of her centrally parted hair. Heavy ear plugs, a choker-style necklace, sacred thread, multiple bangles and anklets, and face paint or tattooing complete her adornment. She stands on a mythical, part-aquatic creature, a *vahana* (vehicle or mount) that may be read as affirming her semidivine status.[4] An inscription that names her Chanda (moon) describes her also as a *yakshi*, a semidivine, nymph-like being associated with forests, foliage, and fertility. She is the epitome of the woman-and-tree motif, which we shall presently explore. What is her function along this railing pillar at the main eastern entrance, where she would be seen by all who entered the stupa enclosure? Her posture is not one of reverence to the Buddha's relics, but seems rather that of a mere spectator. Her modeling recalls a Sanskrit poem of Buddhist content written by Ashvaghosha in the first century, a hundred years or so after this image was sculpted, which speaks eloquently of feminine beauty. It characterizes Sundari, wife of the Buddha's half-brother, Nanda, as "a very lotus-pond in the shape of woman, with her laughter for the swans, her eyes for the bees, and her swelling breasts for the uprising lotus buds."[5] It proceeds to extol the beauty of Sundari, "who with her slender waist and swelling breasts and thighs resembled a golden rift of a mountain with a narrow interior and spurs on each side covered with billowing clouds."[6]

Figure 22. Kubera *yaksha*, sandstone, Bharhut stupa, Madhya Pradesh, ca. 100 B.C.E.

The three-sided pillar against which Chanda *yakshi* is carved carries an inscription stating that it was donated by the reverend Budharakhita, who "has abandoned all attachment." Clearly, this senior monk considered the portrayal of the sensuous moon *yakshi* on this sacred monument as totally appropriate, since he himself commissioned the pillar. Although she does not have her hands in a gesture of adoration, one may still assume that her presence at the stupa is intended to suggest her acceptance of the Buddha's supremacy. The sensuous nature of her modeling and the unspoken link of women with fertility and abundance necessitated the artist's emphasis on sexuality and—in the Indian context explored in chapter 2—the accompanying seductive body. The inner face of this three-sided end pillar carries a full-size, elegant image of Kubera *yaksha*, accepted by both Buddhist and Hindu sources as the guardian of the northern direction (figure 22). Its outer face portrays Ajakalaka *yaksha*, the tutelary deity of the town of Patali.[7] Both *yakshas* are portrayed with smooth body and wide shoulders; they wear a dhoti tied in an elaborate knot below the navel with a folded scarf draped across the torso, and both are richly adorned with necklaces, armlets, and bangles. While Kubera has his palms together in the *anjali* gesture of adoration directed toward the Buddha and his relics, Ajakalaka has his right hand raised, somewhat unexpectedly, in the gesture of teaching.[8]

On the inner face of a double-sided pillar, looking toward the stupa, is a voluptuous female figure labeled Sirima *devata*, a lesser female deity (figure 23). Standing firmly on both feet and directly facing the viewer, Sirima is portrayed with a typical hourglass figure, with large rounded breasts, a narrow waist, and smooth, broad hips. Slung below her navel and held in place with a jeweled *mekhala* is a long skirt, with its elaborately arranged pleats hanging between her legs. Cloth bands wrap around her head, a pendant adorns her forehead, and completing her adornment are heavy ear ornaments, three sets of necklaces, armlets, and rows of bangles and anklets. The heavy sensuality of Sirima's *damaru*-drum-like figure is reminiscent of that of the Didarganj image (see figures 3 and 4). The outer face of this image-pillar carries the figure of Suciloma, patron *yaksha* of the town of Gaya, who joins his palms in the *anjali* gesture of adoration.[9] This pillar featuring Sirima *devata* and Suciloma *yaksha* carries an inscription recording its donation by a Buddhist nun.

Let us consider another two curvaceous pillar figures—which by no means complete the range of this image type. The first is Chulakoka *devata*, who was donated by the venerable monk Pamthaka (figure 24).[10] The second is Sudarshana *yakshi*, donated by the reverend monk Kanaka, a preacher of the law.[11] Chulakoka *devata* stands beneath an *ashoka* tree, heavy with clusters of its characteristic blossoms, in a pose resembling that of Chanda *yakshi* and adorned in a manner similar to both Chanda and Sirima. The elephant mount on which she is poised speaks to her semidivine status. Sudarshana *yakshi* stands on the ground (no mount), her left leg crossed behind her in a casual pose, with her left thumb tucked casually into her low *mekhala* and right hand held at shoulder level.

Figure 23. Sirima devata, sandstone, Bharhut stupa, Madhya Pradesh, ca. 100 B.C.E.

Figure 24. Chulakoka devata, sandstone, Bharhut stupa, Madhya Pradesh, ca. 100 B.C.E.

Much of the railing of the Bharhut stupa is lost, and only forty-nine of its original eighty pillars remain.[12] Among the surviving image-pillars are eight males, mostly *yakshas* or *nagarajas*, and seven female *yakshis*, *devatas*, and unnamed semidivine beings. I have elsewhere estimated that in total about 40 percent of the original sculpted material remains, so it would not be far wrong to estimate that one-third of the imagery surrounding the Bharhut stupa was that of male and female semidivine beings, all portrayed with elegant, sensuous bodies.[13]

The sacred enclosure at Bharhut constituted public space, and its stupa was visited by female and male, old and young, nuns and monks, and laypeople, judging from donative inscriptions. In this context, one has to discard the use of a phrase like "the male gaze," with its inference that the sensuous female figures were created solely for the viewing pleasure of men, for women were responsible for some of these commissions. Moreover, several image-pillars carry full-length portrayals of sensuous male figures. We should ponder the significance of such frank and luscious representation of physical beauty in a space associated with the Buddha's relics, a space open to public viewing, while keeping in mind that the sensuous figures were often gifts from the monastics themselves. While the prime aim of the site was to allow visitors to experience the presence of the Buddha, it was considered important to surround the stupa with carved representations of semidivine beings of more-than-Buddhist significance, several of whom, especially the male *yakshas*, were portrayed as offering their homage to the greatness and glory of the Buddha. A recent study of the popular belief systems surrounding early Buddhism points out that the major *yakshas* revered as the tutelary deities of important towns appear to have been brought together at Bharhut and featured on its image-pillars, presumably to signify the supremacy of Buddhism over this semidivine populace.[14] In this context, it is worth recalling that the newborn Buddha himself was taken to the shrine of the local *yaksha*, Shakya-vardhana, and that the *yaksha*, recognizing the infant as a Buddha-to-be, bowed down to him.

The Buddhist stupa at Sanchi, decorated in stone toward the latter half of the first century B.C.E., has a plain unadorned railing, but four exuberantly sculpted gateways some 34 feet tall. Each gateway is composed of two pillars, extended upward and connected by three curved architraves, and the entire surface is richly carved on both faces with narrative and decorative sculptures that contain references to the biography of the Buddha, his previous lives in the form of the *jataka* stories, as well as later historical events, such as the legends surrounding Emperor Ashoka.[15] Here I shall restrict myself to considering the six luscious images of a woman standing beneath a tree that were carved on each gateway. Two large images are positioned as decorative brackets to connect the pillar uprights to the lowest architrave, while four similar, but smaller, figures of woman-and-tree were placed between the upper two sets of architraves. Each figure, depending on its positioning, has either left or right arm and/or leg

Figure 25. Yakshi bracket, sandstone, east gateway, Sanchi stupa, Madhya Pradesh, first century B.C.E.

wrapped around a tree trunk and the other arm drawing down a branch. The species of the tree varies: sometimes it is the mango; at other times, the *ashoka* (which, as we shall soon see, had strong resonances in Sanskrit literature).

The intact bracket figure on the east gateway is a magnificent piece of carving, with a perfect hourglass contour, full but not overly heavy, while the outward thrust of her body is wholly appropriate to the position she occupies (figure 25). She is clad in an entirely translucent skirt that fully reveals her *mons veneris* and the clear marking of her pudenda; she wears a jeweled *mekhala*, and the presence of the skirt is indicated only by a faint line along her ankles and pleated folds resting against the back of her legs. Her adornment includes fabric bands that cross her head, a forehead pendant, a necklace, and rows of bangles and anklets stacked so as to almost reach her elbows and knees. Sanchi is separated from Bharhut by less than a century, perhaps by no more than fifty years, but the relatively sedate and fully skirted Bharhut females have now been replaced by a more frankly sensual approach. Viewers entering the sacred enclosure and passing through each of the four gateways, as they sought to view its sacred narratives, would have passed beneath these sensuous female figures, twenty-four in all. It is clear that the woman-and-tree bracket was a relatively commonplace adjunct of gateway decoration by the first century C.E., when Sanchi was completed and when the poet Ashvaghosha wrote his *Buddha-charita*, a Sanskrit poetic composition on the life of the Buddha that we encountered in chapter 2. In describing one of the many women in the royal chambers on the night of the Buddha's great departure, the poet compares her to a statue of a woman beneath a tree that adorns a gateway:

Another [woman] lay leaning against the side of a window
with her beautiful necklaces dangling, and seemed with her
slender body bent like a bow as if turned into the statue of
a *shala*-plucker [*shala-bhanjika*, or woman pulling down a
branch of the *shala* tree] on a gateway.[16]

In the context of the Sanchi figures, it is relevant to consider an ivory figurine
of a woman, now in the National Archaeological Museum of Naples, of comparable
modeling, clad similarly in a translucent skirt that displays her clearly delineated pudenda (figure 26). The ivory immediately beyond her limbs is cut away, as if there were
no skirt, so we are surprised to see a set of pleated folds carved beyond the empty space
on either side of her body. Like her Sanchi counterpart, she wears stacks of bangles
and anklets, fabric bands around her head, a forehead pendant, heavy necklaces, and a
jeweled hip-belt, and perhaps served the function of a mirror handle. She was found in
excavations at Pompeii and quite clearly arrived there, as part of Indian trade with the
Mediterranean world, before the volcanic eruption of Mount Vesuvius in 79 C.E. The
ivory figurine emphasizes that the theme we are considering in the context of stone
sculpture, which alone has survived in any quantity, was probably once common, even

Figure 26. Woman with attendants, ivory, Pompeii, first century B.C.E.

ubiquitous, if one takes into account a range of perishable media that includes terra-cotta, wood, and ivory. Painted images of this type, too, must have been plentiful; after all, Buddhist literature contains numerous references to painted halls, including that of King Pasenajit of Kosala, which nuns are forbidden to visit due to the nature of their paintings.[17] The *Sarvastivadin Vinaya*, translated into Chinese in the year 404, contains a similar injunction against nuns visiting painted halls.[18] Early Jain texts also instruct monks and nuns not to go to places where they will view such pleasing forms.[19] Such injunctions, contained in texts written most likely by male monastics, seems contradicted by the donative inscription of the nun who commissioned the sensuous pillar-images of Sirima and Suchiloma.

No fewer than 631 donative inscriptions are found at Sanchi, carved on the very pieces given, whether pillars, railings, crossbars, circumambulatory path slabs, or gateway carvings. Of the 527 records that are sufficiently intact to reveal details, we find 84 gifts from nuns (*bhikkuni*) and 69 from monks *(bhikku)*, indicating that the monastic community was substantially involved in the construction and decoration of the stupa. If the numbers are an accurate reflection, it appears that nuns were more active than monks in supporting construction and renovation. Further gifts come from highly placed monastics with titles like *arya* (noble), *thera* (venerable), *sapurisa* (saint), and *bhanaka* (preacher). The lay community, including householders or landowners (*gahapati*) and housewives or landed women (*gharini*), as well as followers of a miscellaneous range of professions, also contributed generously; in this category, 203 gifts come from men and 171 from women. It might appear that the earlier emphasis on an elite, urbane audience is lost here, but one should note that 616 of the inscriptions are on undecorated, structural parts of the monument. Only eleven donors were responsible for the sculptures at Sanchi, all found on the gateways: two major gifts come from the same wealthy banker, another two from the pupil of a well-known preacher, one from the chief of the artisans of the Satavahana ruler Satakarni, and one from a guild of ivory-workers; two are joint gifts, and three reveal little more than a name. Those responsible for the figurative carving at Sanchi were clearly a more restricted and wealthier group.

In the context of the many sensuous female figures adorning the enclosure of a Buddhist stupa, and the striking fact that a large number of donations come from nuns and lay women, it seems imperative to address the fascinating collection of nuns' hymns known as *Theri-gatha* (*Songs of the Nuns*). They seem to have been transmitted orally for some three centuries before they were written down in Buddhist Sri Lanka, probably toward the end of the first century B.C.E.—the very time these early Buddhist stupas were being constructed.[20] The *Theri-gatha* includes a hymn supposedly composed by Ambapali, a renowned courtesan of the city of Vesali, who frequented the bedchamber of King Bimbisara before she heard a sermon preached by the Buddha and became a Buddhist nun. In a hymn of seventeen verses, Ambapali speaks of the transience of bodily beauty:

My hair was black and curly
the color of black bees.
Now that I am old
it is like the hemp of trees.
This is the teaching of one who speaks the truth.

My breasts were beautiful
high, close together and round.
Now like empty water bags,
they hang down.
This is the teaching of one who speaks the truth.

My thighs were beautiful
like an elephant's trunk.
Now because of old age
they are like bamboo stalks.
This is the teaching of one who speaks the truth.[21]

The verbal picture petrified in stone and chosen to adorn Buddhist Sanchi is of the "before" rather than the "after" conjured up by nun Ambapali. If this causes surprise, perhaps we misunderstand the purpose of the monument. While monks and nuns make up the single largest group of donors who left inscriptions on various parts of the monument, the message of Sanchi was not directed toward those already in the order or, indeed, those aspiring to join.[22] Rather, its message was directed to the many residents of a range of towns and villages who believed in the power of *yakshas* and *yakshis*, of *grama-devatas* (village deities), and perhaps also of the newly emerging and powerful Hindu gods: Shiva, Vishnu, and Devi. To such an audience, the fertility of the field and the fertility of women was *shubha* or *mangala* (auspicious). To appeal to them necessitated incorporating and accommodating some of their most strongly held beliefs.

As we seek to better understand the visual imagery at the early Buddhist stupas of the second and first centuries B.C.E., I believe it is crucial to emphasize the primacy of the concept of fertility, which, in the context of premodern India, clearly signified luxuriance, growth, and plenitude. To consider this an oversimplification or to seek textual proof is to deny the evidence of one's eyes: the Bharhut pillar figures and the Sanchi brackets repeatedly convey the same message. The beautiful, nubile body that signified fertility was a concept whose significance permeated Indian thought, cutting across religious boundaries so that images of woman-and-tree are found in Buddhist, Hindu, and Jain contexts. The reason this motif is first encountered in the Buddhist context is undoubtedly that, for reasons not clear to us, the Buddhists took to the use of stone several centuries before the Hindus, who continued to use brick, terra-cotta, and wood. Thus Buddhist stone alone survives from the earliest period, while the contemporaneous Hindu expression in perishable material is lost. One must mention here the large number of terra-cotta images, both male and female, that have emerged in the past twenty years or so, all modeled in the sensuous style of the stone figures at Bharhut and Sanchi.[23] Made of inexpensive clay, such images would have had a wide circulation and may be taken to represent the widespread emphasis on the body and corporeality. The few images that have emerged from archaeological excavations have been found in houses and not in any sacred context.

It is worth pausing here to repeat and reemphasize a point made in chapter 2 on the closely linked language used to speak of plants, on the one hand, and human bodies, on the other—both considered most beautiful in the period of fresh, tender growth. The beautiful body was one of supple fullness, never of firm muscularity. The connection of the body with swelling plants taut with internal moisture is evident in the constant metaphor of women's tendril-like limbs and bud-like hands, feet, and face. Daud Ali points out that "human limbs in their ideal state were to be smooth and tautly expanded, or 'blown' like the tender and succulent new growth of plants."[24] This repeated aesthetic finds full expression in the concept of *dohada*, the pregnancy longing of plants that is expressed in a wide range of Hindu literary sources. It involves a concept of cross-fertilization between women and plants, both linked by the all-important principle of fecundity.

As an aside, one might note that early feminist studies that pointed out the equation of woman with nature and man with culture, largely in the Western context, served a useful function by alerting viewers to the pervasiveness of certain underlying assumptions.[25] However, the very same equation of woman with nature can result in a totally different set of conclusions in the context of the Indian material. It is true that women, through their biological link with motherhood, suggested nature's exuberance; these evocative overtones emerge in the artists' emphasis, in the feminine figure, on wide, child-bearing hips and full breasts. These features, however, are not regarded negatively; rather, nature's exuberance implied a flow of good fortune that led to women, overflowing foliage, and couples becoming signs of the auspicious, of being a conduit for blessings.[26] It is this association of women with the auspicious that explains, in large measure, their ubiquitous presence on the many monuments of India—whether Buddhist, Hindu, or Jain—and, indeed, their equally pervasive presence on "secular" structures such as wells, pavilions, and palaces. The body of literary evidence regarding the auspiciousness of women is large and continuous, and is relevant also to our study of Hindu and Jain imagery. Yet since the issue of women, trees, and fertility already demands clarification, let us examine the literary motif of the woman-and-tree as it unfolds through time, and then return to complete our exploration of the sensuous body at Buddhist sites.

An Interlude: The *Dohada* Motif

The visual motif of a woman standing beneath a tree, encountered in Buddhist, Hindu, and Jain settings, is repeatedly evoked in literary works—poems, drama, and prose romances—composed over the centuries.[27] The origins of this motif may be traced to the belief that during the springtime, trees were subject to intense longings, similar to those experienced by pregnant women, and that only when such longings were satisfied would the trees put forth new shoots. The term *dohada*, which refers to a form of longing usually associated with pregnancy, was used to describe this condition of trees in the spring, and it was a woman's touch, sound, or sight for which these trees yearned.[28] By their very presence, women could cause a tree to blossom or bear fruit. It was believed that women in a mysterious manner transferred their fertility to the tree and, in turn, their own fertility might be enhanced through contact with the "pregnant" tree. The most popular ancient legend concerned the *ashoka* tree, which blossomed only through the touch of a woman's foot; Bharhut's Chulakoka *devata* stands beneath such an *ashoka* tree, which has elongated leaves and spiky clusters of orange blossoms (see figure 24).

The persistent belief in the importance and efficacy of the *dohada* rite, its continuing popularity in literary texts across the centuries, and its constant presence in the allied traditions of sculpture and painting are all different expressions of the same basic ideal of overflowing growth, with its implications of abundant joy and beauty. True, the literary texts are later than the visual material we have thus far examined, but we have to remember that the texts treat these concepts as well-established beliefs. The renowned poet-dramatist Kalidasa, writing around the year 400 C.E., made reference to the woman-and-tree in the majority of his works. The annual springtime *ashoka* tree rite is central to his play *Malavikagnimitra*, which tells of the love of King Agnimitra for young Malavika. Having hurt her leg in a fall from a swing, the queen had instructed Malavika to take her place in the ceremony of the *ashoka* tree. Accordingly, Malavika's friend adorned her feet with red color and placed the queen's anklets on her feet, saying: "Friend, arise! Perform the command of the queen! May the *ashoka* bloom!" When her gentle kick fails to produce immediate results, Malavika comments: "This *ashoka* is perverse, for it accepts my command to bloom, yet it shows no flowers. I hope our little ceremony won't be for nothing." Behind the scenes, the love-struck king, watching the ceremony, addresses the tree:

> Ashoka!
> You're blessed by the touch of her foot,
> tender as a new lotus shoot,
> and anklets that echo as it moves—
> If you don't burst forth in bloom
> vain will be the pregnant thirsts
> that playful lovers share with you.[29]

It is certain that the audience watching the play, which was staged to celebrate the spring festival when this rite was enacted, would have understood immediately the significance of the *ashoka* tree episode.

In several other works, Kalidasa makes passing references to this rite. In his poem *Kumara-sambhava*, Kalidasa speaks of the *ashoka* tree's response to the appearance of spring (Vasanta) along with Kama, god of love, and his consort Rati:

> At once the *ashoka* tree put out flowers
> and leaves budding straight from the trunk
> not waiting to bloom when a lovely woman's
> foot with her tinkling anklets touches it.[30]

In Kalidasa's *Raghu-vamsha*, King Aja bemoans the sudden death of his youthful beloved and laments:

> This *ashoka* tree in which you awoke the desire to bud forth
> is going to blossom. How can I take its flowers meant to be
> the ornament of your hair and make of them a garland for
> your funeral rite?
>
> O lovely limbed one, this *ashoka* tree, as though remem-
> bering the rare favour which your feet with their tinkling
> anklets granted him, is now mourning for you, shedding the
> tears of his flowers.[31]

In Kalidasa's poem *Megha-duta*, the *yaksha* hero, parted from his beloved, addresses over a hundred verses to a rain cloud that he sends with his message of love. Having described his beloved at length, he refers to her as the cloud's friend in describing a "pleasure hill" in the town:

> On it stands a ruddy *ashoka*, its branches
> swaying, and a lovely *kesara* tree near the bower
> of *madhavi* vines bordered with red amaranth,
> the first tree craving, as I do, the feel
> of your friend's foot, the second wine from her mouth,
> pretending they need these to bring them to blossom.[32]

Just as the listening audience would have understood the reference to the *ashoka* crav-ing the touch of a woman's foot, and the *kesara* pining for wine from the lips of a young woman, so the viewers of the sculpted images at Bharhut, Sanchi, Mathura, and elsewhere would have responded to the visual motif, recalling in imagination the interplay of tree and woman.

Readers of classical Indian literature know that this theme, as a literary motif, continued to be significant well into the sixteenth century, with an increasing number of trees being subsumed into the springtime rites.[33] Since literary and visual scholars do not often work in concert, I take this opportunity to highlight the fact that verbal and visual portrayals of this theme were being produced side by side. Each informed the other and reinforced the resonance and potency of the theme. The seventh-century play *Ratnavali*, attributed to Harsha, monarch of Kanauj, and centering on the love of King Udayana for a young Sri Lankan princess, Ratnavali, was intended for performance at the spring festival. The play carries an elaborate description of the garden where Queen Vasavadatta is about to worship an image of Kama, god of love, placed beneath an *ashoka* tree that she has adorned in saffron with her handprints. The king describes the beauty of the trees, swaying as if intoxicated with wine, and then proceeds to speak of the *bakula*, *champaka*, and *ashoka* trees:

> The wine sprinkled in mouthfuls and collected at the root is, as if, being scented with the shower of their flowers by the *bakula* trees; the *champaka* flowers smile today after a long time, while the moon-like faces of young females are yet red with the flush of wine; and hearing the jingle of the anklets loudly resounding in the act of giving strokes (by ladies) to the *ashoka* trees, an imitation of it is begun, as it were, by swarms of bees with their responsive songs.[34]

A near-contemporaneous prose romance, Subandhu's *Vasava-datta*, in describing the gardens in spring, also speaks of *bakula* trees sprinkled with mouthfuls of wine by amorous girls and of *ashoka* trees delighted by the slow strokes of the lotus-like feet, adorned with anklets, of young women enslaved by love.[35]

The association of the flowering of the *ashoka* tree with the touch of woman's foot became so well established that it was brought into play in the *Saundarya-lahari* (*Waves of Beauty*), a famous poem on Devi, the great goddess, perhaps of eighth-century date and sometimes attributed to the famous philosopher Shankara. Describing the radiance of Parvati's feet, with their enchanting designs in henna, the poet tells us that the gods did not dare to touch them even in reverent homage, addressing her feet only in verbal salutation. The verse explains that this was because Shiva was inordinately jealous even of the *ashoka* (also known as *kankeli*) trees in the forest that craved the touch of her feet:

> Reverence we voice to that eye-delighting pair of your feet,
> whose manifest beauty has been enhanced with liquid lac;

> when it (the *kankeli*) yearns for a kick from that (pair of feet),
> jealous beyond measure is
> the lord of creatures at the *kankeli* [*ashoka*] tree in your pleasure
>   grove.[36]

While readers of classical literature would agree that the *dohada* theme had become a standard literary motif, a routine trope, those who are not literary specialists might be interested to note that this is attested by two influential texts on poetics: the *Kavya-mimamsa* (*Investigation of Poetry*), composed by Rajashekhara around the year 900, and Abhinavagupta's *Locana* (*Eye*) commentary of around 1000 on the earlier *Dhvanya-loka* (*Realm of Suggestion*) of Anandavardhana. Rajashekhara uses the *dohada* motif to illustrate the manner in which negative statements may be presented in the affirmative, while Abhinavagupta cites it to illustrate tragic moments.[37] Both treatises quote a verse of the ninth-century poet Ratnakara, in which women of the vanquished enemy, even when forced to leave their homes, speak to the trees regretfully, saying that they (trees) will no longer experience the joy of interplay with the women; they, the griefless (trees), will be sorrowed and forsaken:

> O amaranth, you will lose the joy
> Of pressing close to our breasts;
> O *bakula* vine, our sweet breath
> Will live only in your memory;
> While you, the griefless *asoka*
> Will be grieved without the touch of our feet.
> Such are the words of his enemies' wives
> As they flee their ancient city.[38]

By the fifteenth century, the *Sahitya-mimamsa* (*Treatise on Literature*) defines the word *dohadika* as different ways of fulfilling the yearning of trees and causing them to blossom.[39]

Finally, toward the end of the sixteenth century, Krishnananda's Sanskrit *Tantrasara* (*Essence of Tantra*) codified these ideas and provided an entire list of trees and the exact action by which women caused them to blossom or bear fruit. This text has never been translated into English in its entirety, but Pratapaditya Pal has published sections of it in translation.[40] The *bakula* and *karnikara* (golden-yellow flowers) trees will blossom if they receive a mouthful of wine from a woman, while the *karnikara* also blooms to the sound of women's conversation.[41] The mango and neem trees will blossom to the sound of women's laughter. The *tilaka* (saffron flowers), *nameru* (*rudraksha* beads), and *piyala* (a type of fruit) will bloom at the sound of a woman singing. The *kuruvaka* and *sindhuvara* trees will respond if a woman embraces them. The orange-flowering *kadamba* and the fragrant *champaka* will blossom if the tree is just touched by a woman.

These examples from a wide range of literary works testify to a widespread belief in the touch of women being life-instilling and auspicious with respect to their counterparts in nature in the form of fruit-bearing or flowering trees. The women, by transferring their richness and fertility to the trees, were believed able to make them sprout and bloom. The association and interplay between the two were celebrated in spring festival rituals and in poetry, prose, and drama, in the context of royal courtly and elite life. Such repeated and widespread cross-references help decode and interpret the ubiquitous presence of women and foliage on all sacred structures, whether Buddhist, Hindu, or Jain. The visual evidence of woman's beauty, sexuality, and desirability testifies as strongly as the literary to the *dohada* theme, and the accompanying fertility and auspiciousness of women. We may assume that the visual motif would resonate as much for the general populace as for the sophisticated and knowledgeable audience of *rasikas*, who might better appreciate the subtleties and the multiple levels of implied meaning of this literary genre.

We may conclude our discussion of the *dohada* theme with J. Ph. Vogel's perceptive article on the woman-and-tree motif, sometimes referred to by the term *shala-bhanjika*.[42] Vogel traces the word to its first use, perhaps in the Buddhist *Avadana-shataka* (*One Hundred Legends*, first century?), where it denotes a festival centered on plucking *shal* blossoms, and he demonstrates how by the seventh century the term meant nothing more than a female statue. Thus the play *Viddha-shala-bhanjika* (*Portrait Statue*), composed by Rajashekhara around the year 900, uses the term solely to identify a female pillar image; it narrates the tale of a king who falls in love with a woman whom he sees first in a dream, then as a painted mural, and finally as a statue carved against a pillar.[43] Vogel suggests that this mutation was possible because the term *shala-bhanjika* denoted both the festival of plucking *shala* flowers and the women who plucked the blossoms. He quotes a persuasive parallel instance from the realm of classical art in which the word "caryatid," from denoting the female dancers at the Artemis temple in Caryae, finally became a technical term to denote any sculpted female figure supporting a cornice or an entablature.

Before returning to the imagery at Buddhist sites, one may comment briefly on the importance of the foliage motif in the decoration of Indian architectural monuments, Buddhist, Hindu, or Jain. Scrolls of foliage—some naturalistically depicted so as to permit identification of their botanical type, and others more stylized and abstracted so as to hide their precise vegetal origin—adorn all ancient architecture. Repeated bands of foliage are seen on every stupa, temple, and shrine (see figure 18). This is not intended merely as ornament, but as an embellishment with deeper levels of meaning. Recall Irene Winter's point that in ancient Mesopotamia, too, vegetal decoration was more than ornament; it was an indication of earthly abundance that was the promise of the monarch, and its very repetition served to intensify the message.[44] In India, foliage, like woman, was in itself a symbol of overflowing fertility, richness, and auspiciousness, and thus an auspicious emblem. Pots filled with overflowing foliage adorn most of the monuments of India, appearing as early as stupa 2 at Sanchi (ca. 100 B.C.E.). Even today, in religious ritual, a water-filled pot brimming with stems of mango leaves serves as a substitute for the anthropomorphic image of the goddess Lakshmi; often a "face" of the goddess is additionally placed against the leaves.[45] So, too, garlands of leaves are hung above entrances to homes, and as wedding decorations, where they are intended to invoke peace, prosperity, and plenty. Foliage and women, emblems of well-being and good fortune, were a recurring feature in the adornment of monuments, both sacred and secular, quite regardless of their religious or sectarian affiliation. As in the Assyrian context, in India their very repetition served to intensify their message. The third motif completing the fertility triad visible on Indian monuments was the couple, to whom we will turn in a Buddhist context; the association of the couple with fecundity, abundance, and growth is too obvious to need special explanation.[46]

Buddhist Sites Again

Little survives intact of the Buddhist monasteries constructed in Mathura during the first and second centuries C.E. We are left primarily with a series of railing pillars that feature women in a variety of stances, including the woman-and-tree motif, as well as several double-sided ornamental brackets, featuring women frontally on both faces (as against the front and rear views seen at Sanchi). The blatant sensuality of artistic expression and the accompanying voluptuousness of these richly adorned women, especially those from Mathura's Bhuteshvara stupa mound, are so overwhelming that some scholars have been impelled to suggest that the women are courtesans.[47] This interpretation was occasioned perhaps by the frank portrayal of the *mons veneris* and pudenda beneath the totally translucent skirt, indicated by a line along their ankles with pleated folds that hang down all the way alongside their legs, and by the carving of prominent nipples on their melon-like breasts. But it may be wise in this context to remember that the gendered body is a social construct that rarely reflects life as it is lived.[48]

One among many image-pillars features a sensual female standing on a crouching, dwarfish male; she is adorned with heavy earrings, a broad necklace, armlets, bracelets, and chunky anklets (figure 27). A wide, ornamental hip-belt holds in place a translucent skirt visible only as a line that connects along her ankles and by its heavy swags, which hang to the left of her lower limbs. She leans exaggeratedly to her right as if to counterbalance the weight of a heavy pot covered with an inverted glass that she holds up with her left hand; her right hand is suspended to hold a bunch of grapes. A railing band above her head serves to separate her from the upper story, which features a couple. The pillar figure gazes directly at the viewer and seems unaware that the man is reaching

Figure 27. Woman on image-pillar, sandstone,
Bhuteshvara stupa, Mathura, first to second century.

down for the glass, presumably to help himself to wine from the pot she holds. No strong reason exists to assign an alternative meaning to these railing image-pillars other than the symbolic association with abundance and fertility.[49] One specific Mathura image-pillar, now in the National Museum in New Delhi, spells out this symbolic meaning of woman as "the source and sustenance of life."[50] Standing on lotuses, the figure cups her right breast with her left hand, and points toward her genitals with her right hand, while the rear of the pillar has been converted into a portrayal of a lotus pond with two peacocks. The auspicious association with life-nurturing breast milk and the life-producing womb is unmistakably portrayed.

The power of the visual motif of woman-and-tree, and the accompanying belief in the potency of woman's fertility and auspiciousness, is reflected in an intriguing manner in the imagery chosen to depict Queen Maya giving birth to the Buddha.[51] The first unambiguous images of Maya giving birth to the Buddha were carved during the first two centuries C.E., more or less simultaneously, at the monastic site of Amaravati in the Andhra region of southern India and in Gandhara in northwestern India.[52] In both regions, artists portrayed Queen Maya standing beneath a tree, with one hand raised to grasp a branch; at Amaravati, the infant Buddha is represented by a pair of footprints on

Figure 28. Queen Maya and the Buddha's miraculous birth, limestone, Amaravati, Andhra Pradesh, second century.

the swaddling cloth held by the gods (an aniconic representation), while at Gandhara we see an anthropomorphic infant emerging from Maya's right hip. A slab that adorned the drum of the stupa at Amaravati is divided into four segments, each depicting an episode pertaining to the Buddha's birth. Its lower-right register portrays the moment after the birth and depicts the sensuous figure of the richly adorned queen standing beneath a tree while four gods hold a swaddling cloth on which a pair of footprints indicates that they have just received the new-born infant (figure 28). Visually, Maya constitutes a figure that at first sight seems interchangeable with the standard woman-and-tree motif; the treatment and positioning of her body, its stack of anklets, and its frank, sensuous quality remind one strongly of the Sanchi *yakshi* bracket.[53] It is of interest to note that Buddhist theology, postulating that any womb inhabited by a Buddha-to-be takes on a pure, fluid-free, crystalline quality, was able to overlook the fact that the Buddha inhabited Maya's womb for nine months. Yet it seems to have decided against the polluting concomitance of a vaginal birth, opting instead for a superhuman experience. The later *Tibetan Book of the Dead* seems to view the process of vaginal entry as the moment when all previous births come into review. Could this belief have had an early origin that might have influenced the theological decision for a miraculous birth?[54] In any case, the ancient sculptors appear quite happily to have drawn on the established artistic model of the woman-and-tree motif to create the setting for the miraculous birth of the Buddha. A combination of the belief in the emergence of new shoots as the response of trees to woman, and Buddhist legend proclaiming that Maya's birth pangs led her to garner support from a branch of the *shal* tree, resulted in a new iconography for the miracle of the birth. That such imagery rapidly became the established mode for the depiction of the Buddha's birth (no variants of any type exist hereafter to represent this miracle) testifies to the immense popularity, effectiveness, and potency of the woman-and-tree theme. In the context of the popularity of the *yakshas* discussed earlier, it is noteworthy that the scene to the left of the birth on the Amaravati drum slab portrays the presentation of the infant, represented by a parasol hovering over the swaddling cloth, to the tutelary *yaksha* of the Shakya clan, to which the Buddha's family belonged.

The theme of the loving couple (*mithuna*), generally portrayed as standing beside each other with the male's hand reaching around the female's shoulder, is seen as early as the Bharhut stupa. To comprehend these images, especially when prominently positioned in the form of larger-than-life-size standing images occupying the veranda space of a Buddhist monastic chapel, we must recall the significance attached to the concepts of fertility and abundance, as well as the primacy accorded to the human form. The Karle rock-cut monastery, not far from Mumbai, belongs to the first century C.E. Located halfway up a hill, some distance from a major township, its chapel was intended not so much for lay worshippers as for the Buddhist monks who resided at the site. These monks lived an austere life, occupying rock-cut residential halls and living in small cells with a raised rock-cut bed, a rock-cut pillow, and a small rock-cut niche in the wall for their few personal effects. The monastery centered on an immense *chaitya*-hall, a Buddhist chapel that extended 125 feet into the rock face and housed a rock-cut stupa at the far end. A row of columns with richly sculpted capitals follows the apsidal shape around the stupa dividing the interior into a central nave and two side aisles. The dimly lit interior, with its barrel-vaulted ceiling rising 46 feet high, creates an aura of shadowy solemnity. In contrast to such mystery, monks entering the veranda of the *chaitya*-hall would have encountered, visually, the images of eight well-built, richly adorned couples (figure 29). The male partner of each frontally portrayed couple has his arm around the shoulder of the female. The women have large, rounded breasts placed high on the torso, a narrow waist, and broad hips wrapped in a translucent skirt slung below the navel and

Figure 29. *Mithunas*, Deccan trap rock, *chaitya*-hall veranda, Karle, Maharashtra, first century.

held by a jeweled belt; the men are clean-shaven and exhibit well-toned torsos. The folds of the women's skirts and the men's dhotis are arranged so as to fall between their legs, and their abdominal musculature allows for the easy flow of breath that is characteristic of the Indian sculptural tradition. The two sets of couples at the far right end of the verandah are gifts from a monk named Bhadasama, and the inscription recording their donation describes them as *mithuna*s.[55] The commission emphasizes that such figures were accepted by the Buddhist clergy as appropriate and auspicious imagery in monastic surroundings. Apparently, the idea that they might generate irreverent thoughts did not arise; rather, the established association appears to have been with accentuated growth, prosperity, and auspiciousness. It is worth noting that the *Sarvastivadin Vinaya*, in its Chinese translation of 404, carries an interesting passage that sanctions decoration on all parts of a monastery. When queried by the devout lay follower Anathapindaka, the Buddha responds that the sole caveat concerns the subject matter of the paintings on the body of the stupa itself: "Save for the figures of man and women coupling, all else you may paint."[56] The implication, of course, is that such sensuous imagery was otherwise accepted subject matter.

Comparable emphasis on the couple as a repeated motif is seen at the Buddhist monastic site of Nagarjunakonda in the Andhra region of southern India, where a series of some twenty stupas were built during the third and fourth centuries. One of the embarrassments of Indian archaeology is the absence of a publication on the clearance and excavations conducted before the flooding of the site after the construction of the Nagarjunasagar Dam, making it impossible to allocate the numerous sculpted slabs from the site to any specific stupa. Fortunately, a mass of inscriptional material exists that clearly tells us the Buddhist monasteries were all constructed by the patronage of the queens and princesses of the Ikshvaku dynasty, while its rulers focused their attention on the Hindu temples at the adjoining capital city. Each stupa has platform projections (*ayakas*) at the four cardinal points, and on each platform stand five *ayaka* pillars that carry the donative inscriptions. Crowning these *ayaka* platforms are a series of long, narrow sculpted slabs that narrate a variety of Buddhist legends, including the life story of the Buddha himself. Each *ayaka* "cornice" slab is bracketed at either end by an image of a woman beneath a tree or occasionally a couple beneath a tree. The length of the slab is divided into four to six framed compartments, each narrating an episode from Buddhist legend and separated from the next by the figures of a loving couple. One slab portraying a different set of stories in its compartments, but intact today along only half its length, is a classic instance of the type (figure 30). Some of the voluptuous *mithuna* couples face the viewer in a more formal frontal view, while others interact with each other so that one or other of the figures presents a rear view to the observer. These cornice-type slabs occupy a prominent position at eye level at the four entrances to each stupa enclosure and would have been one of the first panels viewed by pilgrims to the site. It is apparent that the artists, the queens and princesses who sponsored the monasteries, and the Buddhist monastics themselves found it suitable and fitting to thus punctuate episodes of Buddhist legend with the flowing, sensuous human forms of couples. This only emphasizes how deeply the repetitive theme of fullness and proliferation, and consequent auspiciousness, was ingrained in the Indian psyche; the association was innate and profound so that the possibility of irreverent thoughts does not seem to have been an issue. Additionally, one might think in terms of *alankara* and the need to "dress" or ornament the slab, in this case with figures of couples.

If I appear to give too much attention to the imagery at Buddhist sites, it is partly because some scholars have expressed surprise that the suspicious if not disdainful attitudes toward women, so prevalent in Buddhist texts, are not reflected in the visual arts. One might point out that Buddhist texts were written by monastic scholars who had rejected worldly life in favor of a life devoted strictly to the path of Buddhism, and that their writings reflect the beliefs of a narrowly defined group and not of the Buddhist lay community as a whole. Margaret Miles's observation on the logocentric attitude in European medieval studies, which places much reliance on Christian theological literature produced by educated, male monastics, is worth repeating here. Miles criticizes attempts "to understand a historic community entirely from the study of the writings of a few of its most uncharacteristic members."[57] In India, too, the "ecclesiastic" literature was

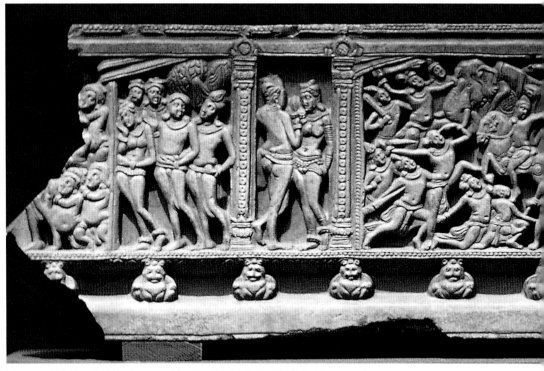

Figure 30. *Ayaka* "cornice" slab, limestone, Nagarjunakonda, Andhra Pradesh, third to fourth century.

largely written by and for the male monastic community, making it more likely that the artistic material at the various stupa sites better represents the widely held beliefs of the lay worshippers who constituted the primary group of adherents to the faith.

In any discussion of early imagery in the Indian subcontinent, it would be best to speak not in terms of a Buddhist art, but of an early Indian art directed toward the adornment of a Buddhist monastery or a Hindu or Jain temple. Doubtless, the same artists worked for different patrons, adjusting their iconography and narratives to the cycle of mythology associated with the deities of various faiths.[58] The auspiciousness associated with the themes of women, couples, and foliage was a common sentiment crossing religious boundaries and language barriers, and hence used to adorn a wide range of the monuments of India.

Hindu Temple Imagery

In its simplest form, the Hindu temple consists of an enclosed sanctum enshrining a deity that is to be viewed through a single doorway from a small adjoining assembly hall. Occupying the center of each of the three outer walls of the sanctum is a deity-niche that houses images relating in one way or another to the goddess or the god enshrined within the sanctum. Between these deity-niches, as well as along the walls of the *mandapa* hall

in front, we find, especially in northern India, a profusion of female figures and *mithuna* couples that echo the same symbolism as the images examined thus far in a Buddhist context. Figural sculpture is noticeably absent on the inner walls of a temple sanctum, decorative treatment being reserved largely for the outer walls. Several thousand ancient Hindu temples exist across the subcontinent, while I have chosen just four temple sites to demonstrate the recurrence of the woman motif on the temple walls. My choice of so few examples from Hindu temple sculpture reflects the fact that this material, in general, is much better known than the Buddhist for its preoccupation with the related themes of woman, couple, and foliage.

The eighth-century Vaital Deul is among the few temples dedicated to the goddess in the temple-town of Bhubaneshvar in Orissa. She is enshrined in its rectangular sanctum in her fearsome form as emaciated skeletal Chamunda and—in an exceptional reversal of the statement that there is no figural sculpture within the sanctum of Hindu temples—is surrounded by other members of her entourage.[59] On the Vaital Deul's exterior, the deity-niche along the long rear wall of the sanctum carries an image of Shiva as Half-Woman (Ardha-nari), while the niches on the two narrower side walls portray eight-armed Durga fighting the buffalo-demon and four-armed standing Parvati. While Ardha-nari is undoubtedly the central deity figure on the rear wall, the niche is not set off in any way from the remaining four niches adorning the wall, nor is the image larger or

Figure 31. Rear wall of Vaital Deul temple, with central deity-niche featuring Shiva as Ardha-hari and flanking niches with women, sandstone, Bhubaneshvar, eighth century.

more prominent than the rest. The four women in the flanking niches are carved as the same size as Ardha-nari and with the same level of attention by the same artist (figure 31). While they adopt different postures—two look into a mirror, one adjusts her scarf-like upper garment, and one is the familiar figure of a woman pulling down the branch of a tree—it is noteworthy that all are given oval haloes that suggest an elevated status. The images of Parvati and Durga on the temple's side walls are more prominent and pronounced; they are immediately flanked by smaller *mithuna* couples and figures of women in varying poses. The repetitive and insistent positioning of figures of women on both sides of all three deity-niches is noteworthy. It seems clear that by the eighth century, the woman-and-tree motif was only one of several poses that women could adopt and still retain their acknowledged status as auspicious figures emblematic of fertility, growth, and prosperity.

Similar in the prominence given to figures of women is the Ambika-mata temple at Jagat, not far from Udaipur in Rajasthan, dated by inscription to the year 969 and dedicated to the goddess Durga as the powerful, multiarmed divinity who destroyed the brutish buffalo-demon Mahisha. Deity-niches on the three exterior walls of the sanctum, and on the two side walls of the preceding hall, carry a total of five dynamic images of the goddess fighting the buffalo-demon. The glorious goddess (see chapter 4) effortlessly defeats Mahisha, who is shown variously as wholly animal, a wholly human male, or a human male with the head of a buffalo. Surrounding the images of the triumphant goddess are female figures in provocative poses (see figure 43). All are slim, elegant, and exhilarating, clad in transparent garments and richly adorned. One tosses her head backward as she strides away from the viewer, another wrings out the water from her long hair, a third strikes a dance pose, a fourth moves in elegant dignity, while the last, in a rare pose, looks directly at the viewer. I would propose that all find a place on the temple walls because all are regarded as conferring auspiciousness.

Setting aside the two small goddess temples at Bhubaneshvar and Jagat, we will turn to consider three large royal temples at Khajuraho in central India, dating between about 950 and 1050, and dedicated to the gods Shiva and Vishnu. All three are exuberantly adorned with female figures and *mithuna* couples, making it quite clear that such imagery, with its connotation of auspiciousness, was used to adorn temple walls regardless of whether a goddess or a god was honored within The Lakshmana Vishnu temple of King Dhanga completed in 954, the Vishvanatha Shiva temple of King Yashovarman completed in 1011, and the Kandariya Mahadeo Shiva temple of around 1050 (which is certainly royal, although lacking an inscription) are all expansive double temples with an inner shrine whose outer walls are adorned like those at Bhubaneshvar and Jagat. Each inner temple with its enclosed sanctum has deity-niches on its three exterior walls that contain images relating to the deity enshrined within the sanctum. And each deity-niche is flanked by images of women in a variety of poses, as well as by *mithuna* couples. A circumambulatory path surrounding the shrine is now enclosed by the outer temple walls, creating a new decorative effect that gives the appearance of having abandoned the three-deity-niche format. This is not so, however, and the standard format may be seen when one enters the temple and performs a ritual circumambulation of the sanctum. The outermost walls of these temples now use the expansive space at their disposal to display images of gods and goddesses, of women, and of couples. The walls of the Kandariya Mahadeo temple are estimated to carry as many as 650 figures. As one studies these outer walls in detail—for instance, its rear walls that enclose the inner shrine—one notes that each band of carved figures portrays a central four-armed god flanked by figures of women. Thus certain portions of the exterior of the Kandariya Mahadeo display twice as many women as deities! If the counterargument is that this is suggestive of the "male gaze," our only response is that such a gaze within the boundaries of a temple seems unlikely, but cannot be conclusively negated.

By the eleventh century, written texts for temple builders contain confirmation of the potency of woman's fertility and its equation with growth, abundance, prosperity, and the auspicious. Reading between the lines of one of these texts, the Orissan *Shilpa-prakasha* (*Light on Art*), dating perhaps to around 1077, one may state that woman seems to have served an apotropaic and hence protective function. Her auspiciousness was transferred to the monument on which she was sculpted or painted, so that such a monument—whether a royal palace, a Buddhist stupa, or a Hindu or a Jain shrine— gained strength and protection through portrayals of the feminine. The *Shilpa-prakasha*, in laying down rules for practicing temple architects and sculptors, categorically states that figures of women are "indispensable in architecture."[60] Emphasizing this, it states: "As a house without a wife, as frolic without a woman, so without (the figure of) woman the monument will be of inferior quality and bear no fruit."[61] Does this in any way suggest a parallel between a temple and, say, an *ashoka* tree? The text lists sixteen types of women who best decorate a monument and instructs the sculptor on how exactly to carve these figures within the confines of an upright rectangle, which he was to divide according to a specified grid. The exact poses and manner of positioning these figures, detailed in the text, find their visual counterpart in the profusion of female images that decorate the walls of temples, such as those at Bhubaneshvar in Orissa and Khajuraho in central India. Although no central Indian counterpart of this text has yet been traced, on the basis of the Khajuraho reliefs one can only assume their onetime existence.

The *Shilpa-prakasha*'s list of sixteen female types commences with the restful, relaxed woman called *alasa*, and the text uses this term rather than *nayika* in a generic sense for "women"; Orissan texts tend to have their own specific architectural terms, too, such as *deul* and *jagamohana* for the more usual *vimana* and *mandapa*. Such a woman could stand behind a door (*torana*), be young and innocent (*mugdha*), be haughty and offended (*manini*), or garland herself with a branch (*dala-malika*). She might smell a lotus (*padma-gandha*), look into a mirror (*darpana*), be pensive (*vinyasa*), adorn herself with *ketaki* flowers (*ketaki-bharana*), or be a lovely mother with her infant in her arms (*matr-murti*). She could hold a fly whisk (*chamara*), turn away from the viewer (*gunthana*), be a dancer (*nartaki*), play with a parrot or mynah bird (*shuka-sarika*), adjust her anklets (*nupura-padika*), or be a drummer (*mardala*). Walls of northern temples display all sixteen types, along with several others—such as a woman fastening her skirt, shooing away a monkey, or playing with a ball—suggesting the existence of textual variants that have not survived (see figure 5).

These evocations of youth, beauty, budding sexuality, and auspiciousness continue to receive praise and acclaim down the ages. In her translation of an eighteenth-century Tamil poem featuring the fortune-teller of Kuttralam, Indira Peterson highlights the poet's joyous, exuberant, and delighted verbal pictures of heroine Vasantavalli playing with a ball:

> The lovely Vasantavalli played ball,
> she played ball with wonderful skill.
>
> Her breasts, high as the Mandara mountains,
> rose and fell,
> her fish-shaped earrings swung to and fro,
> her beautiful eyes darted about,
> her feet danced to the rhythm "tomkat tom."
> The lovely Vasantavalli played ball,
> she played ball with wonderful skill.[62]

The poet conveys to the reader his rapture over this lovely young woman, with ball in hand, to whose lively beauty he pays tribute. Likewise, the Khajuraho artists, as indeed those in Orissa or Karnataka, conveyed to their viewers that same delight in the rotating, whirling, pirouetting figures of young and beautiful women.

Alongside these images of women and deities, placed almost at random on the Khajuraho temple walls, are a certain number of images of loving couples, openly embracing and entwining. If we return to the *Shilpa-prakasha*, we find that it specifies that couples, too, have a decisive role to play in the decorative treatment of temple walls. Suggesting that their inclusion creates an attractive monument, it states that "a place without love-images [*kama-kala*] is known as a 'place to be shunned' [*tyakta-mandala*]."[63] Khajuraho's temple walls contain many such entwining figures, which create striking accents on the walls (see figure 11). In addition, these temples carry sets of figures engaged in a variety of explicit sexual activities; largely positioned on the exterior walls joining the shrine and the hall, at points of juncture, they are the subject of an entirely separate discussion.[64]

At approximately the time when the Kandariya Mahadeo temple was being built at Khajuraho, an extraordinary underground structure known locally as Rani ki Vav, or the Queen's Stepwell, was being constructed in the town of Patan in the western Indian state of Gujarat. It is attributed to Queen Udayamati of the Chaulukya dynasty of Gujarat and was dedicated around the year 1085.[65] In this arid zone, as in many other such areas of India, stepwells were dug deep into the ground, providing water for the township, a cool shelter from the blazing noonday sun, and a *serai* (overnight resting spot) for travelers. It was a descent to plenty. In 1986, clearance commenced of the silted-up remains of the site to reveal an enormous underground structure, built in seven subterranean levels, which measured approximately 215 by 70 feet and contained 292 ornamental pillars. The well was dug down some 100 feet to reach water, and it incorporated an overflow tank for surplus storage when the water table rose. While it was clearly a functional unit, there was much more to the Queen's Stepwell, which is covered with sculpted images, both sacred and secular, of which some four hundred survive. I shall barely touch on the iconographic complexities of the well's sculptural program—which, incidentally, has not yet revealed the logic or method behind its planning. I shall concentrate here only on the proximity of sacred and nonsacred imagery and how they share the same space along the well's perimeter walls, restricting my discussion to just two areas of this stupendous monument.

The walls along the well's terrace on the third level are dedicated to a celebration of the avatars of the Hindu god Vishnu, clearly indicating that the utilitarian character of the well was overlaid by a sacred aspect. And then—to challenge, or to accent, the sacred content?—each avatar is separated from the next by figures of slender, vivacious, provocatively poised women who have little to do with the mythology of Vishnu. The women wear long, translucent skirts wrapped around their hips and held in place with jeweled *mekhalas*, while the pleated folds rest on either side of their legs. Scarf-like upper garments swing away from their torsos to reveal shapely breasts, and the figures are richly adorned with elaborate hair-knots and jewelry that we have noted as typical of the Indian sculptural tradition. Vishnu, as the great snouted boar Varaha who rescues the earth, stands with one foot on a lotus leaf held by two serpentine water beings; the elegant earth goddess sits on his upraised elbow and gently fondles his snout (figure 32).[66] Flanking this powerful vision of the Vishnu avatar are two provocative female figures, both with one arm raised above their heads, thereby affording viewers an unrestricted view of their bodies. To the viewer's right is a richly adorned woman with a water vessel resting on the ground beside her, while to the left is a rare example of an unclothed woman, seemingly a *yogini*, holding in her hand a skull as alms bowl, with a snake wrapped around her and a set of three owls perched on the ledge above.

On the opposite wall of this third terrace, a series of more formally sculpted human avatars of Vishnu is likewise punctuated by sensuous women. The last of these avatars portrays Kalki as the tenth incarnation, the avatar yet to arrive, when Vishnu will appear through the sky riding a white horse and holding a flaming sword (figure 33). The flanking woman to the right holds on to her skirt with one hand while, with the other held above her head, she makes a futile attempt to shoo away a monkey that is pulling at her garment. To the left is an exquisite depiction of a woman with one leg crossed in front of the other, and with a thoughtful look as she raises a morsel of food to her lips. One might note that out of some four hundred surviving sculpted images, as many as two hundred—half the total number—are sensuous females. The actual proportion is probably more in the range of one-third female figures to two-thirds sacred imagery, since several flanking female figures have already been carved in situ while the niche between them remains empty, awaiting the installation of a sacred image that would have been carved in a quarry or a workshop and transported to the site for installation. Whatever the exact numbers may prove to be, the explanation for the repeated presence of women lies in the same deep-seated, instinctive belief in their auspicious and protective role, the identical significance we have seen to apply to such female forms at other sites.

The circular well shaft—covered, like all portions of this amazing monument, with a range of figures of deities—gives pride of place to the popular Hindu creation myth in which the god Vishnu slumbers on his serpent couch on the primordial waters prior to the creation of the world. The image of reclining Vishnu is repeated on the three lowest levels of the well, suggesting that the queen and her architects tried to ensure that regardless of the level of the water table, Vishnu's serpent couch would always rest on the waters. Incidentally, this monument was not open to the sky, as it appears today, but was roofed to afford shelter, as may be seen in several smaller, intact stepwells in the same region. We see here a monument that combines, effectively and imaginatively, a functional element like water, of such enormous importance in the arid regions of India,

Figure 32. Vishnu as Varaha, sandstone, third terrace, Queen's Stepwell, Patan, Gujarat, ca. 1085.

Figure 33. Vishnu as Kalki, sandstone, third terrace, Queen's Stepwell, Patan, Gujarat, ca. 1085.

with symbolic imagery—not only appropriate sacred mythology, but also sensuous images of women—to produce a structure that defies any neat classification. The Queen's Stepwell is a superb example of a seamless weave of sensuous and sacred, of practical and religious, of divine and profane. It emphasizes the importance of the physical body, which was well formed, lithe, and well toned through yogic discipline. It was an auspicious form that spoke of beauty and joy, of fertility and well-being; alternatively, it was a divine body in which beauty of external form spoke of inner spiritual beauty. Most of all, the Queen's Stepwell emphasizes the futility of classifying spaces as sacred or secular, a terminology that is of little help in recognizing and evaluating the range of human activities enacted within architectural spaces.

Temples to the Jain Faith

Temples dedicated to one or other of the twenty-four Jinas (Liberators) of the relatively ascetic Jain faith frequently reveal a decorative scheme with remarkable similarities to that seen on the Hindu temple. Jain monastics split at an early date into the Shvetambara (white-clad) and the Digambara (sky-clad or naked), with the Shvetambara group giving a major role to the worship of images in temples. John Cort demonstrates that a much later subdivision of the Shvetambaras resulted in further subdivision into the Murti-pujak (image-worshipping) Jains, for whom the image and the temple were crucial, and the Sthanakvasi and Therapanthis, for whom image worship played no role.[67] The image enshrined in Jain temples is the renunciant figure of a Jina seated cross-legged and absorbed in meditation with a serene expression on his face. Murti-pujak Jains practice a daily *puja* (ritual worship) and *darshan* (purposeful viewing) of the temple image that in many ways outwardly parallels Hindu practices.[68] One striking point of difference is that while priests, and priests alone, perform the *puja* ritual in Hindu temples, it is the Jain devotee herself or himself who performs *puja* in a Jain temple; in contrast to the high status of the Hindu *pujari* who performs the ritual of *puja*, the Jain temple *pujari* is a mere menial servant who sees to its cleanliness and general maintenance.

Daily *puja* includes prostrating oneself before the image; circumambulating the shrine; offering water, sandal-paste, and flowers to the Jina image; and additional optional *puja* with incense, lamps, food and fruit, bell ringing, and hymns of praise. Unlike Hindu *puja*, where the deity is believed to partake of the food offerings, which are then returned to the devotee as *prasada*, Jain food offerings are not offered for consumption. Indeed, the Jina is addressed during the offering as one who has attained a state of non-consumption of food. Of relevance to our discussion is the sandal-paste offering, which highlights the importance of the Jina's bodily form. We have seen earlier that in the nine-limbed *puja*, sandal-paste is applied to a total of thirteen spots on the body—two toes, two knees, two wrists, two shoulders, and the head, forehead, throat, heart, and navel.[69]

Cort points out that to prevent damage to the Jain *murtis*, many of which are carved from marble, it is customary to inset the image with silver at the spots where the devotees apply sandal-paste. The body of a Jina is one that has renounced the world, yet is celebrated for its finely toned beauty. The nine-limbed *puja* is reminiscent of the Hindu practice of *nyasa*, or touching of parts of the body to activate them. Regardless of Jain theological writings, the beauty of the image seems to emphasize that, as in the Hindu context, spiritual beauty can reside only in a form of physical perfection.

While it is the laity that performs *puja*, the Jain renunciant *sadhus* are also involved in temple activities, at least to the extent that it is they who must consecrate and install an image. Thus involvement with the temple is not solely a lay activity, since the *sadhus* frequently encourage the building of grand temples to honor the Jinas.[70] *Murti puja* is endorsed as leading to *mangala*, *shubha*, and *kalyana*, all words meaning "well-being" and having multiple connotations that include holiness, fortune, prosperity, wealth, good luck, auspiciousness, health, gain, and merit.[71]

Wealthy Jain patrons commissioned numerous temples, which, in western India, were frequently built of expensive marble. Elaborate sculpted ceilings, adorned with a variety of designs, both figurative and ornamental, were constructed over each of the bays of the row of attached mini-shrines that formed a pillared corridor enclosing the main temple. Various portions of a Jain temple were adorned with images of women; pillar shafts frequently display figures of dancing females, while women striking a variety of poses were carved to function as decorative brackets. One such bracket in the marble Luna Vasahi temple at Mount Abu in Rajasthan portrays a pert flutist pirouetting in space so as to treat the viewer to a glimpse of both breasts as well as one well-rounded buttock; the multiple folds of her skirt, and her upper scarf, float around her richly adorned body (figure 34). The extraordinarily ornate ceiling above the temple's *ranga-mandapa* (dance hall) was described in the *Samarangana Sutradhara* (*Heavenly Architect*), the architecture text of the eleventh-century king Bhoja, as a *karotaka* (vision of the cosmos).[72] It resembles some fantastic dream world of lotuses (figure 35). Superimposed on its multiple circular layers are images of the sixteen *maha-vidyas*, Jain goddesses of magical powers, each sensuous goddess being modeled according to the formula seen in the bracket figure. The female form, whether of a flutist or a powerful goddess, was equally celebrated as slender, sensuous, and utterly beautiful.

A Jain temple, like its Hindu counterpart, was in ancient times a place where people congregated for various reasons. Although the main idea may have been to perform ritual worship, to enjoy the sacred atmosphere in the company of fellow devotees, and perhaps to observe silence to meditate, it appears that there were also other reasons to visit a Jain temple. These included admiring the artistic panels and figures on the walls, ceilings, and pillars; watching temple dances; and listening to music. It was sacred space that welcomed devoted worship, solemnity, and serious contemplation, but at the same time accommodated the joyous moments flowing from the external world. An im-

Figure 34. Flutist bracket, marble, Vimala Vasahi temple, Mount Abu, Rajasthan, twelfth century.

Figure 35. Ceiling of *ranga-mandapa*, with *maha-vidyas*, marble,
Luna Vasahi temple, Mount Abu, Rajasthan, thirteenth century.

pression of the atmosphere within a Jain temple during the reign of the twelfth-century monarch Kumarapala is conveyed by the five verses quoted here from Phyllis Granoff's translation of the *Kumarapala-vihara-shataka* (*Hundred Verses on King Kumarapala's Temple*).[73] Written around 1150 by the Jain monk Ramachandragani to describe a temple just erected by his monarch, Kumarapala, the poem actually consists of more than a hundred verses. Cort points out that the reign of this Solanki monarch was a high-water mark for Jain political influence in Gujarat.[74]

> There, in that temple made of dark stone, lovely women had
> to feel their way, and to step quickly only at the door frames,
> which were made of glittering sunstone that threw off the
> light; they smiled upon seeing the female bracket figures and
> felt fear at the sight of the lions adorning the thrones of the
> main images; they were wearied by the crush of worship-
> pers and felt a tingle of pleasure as they brushed against the

bodies of their husbands; they danced to the sound of the drums, and all in all were a delight to the young gallants who watched them.

(verse 68)

In that temple people were always present; faithful Jains came simply as a pious act; those who were seriously ill came out of a desire for a cure; artists came to admire the skill and workmanship; ugly men and women came out of a desire to become beautiful; those who had lost their wealth came out of a desire for money; some who loved music came to hear the singing, and servants came because they wanted to become masters.

(verse 71)

Outside the temple on the street, people craned their necks to stare fixedly at the beauty of the structure which reached into the sky. Not watching where they were going, they bumped into each other and grew so angry that fights and quarrels arose all around.

(verse 99)

There, in that temple, on festival days, when the crowd blocked their way, the cries of the elderly made everyone feel compassion for them as they implored, "Brother! Take me up front and give me a glimpse of the lotus face of Lord Parshvanatha, who grants all wishes."

(verse 107)

There, in that temple, the statue of a lady who struggled to hold fast to her girdle as a monkey untied its knot made young gallants feel desire and confirmed the steadfast in their rejection of sensual delights; it disgusted the pious and made old ladies feel embarrassed; while it made young men laugh and young girls wonder.

(verse 112)

The varying responses of those viewing sensuous imagery; the all-too-natural distinction among the reactions of a grandmother, a young wife, and a teenager; the juxtaposition of devout worship with harmless and joyous dance: all these go to make up a multihued picture of both worship and social interaction in a Jain temple a thousand years ago. The routine of day-to-day life mingled unconsciously and imperceptibly with the sacred and the spiritual, the mundane rubbed shoulders with the otherworldly, once again substantiating the lack of any sharp dividing line between sacred and profane in the Indian ethos.

If we continue to use the phrase "sacred space" for its convenience as a way of classifying architectural spaces, it becomes necessary to clarify its usage in the Indian context. The most obvious purpose of a temple, whether Buddhist, Hindu, or Jain, is to inculcate a desire for the experience of the sacred and to encourage communion with the divine. Indian sacred spaces are dedicated to ritual worship, expressed through *puja* in which all the outgoing senses are harnessed and directed toward concentration on the divine image. Sound, smell, taste, vision, and touch all participate in what often appears to be a noise-filled and disordered affair. In the Indian context, however, there is no distinct break between life in this world and the life of the spirit, the one gradually leading to the next. The temple allowed space for both, while trying to make its visitors constantly aware of its still center, the sacred and the holy. In addition to ritual worship—which does not mandate silence, hushed tones, or solemnity—a variety of other demands are made on temple and monastic spaces, not the least being to provide a daytime meeting place for the priests themselves between *pujas*. The space is used to discuss a variety of matters, such as the nature of rituals, the generosity or parsimony of patrons, the price of specific temple services, even the choice of the sacred hymns to be sung the next day. Once the act of *puja* is over, devotees, too, make use of the space adjoining the shrine as a place to rest, a spot for discussions, or a venue to discuss matters of worldly import. In addition, of course, the temple provides space for several of its own daily, weekly, and monthly festivities, including music and dance, which cause devotees to congregate at temples in large numbers. All these provided proximity to the divine through closely related activities that not only were much simpler to understand and appreciate than the abstract, but also provided recreation, to say nothing of an incipient sense of joy. Architectural spaces in India are not sharply divided into sacred and secular and do, indeed, fulfill multiple roles.

4. TO THE DIVINE THROUGH BEAUTY

Sacred images of gods and goddesses—whether carved in stone, modeled in bronze, or painted in colors—are invariably portrayed throughout the Indian subcontinent as captivating beings with slender, sensuous bodies and exquisite faces. In terms of modeling, gods, kings, and courtiers—like goddesses, queens, and women—share the qualities of idealized figural representation. While in the Judeo-Christian world, one speaks of God having made man in his own image, in the Indian world one may speak, without any disrespect, of man having made god in his own image. Deities, royals, and humans have idealized bodies transfixing in their beauty. It is tricky to come to terms with the concept of the sensuous character of a sacred being. We have to wonder why a sacred icon that is imbued with divinity, a god or goddess intended to be approached with devotion and veneration, is portrayed as adorable in a sensuous aspect. The manner in which viewers react to the allure and intense physicality of the perfect body of a god or goddess is an even more challenging issue.

Equally puzzling, even mesmerizing, are the images of Shiva and Parvati, and of Vishnu and Lakshmi, portrayed as loving couples with the god's left arm reaching around his consort to cup her left breast, and often with a right hand turning his beloved's face toward him to gaze into her eyes. Admittedly, they are partners in a divine marriage, but the sensual nature of their imagery is an extraordinary phenomenon that many feel is a contradiction in terms. Working within the accepted artistic tradition, however, sculptors gave sensuous and stimulating forms to the sacred and worship-worthy images they created.

An appreciation of the sensuous imagery used to portray Shiva, Vishnu, and Devi, deities of daily worship for Hindus, and an assessment of the role of beauty in the evocation of the divine, is enhanced by examining similar material provided by literary and epigraphic texts. The poems, dramas, and epics of court poets over the centuries, as well as the sacred hymns composed by saints and *acharyas* (teachers), show that one easy, direct, and joyous mode of approach to the divine was through reveling in the beauty of the god or goddess, and adoring the sheer splendor of the divine body form. Verse and prose inscriptions of royalty, aristocracy, and wealthy individuals, whether couched in Sanskrit or in a range of vernacular languages, closely parallel the literary works in speaking of the glorious physical aspect of the gods. Furthermore, in openly celebrating the deities' erotic love, both these types of written sources underscore the visual imagery.

Much of the material examined in this chapter pertains to southern India, where festivals that center on beautiful-bodied bronze images were and are most fully and exuberantly expressed. Every temple in the south—and there are several hundred in Tamil Nadu—continues to celebrate the festival cycle with a range of images, some a thousand years old and others made yesterday. The Tamil saints, the Shaiva *nayanmars* and the Vaishnava *alvars*, whose hymns we shall juxtapose with the images, lived between the sixth and the ninth century, before the creation of several of the images on which we shall focus. The saints traveled to the various sacred sites of the south and composed songs at each temple, celebrating the deity enshrined therein. Their striking verbal pictures detailing the bodily beauty of the various forms of Shiva and Vishnu seem to suggest that they were gazing at images. But with the exception of Pallava stone imagery at Mamallapuram and Kanchipuram, little has survived from the many temples of Tamil Nadu celebrated by the saints. We must assume that they were singing in front of images, modeled in clay or carved from wood, that have not stood the test of time. Some of the saints speak specifically of portable images that were taken in procession—of Shiva in his mendicant form, of dancing Shiva—clearly indicating that their verbal pictures were not purely imaginary. The creation of portable bronze images largely dates from the ninth century onward, raising the possibility of early portable images, too, being of wood or clay.[1] The *acharyas*, who postdate the saints, belonged to the eleventh century and onward, their hymns being composed at a time when several magnificent temples with images in stone and bronze were already in place, and more temples and images were being commissioned on a regular basis. The inscriptional material we shall be citing comes largely from the twelfth and thirteenth centuries, and is thus roughly contemporary with the compositions of the *acharyas*; a few epigraphs are of later date.

To place the material in context, it is useful to begin with the concept of *bhakti*, a word that may be translated somewhat imperfectly as "intense devotion to a chosen personal god." Through the ages, many paths by which to approach the godhead have been proposed in India; chief among these are meditation on a formless divine, and the path of *bhakti*, or devotion expressed initially through song and ritual worship.[2] The one entails a withdrawal from home life and worldly interests, while the other proposes life in the world but with the constant practice of *bhakti*. *Bhakti* was and is a joyous path of approach, and one that was not in conflict with life in this world, at least in southern India.[3] The saints of southern India, and the *acharyas* who followed them, demonstrated the efficacy of this approach in their lives, singing songs of praise in which dwelling on the beauty of the god or goddess became in itself a method of recollection that gradually led to surrender, making it an essential ingredient of the path of *bhakti*. Generally, although not invariably, *bhakti* goes hand in hand with the ritual of worship known by the term *puja*; *puja*, in turn, requires images of the deities on which to lavish one's attention and devotion. *Puja* and images are closely associated with *bhakti*, and the understanding of the one component informs the other.

This chapter may be viewed as a series of explications of the manner in which the sensuousness of deities is invoked in sculpture and poetry; they constitute a series of "test cases," so to say. We commence with Shaiva imagery, move to the *archa*-images of Vishnu, and conclude by focusing on the divine couples, both Shiva–Parvati and Vishnu–Lakshmi. My aim is to present readers with a better appreciation of the luxurious, sensuous imagery, both visual and literary, used to portray the gods. Issues arise regarding the viewers' reception of such images. Is it only the art historian and the museum visitor who perceives the dilemma of reconciling the intense physical allure of a sacred image with the fact that it is to be approached with veneration? Does the temple devotee, who encounters such images only after *puja*, when they are totally covered with silks, jewels, and flowers, dwell in a world apart? What of the reaction of that same temple devotee, faced with glorious but "uncovered" images of the deities on the exterior walls of that very same temple? Further, there is the evocative nature of the hymns of the saints and *acharyas*, composed not only in Sanskrit but also in the various vernaculars, which are redolent with similar sensuous phraseology. While such issues will be addressed in this chapter when relevant, we shall leave to the afterword a full discussion of the thorny and problematic issues surrounding the creation and reception of sensuous sacred imagery.

The Shaiva Grouping

Shiva

Chola bronze images of Shiva as Nataraja (Lord of Dance) confront the viewer with a vision of divinity and sensuousness inextricably mingled (p. vi and figure 36). The form of Nataraja—with its exquisite face, elegant torso, perfectly proportioned thighs and legs, and gently curved yet tight behind—is indeed the epitome of beauty. He is the wondrously handsome Lord of Dance, whose dance of joy is imbued with profound philosophic implications. In his dance of bliss, Shiva holds within himself the possibility of dancing the world into extinction, only to re-create it through the same dance. The flaming fire held in one hand bodes destruction, while the sound of the drum in the other foretells creation. The dwarf-like figure on whom Shiva is poised stands for ignorance and darkness that must be destroyed, and Shiva's raised foot bestows salvation on the individual soul. It is a deeply sacred form imbued with immense significance at which I have merely hinted.[4] But it is not this hidden, underlying significance that was celebrated in the songs of the Tamil *nayanmar* saints. Leaving such interpretation to philosophers and erudite commentators, the saints, whose appeal was directed at the devotee, chose to burst into poetic rapture over the beauty of Shiva. The famous, oft-quoted poem of the seventh-century saint Appar, dedicated to dancing Shiva in the temple at Chidambaram, states that so great is the beauty of Shiva's dancing form that

Figure 36. Shiva as Nataraja, Chola bronze, Tamil Nadu, ca. 990.

even rebirth on this earth should be sought, since it affords yet another chance to gaze at that resplendent form:

> If one may see his arched eyebrows—
> the gentle smile upon his lips

115

of kovai red—
his matted locks of reddish hue—
the milk-white ash upon his coral form—
if one may but see
the beauty of his lifted foot
of golden glow—
then indeed one would wish
for human birth upon this earth.[5]

The Nataraja image of the Tanjavur temple, commissioned by Rajaraja Chola at the start of the eleventh century, rests, when not in worship, in a hall within the temple compound, with his limbs tightly swathed in red cotton fabric. Even casual visitors are here permitted to view "the beauty of his lifted foot / of golden glow."

In several verses of the same hymn—one of eight songs in which Appar celebrates dancing Shiva at Chidambaram—the saint describes the form of Shiva and extols him as the one who has entered his heart:

There is the white thornapple flower in the crown of the head,
the glance of the three eyes,
the hand holding the little drum,
the white sacred ash,
the part of the body occupied by the curly-haired one,
the tiger's skin,
and the tinkling anklets of the dancer in the hall of Tillai—
all these occupy the heart of me, the sinner.[6]

Artists commissioned to create images of Shiva modeled his many known forms with a skilled and sensitive touch, creating images of sensuous and captivating beauty. An extraordinary masterpiece of Shiva leaning against his now-missing bull mount was the starting point for this book (see figure 1). The productivity and expertise of the bronze and stone artists of ancient times are astonishing. Responding to the steady demand from temple after temple, they created innumerable images depicting with great sincerity and fervor the extraordinary splendor and magnetism of the form of Shiva. One such is a sinuously elegant Shiva as Tri-pura-vijaya (Victor of the Three Forts), standing in an exaggerated *tri-bhanga* (triple-bent) *contrapposto* pose (figure 37). His face, a perfect oval with full lips and elongated eyes, is the epitome of beauty. His matted hair piled high on his head is adorned with the crescent moon and a serpent, while a few escaping curls lie on his shoulders. An exceedingly slender torso with broad shoulders, powerful thighs, and neatly formed knees and ankles creates an

Figure 37. Shiva as Tri-pura-vijaya, Chola bronze, Tamil Nadu, ca. 950–960.

image of bodily perfection. The elegant gesture of his two front hands represents his grasp of the now-missing bow and arrow with which he released the single arrow that destroyed the cities of the three demons.

In visualizing the glowing form of Shiva at the shrine of Kurankaduturai, Appar introduces a favorite theme, that of Shiva's sweetness:

> My pearl, my precious gem,
> Glittering branch of coral, bright flame—

When I call him, "My father
Who lives in Kurankaduturai
With blossoming groves,"
My tongue tastes an incredible sweetness.[7]

The expression of "sweetness" is repeatedly evoked by Appar, who speaks of Shiva as the beauteous lord who is sweeter than sweet. He addresses Shiva as "sugar" and "honey," terms of endearment that one hears in everyday American talk, as indeed in the speech of other nations. In three consecutive verses, Appar adores Shiva as honey, sugar, and sugarcane:

Honey, milk, moon, and sun,
youth crowned with the celestial white moon,
wisdom incarnate as the fire
that consumed the god of spring—
How should I forget him?

Sugar, sweet syrup of sugar cane,
bright one, brilliant as a lightning flash,
golden one, my Lord who glitters
like a hill of gems—
How should I forget him?

Sugar cane, lump of sweet sugar candy,
bee in the fragrant flower,
light that dwells in the light of every flame,
our Lord who loves flower buds gathered at dawn—
How should I forget him?[8]

Each of the major *nayanmar* saints had his own special mode of approach to the deity.[9] In addition, they also composed hymns in the mode of Tamil love poetry known as *aham* (interior). For instance, the seventh-century child saint Sambandar sang in the voice of the young woman pining for her beautiful lover, asking the birds and bees, the clouds and the waves, to speak to her beloved Shiva of her love-stricken state and bring him to her:

O king of bees
you and your lady-love
are drunk with honey from the water-lotus—
your humming song echoes the waves.

Fly to the lord of sacred Tonipuram
master of the Panduranga dance
the lord who sports the crescent moon
and wears a necklace of bones
Speak to him of my distress.[10]

The artist expressed the beauty of Shiva in direct terms by modeling an image of such physical charm that it transfixed its audience with wonder and delight. The poet, however, often captured the beauty of Shiva by spelling out its effect on those women who longed to view him.

In another song, Sambandar sings as the friend of the heroine who has fallen madly in love with the lord:

"O god with matted hair!" she cries,
"You are my sole refuge!" she cries,
"Bull rider!" she cries, and faints in awe.
O lord of Marukal
where the blue lily blooms in field water,
is it fair
to make this woman waste from love's disease?[11]

Shiva's manifestation as Bhikshatana (Enchanting Mendicant), forced to roam the earth with alms bowl in hand, held strong appeal in southern India, and presents a unique instance of the "naked body adorned." While the form is of lesser importance in the north, it is sculpted in stone on the walls of temple after temple in the south, where it is also cast in bronze as a processional icon. One exquisite bronze, to which a set of gold ornaments was given in the year 1048, was commissioned for the temple at Tiruvenkadu, near Tanjavur, perhaps during the reign of the Chola emperor Rajendra (figure 38).[12] Four-armed Shiva is shown naked, with a serpent knotted around him supposedly to serve as loincloth, but the serpent sways sinuously to fully reveal his nakedness. Another serpent peeps out from his matted hair, which is adorned with the crescent moon and arranged in an elaborate halo-like formation around his head, being held in place by a jeweled headband above which rests a human skull. His ornamentation in bronze consists of multiple necklaces, a waistband, sacred thread, armlets, elbow bands, bangles, anklets, and rings on all ten toes and fingers. Unlike the standard barefoot treatment of all other forms of Shiva, and indeed of all other deities and human beings, this "wanderer," with his pet antelope leaping playfully by his side, wears wooden clogs on his feet. The sensuous nature of naked Shiva is well brought out by the manner in which the sculptor has modeled the elegant torso and the rounded buttocks of the image to create the vision of a bodily manifestation in which Shiva stole the hearts of all the women who came to give him alms.

Figure 38. Shiva as Bhikshatana, Chola bronze, Tiruvenkadu temple, Tamil Nadu, ca. 1040.

Confronted with the problem of how to express effectively the magnificent radiance and bodily glory of Shiva as the Enchanting Mendicant, several poet-saints resolved it by describing his compelling effect on the women who gazed at him. Saint Sundarar (ca. 800) placed each verse of a Bhikshatana hymn in the lips of one of the women who came to fill Shiva's bowl with food; fully aware of the incongruous nature of his beauty, they were nevertheless enamored of him:

What strange attire is this of yours?
The music of the Tamil tongue
adorns your speech
The while,
the serpent dances on your hand—
We bring you alms—
But how to give it to you
When your serpent hisses?
Pray tell us
Handsome One of the forests
You of Painnili
where fragrant groves abound
Does not the radiance of your form
mock the glory of the setting sun?

Wild golden cassia adorns your hair
your ornaments are graveyard bones
the dark dense forest is your home
and the bowl in your hand
is a skull—
We women in love
what can we hope to gain from you?
The groves of Painnili resound
with the song of humming bees
Pray tell us handsome one of the forests
are you too versed
in music and dance?[13]

Saint Appar expresses much more directly the passionate longing of the women for physical contact with Shiva, introducing a strongly erotic element to his celebration of Bhikshatana's entrancing form. In a song that adopts the conversational mode, a love-struck woman speaks thus to her companion:

Listen my friend,
yesterday in broad daylight
I'm sure I saw a holy one—
As he gazed at me
my garments slipped, I stood entranced,
I brought him alms

Figure 39. Shiva as the *vina*-playing Enchanting Mendicant,
Chola bronze, Valampuram temple, Tamil Nadu, ca. 1178.

but nowhere did I see that Cunning One—

If I see him again

I shall press my body against his body

never let him go

that wanderer who lives in Ottiyur.[14]

A variation on the naked Enchanting Mendicant Shiva is seen in a bronze image
in the temple of Valampuram (today's Mela-perum-pallam), where the deity is clothed in
silk and plays the lute-like *vina* (figure 39). The image is an exquisite casting that portrays
an elegant and slender Shiva, richly adorned, with two front hands poised to hold the
now-missing *vina*. He stands in *tri-bhanga*, resting his weight on his left foot, which is
placed slightly ahead of his right to suggest a walking gait. His snake dances on his hand,
his antelope leaps playfully against his right leg, while a dwarf *gana* attendant stands
to the other side. An inscription in the temple speaks of the commission, in the year
1178, of a bronze image of Shiva as "the lord who walked with swaying gait" (*vattanaigal
padanadanda nayakar*). The phrase mystified scholars until R. Nagaswamy identified it
as one used by Saint Appar in his poem dedicated to the Shiva of Valampuram in the

unique form of the *vina*-bearing, silk-clad Enchanting Mendicant.[15] Appar's verses are once again placed in the lips of the women who encountered Shiva:

> He came holding the *vina*
> the smile upon his lips
> swept my heart away,
> he did not turn back to look at me
> he spoke enchantingly
> he came to Valampuram—
> there he abides.

> Clad in silk,
> fresh sandal paste upon his form of coral hue,
> heel to toe
> he placed his feet in dancing steps,
> I asked
> "My lord, which town is yours?"
> The piercing eyes that gazed
> cast a spell upon me;
> As if to go elsewhere
> he walked with enchanting gait [*vattanaigal padanadandu*]
> he came to Valampuram—
> there he abides.[16]

In these lines (a verse and a half), Appar found an effective way of describing the beauty of the lord by focusing on the mesmerizing effect it had on the viewer. The vivid evocation clearly left a lasting impression on one ardent lay worshipper, who, in the year 1178, commemorated Appar's vision by commissioning a bronze image. By including Appar's exact phrase describing Shiva's seductive walk in his donative inscription, he left behind a clue to his specific inspirational source.

An innovative stone carver decided to evoke Shiva as the Enchanting Mendicant by combining the direct expression of the beauty of the deity with the poet's strategy of emphasizing its effect on those gazing at him. He created a dramatic and transfixing full-size tableau in granite with Shiva at the center flanked by seven women to one side and seven *ganas* to the other. The images, exhibited today in the Tanjavur Art Gallery, were positioned within the spacious pillared colonnade that runs around the Shiva temple at Darasuram, built during the reign of Chola monarch Rajaraja II (r. 1146–1173). Beautiful Shiva, clad in silk with a *damaru*-drum in his two front hands, stands at the center of a crescent-shaped rocky formation with his antelope leaping up on his right and a *gana* against his left leg. To Shiva's left,

Figure 40. Two adoring women from a Bhikshatana group, granite, Darasuram temple, Tamil Nadu, twelfth century.

the unknown master artist carved six more captivating little *ganas* playing various musical instruments. Seven women who come to give him alms stand on the opposite side, several with ladles in their hand, and one with a finger held to her lips to express astonishment at the wondrous vision of Shiva. The two women closest to Shiva, carved from a single piece of stone, stand against each other; the clothes on the woman with her back to the viewer slide off her hips to reveal her buttocks (figure 40). One can imagine her speaking to her friend in the manner of Appar's conversational verse that we just encountered: "As he gazed at me / my garments slipped, I stood entranced." This stone tableau was not enclosed within a shrine and does not appear to have served as a specific focus of worship. Devotees visiting the Darasuram temple probably would have admired the images much as we do today, viewing their fluid forms without the cloth, jewels, and flowers that are an integral part of worship.

The conjoint form of Shiva as Ardha-nari (Half-Woman), popular throughout India, was generally celebrated as the form resulting from Shiva taking Uma as one-half of his body. Occasionally, the suggestion is made that Uma initiates the conjoint form, as in this verse from an eleventh-century Paramara dynasty inscription from the Gwalior region:

> May Parvati grant you prosperity—she who out of jealousy,
> as it were, of Ganga who rests on Shambhu's [Shiva's] head,
> firmly clings to one half of his body, joining hers (to his), and
> who feels pleasure in every limb when she sees the subjection of her lord.[17]

A conjoint form may not seem best suited for displaying bodily perfection or arousing utter adoration, yet master artists across India were able to fuse the masculine and feminine aspects of the deity into a seemingly harmonious whole that is captivating in its sensuous characterization. One such compelling image is a bronze from the Tiruvenkadu temple, probably commissioned during the reign of Rajendra Chola (figure 41).[18] Uma's jawline is gently curved, while Shiva's displays a straighter, firmer profile; similar distinctions are carried right through the image with the rounded breast, narrow waist, and gently curved hip of the female half contrasting with the broad chest, straight waist, and firm hip profile of the male side. Ornament and dress, too, are different, all the way from the hairdo and earrings to the long-skirted, slender female leg and the short-waist-cloth-clad male thigh. Shiva has two arms, one holding a battle-ax and other poised to rest the elbow on the now-missing bull, while Uma has a single hand raised to hold a lotus blossom. The seventh-century child saint Sambandar sang in praise of this entrancing form of Shiva at the temple of Pundurai, choosing to stress the female aspect of the image:

> Smooth and curved her Venus mound
> like a snake's dancing hood,
> her flawless gait
> mocks the peacock's grace.
> With feet soft as cotton down
> and waist a slender creeper
> Uma devi is one half of Shiva
> Lord of sacred Pundurai
> where bloom the lotus and the water lily
> where live holy Brahmins
> chanting Vedic verses[19]

Figure 41. Shiva as Ardha-nari, Chola bronze, Tiruvenkadu temple, Tamil Nadu, ca. 1040.

Describing the breasts of the goddess in sacred hymns was far from taboo; rather, it appears to have been considered an entirely appropriate tribute to her beauty. A verse from the same hymn speaks thus of Uma's breasts:

> Fresh, as new-born lotus buds
> lustrous like *kongu* blossoms
> honeyed like young coconuts
> golden *kalashas*,
> filled with the nectar of the gods
> are the breasts of resplendent Uma.
> She is one half of the silvery glory

of Shiva of Pundurai
where rare birds roost
and fine flowers bloom
in shady groves of green[20]

It will be evident to the reader who has traveled with me thus far that the appreciation of the deity's bodily beauty was one of the customary approaches to the divine in the multiple and varied expressions of devotion covered by the term *bhakti*. Joyous recollection of Shiva's sheer perfection of physical form was considered a prerequisite for the outflow of his inner beauty and spiritual supremacy, thus becoming inseparable from the approach to the divine through the love, devotion, and adoration that are concomitants of *bhakti*. While devotees did not actually view the physical beauty of the image of worship, adoring only its ornamented form, we must give a place to imaginative evocation, specially since closely similar images could be seen in all their bodily beauty on the outer walls of the temple as devotees performed the repeated ritual of *pradakshina* (circumambulation).

Goddess as Uma-Parvati

Shiva's consort, the beautiful goddess Uma—known also as Parvati, especially in northern India—is visualized and invoked by artists and poets in a comparable manner. Images of Uma invariably reveal her as a woman of great beauty, as in a Chola bronze of the early eleventh century from the Kaveri basin (figure 42). Wearing a tall, conical crown, she is a slender figure, sensuously modeled. Her breasts are heavy but softly sculpted, and the flowing curve of her stomach with its illusive look of flesh contrasts with the details of the jewelry that adorns her. The bronze imparts a heightened awareness of form and a swaying sense of movement. The image is so evocative in its sensuous perfection that one must remind oneself that this is not a portrayal of just any courtly beauty but of the great goddess herself, Uma, the consort of Shiva.

As early as the fifth century, the court poet Kalidasa celebrated the bodily beauty of the goddess, devoting a series of fifteen verses in his *Kumara-sambhava* to a foot-to-head (*padadi-kesha*) description of Parvati's body.[21] Here are some brief selections:

> She had thighs so lovely, rounded and even
> and long but not too long . . .
>
> (verse 35)

> Since the trunk of an elephant has too harsh a skin
> and the plantain stalk is always cold,
> those similes the world offers to express flowing,
> ample curves were useless for those thighs.
>
> (verse 36)

Figure 42. Goddess Uma, Chola bronze, Tamil Nadu, ca. 1012.

She with her eyes like dark waterlilies had full breasts
and they were of light color, with black nipples,
and pressed so closely together not even
the fiber of a lotus could find space between them.

(verse 40)

Lightly moving and black as if painted in by pencil,
the long lines of her eyebrows drew desire . . .

(verse 47)

Here, too, one has to call up awareness that this lengthy description of a nubile body refers, in fact, to the great goddess Uma-Parvati and not to a human woman.

The language used by Kalidasa in evoking the sensuous bodily beauty of Parvati, and of Shiva, may be understood perhaps as fitting the style of court poetry. More intriguing is the unabashedly sensual language used by the Tamil *nayanmar* saints in what are certainly sacred hymns. The sensuous verbalization of the form of Uma is seen, for instance, in a song by Saint Sundarar (ca. 800) in which he evokes Shiva accompanied by Uma. Each verse commences "Shiva passed this way," and following the main reference to the god comes a phrase to describe Uma:

> He passed this way . . .
> together with the young woman whose soft breasts
> fill her taut bodice
>
> He passed this way . . .
> together with the woman whose smile is white
> as pearl
>
> He passed this way . . .
> together with the woman, perfectly adorned
> whose mound of Venus is veiled in cloth
>
> He passed this way . . .
> with the woman whose brow
> is the crescent moon.[22]

Apparently, the sensual phraseology was considered totally appropriate by Sundarar, who saw only the divine aura that exuded from the beautiful Uma, she who was one with Shiva. In turn, the devotees of that period, the "there and then," did not question the appropriateness of the "sensual" imagery evoked by the poetry because their faith in, and acceptance of, these saints was unquestioned. To us, although presumably not to them, it involves an entirely unusual way of looking at sacred images, involving a sort of control though not rejection of body-consciousness.

Goddess as Durga; Goddess as Kali

While Uma-Parvati is the name by which the goddess is known in her role as consort of the god Shiva, as a powerful deity in her own right she is addressed as Durga (Impassable One). Famed as the killer of the fierce buffalo-demon Mahisha, and of the dreaded demon brothers Shumbha and Nishumbha, Durga is worshipped all over India. Everywhere, she is portrayed as a lithe, beautiful, young, and fearless goddess, richly adorned, who takes on gross, fearsome, and powerful enemies whom she defeats effortlessly at the end of long-drawn-out and horrendous battles.

The Ambika-mata temple at Jagat, near Udaipur in Rajasthan, has five depictions of Durga clearly displayed on its outer walls, two along the *mandapa* and three around the exterior of the sanctum. All portray her as a gorgeous figure who tears at your heartstrings while you watch her dispatching Mahisha (figure 43). Tall and elegant, with smoothly rounded breasts and broad hips, the long-eyed beauty stands with one leg placed on the rump of the buffalo that she has just decapitated. Among the weapons in her multiple hands is an upraised sword, which she brandishes against the human demonic form who has emerged from the buffalo and whom she grasps by the hair. She is entrancing in her sensuous beauty. At the Khiching temples in the eastern state of Orissa, from a similarly placed exterior niche clearly visible to all, she is portrayed as a statuesque, richly adorned, eight-armed beauty in total command of her opponent; having emerged from the decapitated buffalo's body, Mahisha cowers helplessly at Durga's feet before her sword (figure 44). The effortless victory of the goddess is well conveyed in a Gupta inscription: "May the foot of Devi . . . surpassing in radiance all the beauty of a full-blown waterlily, which was disdainfully placed, with its tinkling anklet, on the head of Mahishasura, reward your supplication."[23]

Figure 43. Durga victorious over Mahisha, sandstone, Ambika-mata temple, Jagat, Rajasthan, ca. 960.

130

Figure 44. Durga victorious over Mahisha, sandstone,
Khiching temple, Orissa, tenth to eleventh century.

At the southern Indian site of Mamallapuram, where Durga occupies the entire side wall
of a cave named after her, a lithe, young goddess sits astride her lion, brandishing weapons
as she battles the monumental buffalo-demon together with her female warriors and a
group of *ganas* (figure 45). Although the battle is far from over, the retreating stance of the
gigantic male demon with a buffalo head, and of his fallen army, foretell Durga's victorious
outcome. As light falls on the fluent lines of her body, all may marvel over her effortless
dispatching of her oversize opponent. By contrast, within the sanctum of the Brahmor
temple in the Chamba foothills of the Himalayas, she is the victorious goddess, adorable
and beautiful, cast in bronze, but fully swathed. If you are able to move aside the silks draping the serenely confident figure, you will see that she stands with one foot on the head of
the vanquished buffalo-demon, into whom she plunges her trident, while with her other
hand she grasps the helpless buffalo by the tail, lifting him partly off the ground.

    In each of these locations—and, indeed in numerous others where she is celebrat-
ed—one may profitably recall the words of the *Devi-mahatmya* (*Glory of the Goddess*), a decisive sixth-century text that celebrates the feats of Durga, whom it distinctly identifies as being
the same as Parvati, consort of Shiva. The text narrates that the goddess is so stunningly beautiful that the two generals Chanda and Munda, who come across her after she has destroyed
the buffalo-demon Mahisha, report thus to their master, the demon Sumbha:

Figure 45. Durga fighting Mahisha, granite, Mahishamardini cave, Mamallapuram, Tamil Nadu, seventh century.

O King, a certain woman dwells (there),

Exceptionally beautiful, causing the Himalayas to glow.

Such a form has never been seen anywhere by anyone.

You should find out who this goddess is and seize her, O king!

She is a jewel among women; with the most beautiful limbs,

    illuminating all directions with her lustre,

She abides there; O lord of demons, you really must see her![24]

Artists sculpting images at the various temples dedicated to the goddess, or indeed to Shiva or Vishnu, happily portrayed Durga as a "jewel among women," whether the image was to be displayed on the temple's outer walls or enshrined within its sanctum.

It is important to consider the visualization of the goddess as she is celebrated in the *Saundarya-lahari*, an important sacred poem in a hundred verses, which may have been composed around the year 800 and is sometimes attributed to the great philosopher Shankara. The poem is considered of immense significance for goddess worship, and its first verse hails her as the feminine power, Shakti, without whom the god Shiva cannot even move. In successive verses, she is hailed as the Immanent One, Permanent One, Wave of Consciousness, the Refuge, and Supreme Power.[25] However, from verse 42 onward, the poet alters his strategy and adopts the head-to-toe mode of the Indian poetic tradition, providing a description of her bodily beauty, starting with her crown and ending with her feet.[26] The following verse, which celebrates her navel, illustrates the strategy whereby the bodily beauty of the goddess, and her sexuality, is hailed as an apparently essential feature of her glory and power:

> Oh daughter of the Mountain,
> your navel flourishes as the still current of the river Ganga,
> as the bed for the hair creeper supporting the lotus-buds of your
>   breasts
> as the firepit for the flame of Cupid's magnetism
> as the sport resort of Rati, Cupid's wife
> and as the entrance to the cave where the penance of the eyes of
>   your Lord attains its goal.[27]
>
> (verse 78)

Within the Indian artistic tradition, a rare exception to the model of the sensuous body is provided by the fearsome and skeletal goddess Kali, who represents the darker side of Durga's power.[28] The word *kala* means both "black" and "time," giving Kali the epithet Dark One and suggesting that she represents time, which brings all things to an end. Either way, she conjures up a vision of awesome power and potency, and powerful images of her were created across the subcontinent. A ninth- or tenth-century bronze from Nepal—with sunken stomach, sagging breasts, skeletal limbs, and clearly delineated ribs—is a vivid evocation of emaciated three-eyed Kali (figure 46). With hollow cheeks, sunken eyes, and fanged mouth, she wears a garland of human heads and holds a severed human head in one hand and various weapons in her other eleven hands. She is richly ornamented with a tiara, large earrings, necklaces, armlets, bracelets, anklets, and a hip-band that holds her long skirt in place. An unknown master artist created this awesome image of spell-binding intensity, which seemingly represents an anti-auspiciousness of sorts. Seated with both feet planted on the ground, the metal image is an arresting, if macabre, portrayal of this powerful goddess.

The *Devi-mahatmya* text tells how Kali emerges from the enraged fury of Durga and at her command works for her by drinking blood, severing heads, and killing whole armies of demons:

> From the knitted brows of her forehead's surface immediately
> Came forth Kali, with her dreadful face, carrying sword and
>   noose.
> She carried a strange skull-topped staff, and wore a garland of
>   human heads;
> She was shrouded in a tiger skin, and looked utterly
>   gruesome with her emaciated skin,

Figure 46. Kali, bronze, Nepal, ninth to tenth century.

Her widely gaping mouth, terrifying with its lolling tongue,
With sunken reddened eyes and a mouth that filled the
    directions with roars.[29]

Beautiful and elegant Durga enters the battle in its final stages and, with dignity and heroism, dispatches the dreaded demon brothers Shumbha and Nishumbha. Kali is worshipped and revered all over India and is generally portrayed in art as an emaciated figure, often with a scorpion positioned on her sunken stomach. We see her thus in Orissa in the east and Gujarat in the west, in the Himalayan valley of Kathmandu in Nepal, and in the Karnataka region of the south. But in the Tamil region of southern India, while retaining her awesome powers, Kali is transformed into Bhadra-kali (Auspicious Kali) and is depicted as a beautiful young woman with uplifted breasts, smooth limbs, and a finely structured face. The only concession to her fearsome role is the fangs depicted at the corners of her mouth; in other ways, she closely resembles the beautiful Durga. Evidently, the absence of physical beauty was a concept that did not fit too comfortably with the general vision of the divine, at least in the Tamil country.

Alankara of the Divine Image

A tenth-century bronze of Shiva as Tri-pura-vijaya, considered earlier, is a perfect illustration of the primacy given to ornamentation in the creation of divine images (see figure 37). The beautiful-bodied bronze image of Shiva is elaborately adorned in the bronze itself by a tall sumptuous, crown-like arrangement of matted locks, a jeweled forehead band, multiple strands of exquisite jeweled necklaces, a sacred thread of many strands, a waistband, a richly patterned short *veshti* (waist cloth) held by a jeweled hip-belt, large ornamental armlets, elbow bands, rows of bangles, anklets, and rings on all ten toes and fingers. The image of Uma, equally exquisite in form and ornamentation, stands as a fitting consort for her lord.

A comparable emphasis on the elaborate adornment of Shiva is contained in a literary text from the same region, written perhaps a hundred years before the casting of the bronze. The Tamil *Tirukkailaya-nana-ula* (*Procession of the Lord of Kailasa*), translated by Blake Wentworth, details the elaborate adornment of Shiva by Uma, before Shiva's public emergence in procession. It is Uma's intervention that creates the beautiful, ornamented, processional form of Shiva:

> She adorned him with a garland fashioned by the irrepressible
> god of love
> and dusted him with wholesome fragrant powders;
> taking up cool sandalwood
> prepared by ladies accomplished in their arts
> she applied it to his worthy chest.
> She clothed him in silk
> redolent with the scent of wish-giving trees
> and tied golden anklets about his feet,
> she placed a crown set with a radiant crest-jewel on his head
> and on his forehead a shining plate

sparkling with gems.

She ornamented his ears with fish-shaped earrings made of un
pierced ruby

and taking up a beautiful diamond necklace, a strand of gold,

a well-crafted necklace of enormous pearls and a shining garland
of victory,

she wreathed his holy chest

and it shimmered in their light.

She fastened brassards around his eight mighty biceps

and tied on a belt which delights all who see

she bound a waist-cord about him

placed bracelets on his hands

and adorned his body with elegant designs.[30]

The poem is traditionally attributed to Ceraman Perumal, king of Kerala, and himself one of the sixty-three *nayanmars*, a contemporary and friend of Sundara *nayanar* who lived around the year 800.[31]

That bronze images, both male and female, are already richly ornamented in the cast bronze itself did not eliminate or even diminish the necessity for further adornment with gold and gemstones; obviously, you could not have too much of a good thing. Tamil temple inscriptions provide abundant testimony of the adornment of the processional bronze images of gods and goddesses with gold and gems. Vast numbers of jeweled ornaments were given to temple bronzes, and the inscriptions that record these gifts provide details of the ornaments, the number and quality of the precious stones each one contained, and the weight of the gold that served as the base for the inset stones. One example pertains to a *mekhala* (hip-belt) given by Kundavai, sister of Emperor Rajaraja Chola, to a bronze image of Uma:

> One sacred girdle adorning the hips (*tiru-pattigai*), containing gold weighing 521.9 grams [1.1 lb]. Six hundred and sixty-seven large and small diamonds with smooth edges set into it, including such as had spots, cracks, red dots, black dots, and marks as of burning, weighing 12.5 grams. Eighty-three large and small rubies—twenty-two *halahalam* [a type of ruby] of superior quality, twenty halahalam, twenty smooth rubies, nine bluish rubies, two *sattam*, ten unpolished rubies . . . weighed 60.3 grams. Two hundred and twelve pearls including round pearls, roundish pearls, polished pearls, small pearls, *nimbolam*, *ambumudu*, pearls of brilliant water and of red water, weighed 97.5 grams.

Altogether the girdle weighed 684.4 grams [1.5 lbs], and was val-
ued at 4500 gold *kashu*.[32]

The jewels given to temple bronzes of Shiva were as abundant and sumptuous as those
given to the goddess Uma, reinforcing the fact that male and female images were equally
adorned. A Tanjavur bronze of Shiva as Tri-pura-vijaya, standing almost 3 feet tall, and
of a size and form comparable to the image just considered, was given twenty-two gold
jewels. These comprised one long garland strung with *talis* and weighing over 1 pound;
four single-strand necklaces set with pearls, coral, and lapis; a *shrichanda* ornament set
with 2,524 pearls and weighing 1.2 pounds; an elaborate hip-girdle strung with 2,339
pearls with a clasp studded with diamonds and crystals and weighing almost 1 pound;
a pair of earrings of dangling pearls; two armlets; eight bracelets; and four anklets. The
jewelry given to a Tanjavur bronze of Uma as consort of dancing Shiva, although more
numerous (thirty-three items in all) seems less sumptuous, in part because the image
is of smaller scale, being female. The ornaments include a crown, a garland, a pendant,
seven pairs of earrings, a string of beads for the marriage *tali* pendant, five necklaces, six
pairs of armlets, three sets of bracelets, two ornamental hip-girdles, four sets of anklets,
and two complete sets of ten toe rings.[33]

    In this context, *puja* directed at the deities, with the accompanying *alankara* of
images by the priests before opening the sanctum to public view, is a crucial factor that
was noted briefly in chapter 1. Today, visitors to a temple know full well that they may
have to wait for their *darshan* (viewing of the deity) until *alankara* has been completed
and the image is considered ready for public viewing. *Alankara* equips the image to display its auspiciously ornamented form in public; devotees, by the purposeful act of *darshan*, and admiring its beauty, make themselves ready to receive the transfer of grace. We
noted also that another word for "ornament," *abharanam*, with its roots in the concept
of an irresistible, almost magical attraction, conveys vividly the critical role of ornament.
The ancient derivation of this crucial concept is indicated by the many verses addressed
to deities enshrined in individual temples that invariably describe their rich adornment.
Occasionally, inscriptional material, too, testifies to the practice of placing gem-studded
jewelry on images; one such instance is recorded in a set of Rashtrakuta copper-plates
of the eighth century that speaks of the rock-cut Kailasa temple at Elapura or Ellora.
It describes the beautiful Shiva, adorned with the Ganges, the crescent moon, and the
poison held in his throat, and informs us: "Although he was already adorned by such
supremely marvelous ornaments . . . the image of Sambhu (Shiva) who stood there was
further ornamented . . . with all manner of wealth in rubies, gold, and the like."[34] While
the inscription seems to refer to a manifest form of Shiva, the Kailasa temple sanctum
enshrines a *linga*; to this day, *lingas* in temples are richly adorned and prepared for the
ritual viewing of *darshan*. The devotee's experience of a sanctum image is restricted to

[handwritten marginalia: Part of the reason for the adornment?]

admiring its adorned form; the priests alone know the exact dimensions, contours, and beauty of the enshrined stone image. Yet there is no doubt that for all concerned, the image had to be flawless and perfect in every way; after all, in the Shaiva context the image was seen as the temporary home inhabited by the divine upon appropriate invocation by the priests.

The crucial importance of the corporeal body of the deity is further reinforced by the sixteen *upacaras* (ceremonial formulas) of *puja*, the majority of which are related to physical ministrations to the divine body.[35] Commencing with the invocation of the deity with mantras, it proceeds with providing a seat for the deity, washing the feet, washing the hands, and offering water, followed by ritual bathing with a variety of liquids that include milk, curds, ghee, honey, and sugar, and clothing with vestments and adornments. It proceeds with further ornament with sweet-smelling sandal-paste and flowers, invoking each one of the limbs of the deity in succession.[36] Then come offering lights, food, and betel leaf; circumambulation; and the final honor of praise with fanning, holding a regal parasol, and the concluding chant of mantras as an expression of the devotee's total surrender. *Puja* is concerned with pleasing the deity's senses with the smell of sandal-paste, flowers, and incense; the sight of the waving of oil lamps; the sound of chants of praise; the taste of food and betel leaf; and the touch of the feet and hands. The importance of the corporeal body of god is clearly accentuated by these sixteen rites, which complete the *puja* ritual.

Vaishnava Imagery

An exceedingly youthful Vishnu standing in three-quarter view was carved by a granite sculptor as one of the images adorning the walls of a Chola temple at Pullamangai, belonging to around the year 915 (figure 47). The gently curved contours of his slender body are quite alluring, as is his beautiful face with strongly arched eyebrows and full, sensuous lips. In the two rear hands, he holds the conch and discus, while one front hand rests on his hip and the other holds a damaged and hence indeterminate object. The distinguishing tall crown, forehead band, *makara* earrings, necklaces, sacred thread, armlets, bracelets, waistband, hip-belt, and anklets complete his adornment. He stands facing the viewer, presenting himself as an easily approachable figure.

Southern Indian Vaishnavism conceived of five potent forms of Vishnu—ranging from *para*, the supreme form that is seen only in heaven; through the avatars; to the *archa*, or image of worship. Far from being considered a lowly form, the *archa* image was thought of as capturing the essence of Vishnu and as being "a bit of heaven on earth."[37] Songs of the saints and *acharyas* were addressed directly to cultic icons in specific temples. C. J. Fuller's comment on *puja*, in which "worship is addressed to a deity whose power is *in* an image and also to a deity *as* an image," succinctly covers both Shaiva and Vaishnava approaches.[38]

Figure 47. Vishnu, granite, Chola temple, Pullamangai, Tamil Nadu, ca. 918.

Stone and bronze sculptors across India created glorious images of Vishnu, tall, slender, and elegant, wearing a high crown, a long *veshti*, and rich adornment. Ecstatic poet-saints and *acharyas* wrote that so great was the luminous beauty and radiance of Vishnu that even gemstones sought to increase their own brilliance by being placed on his body.[39]

Roughly contemporaneous with the sixth- to ninth-century *nayanmars* of Shiva in Tamil Nadu were a group of twelve Vaishnava *alvar* saints who likewise approached their lord Vishnu through the path of beauty. Just as Saint Appar insisted that the inexpressible beauty of the form of dancing Shiva merited rebirth on earth, so did the Vaishnava poet-saints sing of the blessings of being born on earth where one could enjoy endlessly the beauty of the image of Vishnu. The untouchable saint, Tiruppanalvar, composed a rapturous Tamil poem extolling the enthralling beauty of Vishnu from foot to head, and speaking of it as causing physical reverberations in him. He is believed to have sung the song standing before the image of reclining Vishnu in the sanctum of the hallowed Shrirangam temple near Tiruchirapalli in Tamil Nadu. Here are the closing phrases of five of his verses:

It seems as if his lovely lotus feet
    have come and entered
    my eyes!

(verse 1)

Ah! My mind runs
    to the red cloth
he wears on his waist!

(verse 2)

The waist-band around
    his lovely belly
    strolls in my mind!

(verse 4)

Ah! My mind is ravished
    by his red lips!

(verse 7)

My God! His lovely dark body
    of unfading beauty,
strung with pearls
    and big dazzling gems
fills my heart![40]

(verse 9)

When a woman sings in the love-poem mode, we have to exercise extra caution in our interpretative strategy. A set of fourteen Tamil poems, the *Nacchiyar Tirumoli* (*Sacred Words of the Lady*), allows us to accompany Andal, the only woman among the twelve Vaishnava *alvars*, on her spiritual journey to achieve union with the god Vishnu. She commences by proclaiming that she is the promised bride of Vishnu, plays out the wedding ceremony in poem 6, and progressively suffers the intense anguish of separation from the lord. Using the mode of the messenger poem, she addresses the rain clouds:

Tell him I will survive
only if he will stay with me
for one day—
enter me
so as to wipe away

> the saffron paste
> adorning my breasts.[41]

Andal's erotic allusions are clear, and she makes reference in her poems to her body, her shapely breasts, and her slender waist; yet the "I" of the woman and the "I" of the mystic are inextricably interwoven. One might refer in this context to the erotic mysticism of Saint Teresa of Ávila, who saw Christ as Bridegroom and longed to be united with him. Her poem "Vuestra soy, para Vos naci" (I Am Thine, and Born for Thee) addresses Christ as "Sweetest Love" and "Sweetest Spouse."[42] However, Teresa is well aware that she will have to die to be united with her lord, while Andal plays out her longings in terms of the here and now of life on earth.

Around the start of the twelfth century, two *acharyas*, Bhattar and Kuresha, immediate disciples of the great Vaishnava teacher Ramanuja, converted into Sanskrit *kavya* this ecstatic Tamil longing for a vision of the beautiful lord. In Nancy Nayar's translation, we see how Bhattar used the metaphor of "drinking in with the eyes" the beauty of the lord, referring specifically once again to the sanctum icon of reclining Vishnu at the Shrirangam temple:

> We drink in with our eyes
> the [Lord] who sleeps in Shrirangam—
> > Who is like a stream of ambrosia
> > flowing into the minds
> > of those who see [Him]—
> with [His] long, gentle and attractive, limbs
> > reclining on [the Serpent] Sesha,
> and with the splendor [of every part of His body]
> > growing greater and greater
> from [His] *makara*-shaped crown jewel
> clear down to [His] feet.[43]

Kuresha, too, speaks of "feasting the eyes," but his longing to see the lord as a physical presence is so intense that it causes an overwhelming and fanatic longing in all his bodily senses, his skin and eyes, his tongue, ear, and nose:

> My skin and eyes desire
> to drink [You in]
> while my tongue is distressed
> at not being able to hear [You]
> like an ear.
> My nose too, is in that same condition

regarding You.
O Lord of the Elephant [Gajendra]
How in the world can I reach the state
[that I so long for]!⁴⁴

This passionate approach to the deity seems to reach an electrifying culmination in the poems of the twelfth-century poet-*acharya* Vedanta Desikar, who wrote in Sanskrit and Tamil, and also in the *Prakrit* Maharashtri.⁴⁵ *Singing the Body of God*, the title chosen by Steven Hopkins for his book on Desikar's literary corpus, expresses succinctly the character of that sacred poetry. The Sanskrit poem *Bhagavad-dhyana-sopana* (*Ladder of Meditation on the Lord*) is a supreme example of the ecstatic mode of approach to a deity whose beauty enraptures and totally enslaves the devotee. The four verses quoted here from its toe-to-crown adoration of Vishnu incorporate the very special Indian concept of bodily beauty that rivals and outdoes the beauty of nature, and demonstrate the application of the language of erotic love to a cult icon within the Shrirangam temple:⁴⁶

O Lord of Ranga!

I see the exquisite curves of your calves,
the luster of anklets bathes them in colors;

swift runners between armies in time of warlong ladles to
    catch the liquid light of your beauty—

their loveliness doubled by the shade
of your knees:
seeing them,
my soul stops running
the paths of rebirth.

(verse 3)

They seem like firm stems of plantain
growing in a pleasure garden;

wrapped in the linen cloth, on fire
in the dazzle of the jeweled belt,

they are pillows for his wives,
Kamala, Bhumi, Nappinnai;

Ah! my mind plunges into the mysterious depths
of Ranga's young thighs

as into a double stream of beauty.

(verse 4)

His half-smile, that just-blooming
    flower, as if he were about
to say something—his pouting
    lower lip, red
as a ripe bimba fruit.

His up-turned glance, as if fixed on a distant
    horizon, holds in one thrall
all those who long for an end to their grief—

this lovely face of Ranga's Lord,
    adorned with a golden
tilaka—

his welcoming eyes cling close to my heart
    and will not let me go!

(verse 8)

So my mind touches the lotus feet of Ranga's Lord,
    delights in his fine calves, clings
to his twin thighs and, slowly
    rising, reaches
the navel.

    It stops for a while on his chest,
then, after climbing
    his broad shoulders,
drinks the nectar of his lovely face
    before it rests at last
at the crown's flowery crest.

(verse 10)

Desikar's poetic effusion is an almost delirious contemplation of Vishnu as a temple icon; the image enthralls and mesmerizes him, evoking an insatiable yearning to continuously gaze at the exquisite beauty of Vishnu at Shrirangam. The poet assures us that those whose minds are immersed in the glory of the lord's body will not be born again; as Hopkins phrases it, Vishnu's beauty is a "beauty that saves."[47] In the poem's final signature verse, Desikar speaks of composing the verses at the Shrirangam temple "for those who long to climb, with ease, the hard path of yogis."[48] Thus he clearly maintains that the path of ecstatic contemplation and unswerving absorption in the bodily beauty of Vishnu is a path of meditative recollection (*bhagavad-dhyana*), an approach to the lord that is natural and rich, and easy to achieve compared with the difficult path of the yogis. In the context of this chapter, we may note that the sanctum image of reclining Vishnu at Shrirangam is invariably fully draped, ornamented with a range of jewels and metal body-plates known as *kavachas*, and smothered in floral decoration. The devotee must recall the bodily beauty of Vishnu from having seen the many stone images on temple exteriors or must conjure up its physical glory from the songs of the saints and *acharyas*.

The Divine Couples

Down the ages and across the country, the Indian artistic tradition has taken pride in portraying the love of the god and his consort, whether it is Shiva and Parvati, whose marriage and conjugal love are detailed in numerous literary sources, or Vishnu and Lakshmi, about whose marriage the texts are relatively silent. Walls of temple after temple carry stone relief images of the divine couples, either standing beside each other or seated together on a throne, exquisitely highlighting their interaction and tender intimacy.

Shiva and Uma-Parvati

A series of large slabs from the eastern region of Orissa demonstrate admirably this focus on the loving relationship between Shiva and Parvati. In one such slab of twelfth- or thirteenth-century date, carved in deep relief, the bodily forms of the divine couple have been cut away completely from the background so as to stand out in prominent display (figure 48). Framed by an elaborate arch topped with a *kirtimukha* motif, Shiva sits on a lotus seat in the *lalitasana* position of ease, with one leg pendant while the other is bent and placed along the seat, to accommodate Parvati, who sits on his knee. Exquisitely adorned, smiling Shiva is seated in three-quarter profile, turned toward Parvati, with one front hand cupping her left breast and the other holding a lotus bud, while the two rear hands hold a trident and a rosary. Parvati, with her hair gathered up as an elaborate rounded knot placed to one side of her head in the typical Orissan fashion, places one arm around Shiva's

Figure 48. Shiva and Parvati, schist, Orissa, twelfth to thirteenth century.

shoulder while holding a mirror with the other. A host of semidivine flying beings, several holding garlands, occupy the upper register on either side of a trefoil arch that serves to frame the faces of the divine couple. Attendants with fly whisks and adoring worshippers are carved along the sides, while below their feet are their bull and lion mounts; their two sons, Kartikeya and Ganesha; and vessels and stands for ritual worship. Both god and goddess are richly adorned and draped in the manner now familiar to us as they radiate charm and allure in their absorption in each other.

The Chola temples of southern India likewise carry a series of stone images carved in deep relief, both sitting and standing, that focus on the conjugal love between Shiva and Parvati. From the Kilaiyur temple of late-ninth- or early-tenth-century date comes a slab, now in the Tanjavur Art Gallery, that shows Parvati turning somewhat hesitantly away from Shiva, who draws her back toward him with one front hand and caresses her breast with the other (figure 49). A closer look reveals the reason for Parvati's stance; with his rear right hand, Shiva holds out a lock of hair on which the heavenly river goddess Ganga is perched. Parvati's

Figure 49. Shiva and Parvati, granite, Kilaiyur temple, Tamil Nadu, ninth to tenth century.

jealousy of the Ganges, and in turn the river goddess's envy of Parvati, is a well-known trope that found frequent poetic expression in inscriptions and literary works. A thirteenth-century invocatory verse from a rock inscription of the Chandella king Viravarman from Ajaygadh illustrates this rivalry, making reference to the conjoint form of Ardha-nari:

> May the divine Ganga on Shiva's head protect you—(she who
> is) attenuated as it were with jealousy, at seeing half his body
> appropriated by the daughter of the mountain.[49]

The later Chola temples—whether at Tanjavur, Gangai-konda-chola-puram, Melaikad-ambur, or elsewhere—carry similar portrayals of this divine couple, either standing joyously content beside each other or sitting together, with Shiva turning Uma's face toward him with one hand and caressing her breast with another. Similar images of Shiva and Parvati as the joyously blissful couple may be found in just about every part of the Indian subcontinent.

In literature, too, the conjugal love of Shiva and Uma, and their delight in each other's physical beauty, was a theme for joyous celebration. Kalidasa's *Kumara-sambhava* of the fifth century, in which we encountered a head-to-toe description of the body of Parvati, likewise celebrated the Shiva–Parvati theme. Its eighth canto, currently its last, and titled "The Description of Uma's Pleasure," consists of ninety-one verses describing the lovemaking of the divine couple, commencing with the shy bride and following her progressive experience in lovemaking. One verse presents a sensitive description of the new bride's discomfiture:

> Alone together, before she would let the robe fall,
> she would cover Shiva's eyes with both palms,
> but she was left troubled then by that useless effort
> as the third eye in his forehead looked down at her.[50]

Kalidasa describes Parvati losing her initial hesitancy and, under Shiva's tutelage, rapidly gaining experience in the art and joy of lovemaking:

> Though, as they loved, the moon suffered when she seized
> his hair and they tried to outdo each other scratching
> where nailmarks should not be made and Parvati's belt-string
> easily opened to him, still he was never satisfied.[51]

It should be mentioned here that much of the later Kashmiri commentatorial tradition of literary criticism disapproved of the canto for what it regarded as an improper portrayal of the intimate activities of the divine couple.[52] The *Kumara-sambhava* allegedly deals with the birth of Kumara, a point it never reaches, suggesting that Kalidasa may have left the work unfinished.[53]

The *Saundarya-lahari*, the sacred poem on the goddess that we encountered earlier, speaks in uninhibited terms of the union of goddess and god. In one of many verses that describe the glory of the feet of the goddess, the poet refers to her "lotus-like feet that strike the lord on the forehead during love-play."[54] In the Indian context, anyone's feet touching any part of the body of another, let alone the forehead, is something so inappropriate as to be taboo. Its inclusion in this poem can only indicate the deep significance, for devotees, of the ecstatic union of goddess and god.

The vast corpus of copper-plate and stone inscriptions introduces us to a parallel and equally intriguing phenomenon. We have seen that these inscriptions proclaim royal genealogies, record the gift of lands or money to a Brahmin or a temple, and frequently provide the date of the grant, the name of the composer of the eulogy, and the name of its scribe. It is quite remarkable that the invocatory verses of these public documents frequently use overtly sensual language to describe not just the bodily beauty of the gods, but also the nature of their amorous dalliance.

The introductory verse of the Sanskrit Pattadakal Pillar inscription of Kirtivarman II, dating to the year 754, commences with a verse extolling Shiva and Uma, referred to here as Hara and Gauri. The verse does not praise their power and glory, their wisdom and insight, their mercy or compassion; nor does it praise their physical beauty alone. Rather, the verse extols the union of god and goddess, and stresses their intimacy:

> Om! Om! Reverence to Shiva! Victorious, victorious, be that
> union of (the god) Hara and (the goddess) Gauri, in which
> the face and breasts (of the goddess) are passionately kissed
> by the left arm (of the god); in which the fingers (of the god)
> separate themselves among the curled tresses (of the goddess) that imitate the quivering movements of a swarm of
> black bees; (and) which resembles in beauty a fully expanded
> white waterlily (i.e., the god), enhanced by the sweetness of
> a yellow waterlily (i.e., the goddess) brought to maturity by
> the rays of the sun![55]

This epigraph, inscribed twice on the pillar, once in the *nagari* script and then repeated in a local script, is familiar to art historians, since it provides the authorship of three major Chalukyan temples at Pattadakal: the Sangameshvara, built by Vijayaditya; the Virupaksha, by Vikramaditya's chief queen, Trailokyamahadevi; and the Mallikarjuna, by Vikramaditya's second queen.

The column that carries the record was erected at the center of the three temples by *acharya* Jnanasiva to commemorate his gift of a village and its produce to a brahmin to enable the continued performance of temple rites, the convening of learned discourses, and the like. It is fascinating that a public record of this nature should be prefaced by a verse that so openly alludes to the amorous activities of the deities. It is an evocation of sensual beauty that is rooted in body-consciousness, and may be interpreted as emphasizing that spiritual magnificence expresses itself most effectively and emphatically through the beauty of bodily perfection. Conversely, physical beauty is viewed as an invariable concomitant of divine glory.

A Sanskrit inscription of the Paramara monarch Chamundaraja of the year 1080, which records the founding of a temple in Rajasthan, devotes its invocatory verse to Parvati's joyous anticipation of marriage to Shiva:

> May the glances of Devi at the time of her marriage protect
> you—(glances) confused with excitement, budding forth
> with pleasure, quivering with delight, made slow by modes-
> ty, as in terror at the hissing of the snakes clinging to his arm
> she clenched her hand, which was drawn back by the old
> ladies, for Shambhu who seized it eagerly in firm grasp![56]

A more suggestive sentiment is evoked by the Ratanpur Sanskrit stone inscription of the year 1163, which records the construction of a Shiva temple, and other shrines and stepwells, by a feudatory prince named Brahmadeva. It commences with this verse in praise of god Shiva:

> May the divine half-moon crested (Shiva) increase your
> welfare!—(he) who has three eyes as if because of his desire
> to see simultaneously, at the time of playful amorous enjoy-
> ment, the pair of gold pitcher-like breasts and the lotus face
> of Parvati, daughter of the mountain.[57]

One is irresistibly reminded of the shy bride of Kalidasa's *Kumara-sambhava*, who uses both hands to close Shiva's eyes, only to find him gazing at her with the forehead eye. Still, one must admit that it is indeed an amazing conceit to conjure up so fanciful a reason to account for Shiva's third eye!

The Puri copper-plates of Madhavavarman-Sainyabhita, a Sailodhava ruler of Orissa, dated to the year 1164 and issued to record the monarch's revenue-free grant of a village to a Brahmin, conjures up a similar scene of divine erotic play. The first verse of this Sanskrit record invokes Shiva's matted locks in laudatory phrases and speaks of their disheveled nature due to Parvati's loving grasp of his hair:

> May the matted locks of hair of Shambhu, in which the par-
> ticles of ashes are separated by the overflowing waters of the
> Ganga (on his head), which are touched by the soft rays of the
> moon (also on his head) as if by white lotus fibres, of which the
> luster is daubed by the red rays of the entwining snakes bear-
> ing sparkling gems on their hoods, and which are slackened
> because of their knot being set aside on account of Parvati's
> union accompanied with a grasp of His hair, protect you![58]

In its invocatory verse, a Bengal Sena Sanskrit inscription of the end of the eleventh century carries its vision of the lovemaking of Shiva and Parvati a stage further:

> Triumphant are the faces of Sambhu, which smile, when by
> the rays of the moon they see the shame-contracted coun-
> tenance of Devi who, frightened at the withdrawal of her
> breast-cloth, pulls down the wreath on her head and extin-
> guishes with it the lights of the hymeneal chamber.[59]

The purpose of this finely engraved stone inscription, in thirty-six Sanskrit verses, each
composed in a different meter, is to record that the Sena monarch Vijayasena built a
magnificent temple to Shiva, topped with a golden cupola, and created a lake beside it.
The epigraph specifies the name of the poet, Umapatidhara, as well as the name of the
engraver, Ranaka Sulapani, who belonged to the Varendra guild of artists.

A Sanskrit inscription on a stone slab, engraved around 1191 during the time of the
Chedi prince Prithvideva, now in the Nagpur Museum, records the gift of a Shiva temple by a
certain Devagana, who also composed its eulogy. The partly damaged invocatory verse of the
poem portrays Shiva soothing Parvati's fears that their lovemaking may have been observed
by the crescent moon or the serpent, both of whom adorn Shiva's matted locks:

> May Rudra protect you!
> He who at the time of sexual enjoyment eagerly speaks
> (thus) to (Parvati) the daughter of the mountain: "How
> should that lord of serpents, who uses his eyes as ears, be
> able to see us? And (how should) this crescent moon (too,
> reduced to a state of infancy) . . . ![60]

A similar picture in which Parvati wishes to hide from the light of the crescent
moon in Shiva's locks is conjured up in the introductory verse to the Kalinjar Sanskrit stone
inscription, which celebrates the foundation of a temple to Shiva in Uttar Pradesh in 1201:

> May Ishvara, who experienced the delight of an embrace
> from Parvati, multiply your excessive delight; she who when
> the knot of her garment was undone (by Shiva) extinguished
> the lamp at once with the lotus which she wore in her ear, but
> becoming anxious because of the spreading of the light of
> the moon in Shiva's locks, took recourse to the dark neck of
> Shiva which was like the formation of new clouds, thinking
> that it was the darkness.[61]

The many images and inscriptions invoking Shiva and Parvati in forms of conjugal lovemaking beseech their blessings to effect a transfer of such bliss to the devotees
themselves so as to increase their own happiness and prosperity. As the Kalinjar inscription explicitly states: "May Ishvara, who experienced the delight of an embrace from
Parvati, multiply your excessive delight." Happiness and prosperity are transferred from
and through contemplation of the bliss of the divine couple.

Vishnu and Lakshmi

A close parallel in portrayal to images of Shiva and Parvati, created in equally
varied parts of the country, are the images of Vishnu and Lakshmi enjoying each
other's physical proximity. In slabs from Orissa, the only difference from Shiva–
Parvati imagery lies in the incorporation of the Vaishnava attributes of conch and
discus instead of the trident and in the placement of Vishnu's divine eagle, Garu-
da, at the center of the pedestal. The temples at Khajuraho in central India carry
closely similar portrayals of Vishnu and Lakshmi, on the one hand, and Shiva and
Parvati, on the other. The identity of the divine couples is established almost exclusively by the attributes held by the god and by Vishnu's crown as against Shiva's
piled-up matted locks. In all other ways, including bodily contours and conjugal
intimacy, the images are closely similar. A high-relief carving on the walls of the
Parshvanatha Jain temple at Khajuraho depicts the well-formed and voluptuous
figures of Vishnu and Lakshmi, in which the god draws the goddess close against
him and cups a breast in his palm (figure 50). In the context of the images adorning the walls of a Jain temple, one might note that Jain tradition considers Vishnu,
in his Krishna avatar, to be the cousin of the Jina Neminatha, whose attribute is
also the conch. The Vishnu–Lakshmi imagery on the Jain temple speaks of the
close links between various Indian belief systems and the overall acceptance by
each of the values adopted by the other.[62]

In inscriptional eulogies as in sculpted images, the lovemaking of the god
Vishnu and his consort Lakshmi is celebrated with enthusiasm. The Karhad San-

Figure 50. Vishnu and Lakshmi, sandstone, Parshvanatha temple, Khajuraho, Madhya Pradesh, ca. 955.

skrit copper-plates of the Rashtrakuta king Krishna III, dated to 959, commence with two verses, the first in praise of Vishnu and the second of Shiva. The purpose of the inscription is to record the grant of a village by the monarch to a certain Gaganashiva, pupil of Isanashiva, for the maintenance of the ascetics who lived in that area of Maharashtra:

> Om. Triumphant is the leaflike hand of (Vishnu) the enemy
> of Mura, which, being placed on the jarlike breast and face
> of Lakshmi, that are marked by shining particles of nectar-
> water, proclaimed the entrance of the world on a joyous
> festival.
>
> (verse 1)

> And triumphant is the rampart-like shoulder of (Siva)
> the conqueror of the three cities, which is adorned by the
> coloured figures impressed on it by (the close contact of) the
> cheek of (Parvati) the daughter of the mountain, and which
> thus bears, as it were, through regard for his beloved, an edict
> promising safety to the god of love.[63]

To stress the intimacy of Vishnu and Lakshmi, a Sanskrit stone inscription of the twelfth-century Chandella ruler Madanavarman, from Mau near Jhansi, that records the erection of a Vishnu temple and the building of a tank by Gadadhara, minister of the monarch, uses the analogy of the impress of color by contact that we encountered with Shiva and Parvati. Engraved on a 4- by 3-foot slab, in twenty-nine lines with some damage at the end, it provides a genealogy for both the Chandella ruler and the minister. The second verse of the charter reads thus:

> May the undulating lines of paint . . . protect you, which,
> from the round breasts of the impassioned Lakshmi, trans-
> ferred unto the rock-like chest of Shridhara, are like a beauti-
> ful eulogy, set down by the god of love in clear characters, a
> record of ecstatic amorous dalliance.[64]

Occasionally, as in the case of the inscriptions of the Gahadvala rulers of Kanauj (roughly 1000–1200 C.E.), every inscription of a dynasty commences with the identical invocatory verse. Those of the Kanauj rulers speak of the lovemaking of Lakshmi and Vishnu in terms as graphic as those that tell of the dalliance between Shiva and Parvati. One such Sanskrit inscription, among dozens that commence with this repeated verse, is from the village of Kotwa in Uttar Pradesh; it is dated to 1197, during the reign of Harish-chandra of Kanauj, and records the various taxes to be paid to the monarch:

> Om. May Lakshmi's hand which is caressing, in the course
> of a turbulent sexual act, the neck of Vishnu whose ardour is
> undiminished, grant you happiness.[65]

The alliterative sound of the original, impossible to reproduce in English, is worth recording for those who might like to read it out loud:

> *Akunthotkantha-vaikuntha-kantha-pitha-luthat-karah*
> *samrambhah suratarambhe sa shriyah shreyasestu vah*

From varying parts of India and across the centuries, Vishnu in his incarnation as the giant boar Varaha, who rescued Bhu, the earth goddess, when she was in danger of drowning, is frequently invoked as her lover. A stone image we encountered earlier at the Queen's Stepwell at Patan suggests their love by portraying the delicate and elegant earth goddess, seated on Varaha Vishnu's upraised arm, lovingly stroking his boar snout (see figure 32). A fifteenth-century Sanskrit inscription of the time of Krishnaraya of Vijayanagar, in 257 lines written in the Telegu script on a pillar at Mangalagiri, elaborates on this theme in its two invocatory verses:

> May the primeval boar protect you, he who lifted the earth
> that was wet as if it (were a woman that had fallen in love
> with him and) were in violent perspiration on account of the
> touching of his body!
>
> (verse 1)

> Let this primeval boar devise what is propitious! When he
> had lifted the wet earth from the flood of water, he held it
> with great force for fear lest it should slip down and (thereby)
> hurt a little the lower part of it with his tusk (like a lover who,
> when he has lifted his mistress in excess of passion, bewil-
> dered by contact with her body, squeezes her with great force
> and inflicts a little wound to her lower lip with his tooth).[66]
>
> (verse 2)

The purpose of the pillar inscription is to record that Salva-Timma, prime minister of the king, was assigning a village given to him by the monarch for the upkeep of a Shiva temple (not one dedicated to Vishnu Varaha, as the invocation might cause us to assume). It further proclaims the generosity of his sons and painstakingly records three gifts made by his son Gopa and nineteen by his son Appa.

As with Shiva and Parvati, the innumerable visual and verbal invocations of the erotic delight of Vishnu, played out with either Lakshmi or Bhu, served as a prayer for their transference of grace in the form of well-being, happiness, and prosperity. These visual portrayals and verbal prayers may be considered in a context paralleling the transference of blessings through flower or food offerings, the *prasada* of temple ritual, which is returned to the devotee. However, such specific visualizations of divine togetherness are vastly more potent because they evoke contemplation of the power of divine love, transmuted here into divine "bliss" in the context of conjugal eroticism.

Buddhist and Jain Imagery

The earliest images of the Buddha, examined in chapter 2, accented his role as a *chakravartin* (universal monarch) and emphasized the strength and robustness of his bare torso with a robe that merely lay in folds across one shoulder. Later images of the Buddha as teacher and savior also emphasize the beauty of bodily form, but in a manner somewhat different from that of the Hindu gods. The Buddha is portrayed as a slender, elegant figure with a monastic robe wrapped across his entire body, which nonetheless reveals the smoothly modeled outlines of his form as well as the ridged waistband of his long, dhoti-like undergarment. His commanding presence and exquisite face, often modeled with slightly lowered eyelids suggestive of introspection, inspired the magnificent Buddha images of the Gupta period.[67] They, in turn, served as the ideal model for all future sculpted images of the Buddha produced within the boundaries of India as well as in surrounding regions, such as Nepal, Sri Lanka, and Thailand. Adorning the image of a divine being, with a view to its beauty attracting the admiration and attention of devotees, was a pan-Indian phenomenon that was as much Buddhist as it was Hindu or Jain. For instance, a Sanskrit inscription of the monarch Vipula-shri-mitra (eleventh or twelfth century) from Nalanda specifies: "In order to turn the populace toward enlightenment, he gave to the Buddha a wondrous gold ornament [*hemabharanam vichitram*]."[68]

With the enlargement of the Buddhist pantheon and the introduction of images of divine *bodhisattvas* and female deities, sensuous sacred beings began to proliferate within the Buddhist world. In an earlier context, we made reference to an extraordinarily beautiful Nepalese image of the future Buddha Maitreya as representative of this development (see figure 9). Here we may point briefly to the many earthy and sensuous depictions of the goddess Tara, one of the most important deities of the later Buddhist pantheon, represented and celebrated across the Buddhist world. Cave 7 of the Bud-

Figure 51. Buddhist goddess Tara, Deccan trap rock, cave 7, Aurangabad, Maharashtra, seventh century.

dhist rock-cut monastery at Aurangabad, which contains a shrine housing a solemn and monumental seated Buddha, carries four vibrant sculpted images of Tara. On either side of the entrance to the shrine, in panels that extend from floor to ceiling, is a voluptuous Tara flanked by equally seductive female attendants. Clothed in a translucent skirt and adorned with rich and varied jewelry, Tara stands in a provocative *tri-bhanga* posture, holding a full lotus bud in one hand. She is an alluring figure, portrayed with melon-like breasts, a narrow waist with three folds, a smooth rounded stomach, and well-formed robust thighs. Her elaborate hairstyle with curls, ringlets, flowers, and jeweled ornaments, framed by a halo, certainly attracts attention.

Within the sanctum, once the visitors' eyes grow accustomed to the dim light and they turn their attention from the central Buddha to the side walls, they will encounter two more images of Tara. To the right, she stands as dazzling savior next to an image of the protective *bodhisattva* Avalokitesvara. To the left is a flamboyant portrayal of Tara striking a seductive dancing pose, flanked by musicians, three on each side, playing the flute, cymbals, tambourine, and drum as they accompany Tara's dance in honor of the Buddha (figure 51). She stands with both knees flexed in an elegant dancing posture, with her left hand resting on her hip and her right held in a graceful gesture. To complete the portrayal, she exhibits large rounded breasts, and exquisitely contoured face, and an elaborate hairdo adorned with blossoms and jewels. While the artist has allowed the figures of the musicians to recede into the rock walls, he has almost fully extracted Tara from the rock, thereby highlighting the magnificent contours of her body. In the portrayal of Tara, we see at work a pan-Indian sensibility that is neither Hindu nor Buddhist.

Rather, it seems that all deities were portrayed according to the same aesthetic criteria that visualized them as young, beautiful, and richly adorned. Cave 7 at Aurangabad is as much a testament to the eminence assigned to the Buddhist goddess Tara as it is to the workings of a pan-Indian aesthetic.

The Liberators (Jinas) of the Jain faith, much more than the saints and *acharyas*, were living examples of renunciation and penance, and yet the imagery portrays a Jina as a beautiful and youthful male modeled with smooth unbroken planes, with long arms and legs. He is either clothed in a dhoti or completely bare, depending on whether the image was commissioned by members of the Shvetambara (white-clad) or the Digambara (sky-clad) order. As noted earlier, Jain devotees perform a nine-limbed *puja*, in which sandal-paste is applied to nine parts of the Jina's body, emphasizing, once again, the primacy of the bodily form of a sacred image.

With the expansion of the Jain pantheon, a range of additional deities, both male and female, enlarged the visual vocabulary and were carved within the precincts of Jain temples. One such important group comprises the sixteen *maha-vidyas*, female personifications of magical chants known by the term *vidya*. First mentioned as deities in a text that dates to around the year 500, they became an established grouping of potent Jain deities over the next two hundred years. Texts describe these powerful goddesses as shining like lightning, wearing divine garments, and being adorned with a rich array of ornaments. Earlier we encountered the magnificent ceiling of the dance hall (*ranga-mandapa*) of the Luna Vasahi temple at Mount Abu, which honored a standing group of sixteen *maha-vidyas* (see figure 35). These goddesses were honored individually, too, and a ceiling panel from the same temple portrays Mahamanasi, the sixteenth *maha-vidya*, flanked by two multiarmed male demigods (figure 52). The voluptuous but solemn goddess has an exquisite face with arched eyebrows, a sharp nose, well-defined lips, and a lightly pointed chin. She sits on her lion mount in the *lalitasana* pose of ease, with one leg folded on her lion-seat and the other pendant. Her two main hands make the gestures of protection (*abhaya*) and wish-granting (*varada*), while her remaining eighteen hands hold various items that include, on one side, a water vessel, a battle-ax, a conch shell, the *vajra* thunderbolt, a sword, and a shield, and on the other side, a club, a snake, an elephant goad, a flute, a trident, and an arrow. The sensuous body of the goddess was readily visible on the low ceiling some 3 feet above the visitor's head; clearly, the seductive form was not viewed by devout Jains as detracting from her supernatural might and power or as a distraction for individual worshippers.

It is in this complex milieu—sociocultural, literary, religious, and artistic—that we must evaluate the visual imagery chosen to depict the sacred form, Hindu, Buddhist, and Jain. Sanctum images, whether commissioned in the seventh century for a shrine like the Devi temple at Brahmor or in the twenty-first century for a diaspora temple, are created with exquisite bodies, whether or not that beauty would be seen and admired by

Figure 52. *Maha-vidya* Mahamanasi on ceiling panel, marble, Luna Vasahi temple, Mount Abu, Rajasthan, thirteenth century.

all. Although the sanctum image would be admired by devotees only after it had been covered with silks, jewels, and flowers, the beauty of the body of god was readily visible in the many manifestations of the deity carved prominently along the outer walls of the temple. We must conclude that sensuous beauty, delineated and emphasized in physical form, was an indispensable clue to the presence of the formless beauty and perfection of the spirit. The images created by the artists, the poems composed by the saints, and the worship of the beautiful, adorned deity testify to the belief that the experience of the one—external beauty of bodily form—would become the path to the other—beauty of the spirit and the inner self. The repetition of the sensuous body over the centuries ultimately resulted in the creation of a norm that was transformed into a motif of consequence, albeit one whose original signification has been all but lost.

5. INSERTING THE GODS INTO THE WORLD OF MEN: RAJPUT PAINTED MANUSCRIPTS

Illustrated manuscripts were a relatively late development on the Indian subcontinent, the earliest being created during the twelfth century, a millennium or so after the production of written manuscripts. Painted on the long, narrow leaves of the *palmyra* palm, these first manuscripts were produced in the Buddhist and Jain contexts. When paper replaced palm leaf, from the fourteenth century onward, it largely retained the horizontal format in the Rajput courts, while the Mughal tradition adopted the vertical page format of the Persian courts. From the start of this painted tradition, the emphasis is on the sensuous body adorned, as seen in the *Vasanta-vilasa* (*Sports of Spring*), painted in Ahmedabad in the year 1451 in the unique format of a vertical cloth scroll.[1] Verses in old Gujarati, accompanied by selected Sanskrit and Prakrit verses of appropriate mood and tone, accompany the paintings. Female figures—pert, slender, and poised in elegance; clothed in richly patterned fabrics; and adorned with variegated ornaments—present a picture of youth, beauty, and sensuality. Long, plaited braids of hair intertwined with blossoms sway outward, following the vivacious movements of their limbs. The manuscript, which heralds the arrival of spring, focuses on the women who embody the joys and pleasures of springtime—a theme the reader might by now have come to expect of the tradition of premodern India.

This chapter introduces the world of painted manuscripts and, in particular, a genre of paintings that do not merely blur the lines between the sacred and the profane, but seem to gloss over the distinctions between the two. The act of inserting the gods—primarily Krishna, but occasionally other deities, too—into the world of men and substituting them for the courtly *nayaka* (hero) appears to dissolve any boundaries that might have been thought to exist between the sacred and the "secular." These paintings seem to present us with the flip side of the scenario encountered in chapter 2, in which the well-formed and sensuous figures of aristocracy and royalty were extolled in terms of the divine: here, divinities stand in for human heroes.

Commencing in the sixteenth century, the many Hindu Rajput courts in the plains of Rajasthan, as well as those in the foothills of the Himalayas, began to commission painted manuscripts devoted to a series of courtly themes with no direct sacred connotations. These princely states, which coexisted with Mughal power at the imperial center of Delhi, varied in size from the expansive plains state of Mewar, with its capital at Udaipur, to the tiny hill state of Basohli, measuring a mere 20 miles long by 15 miles wide, situated in the Himalayan foothills.[2] For the sophisticated patrons at these courts, artists created a variety of painted manuscripts depicting the beautiful *nayika* (heroine) and the handsome *nayaka* (hero), placing them in well-furnished mansions with rugs and silken cushions, or on marble terraces and pavilions appointed with equal luxury. Often the background is merely a wash of a deep primary color like red or mustard yellow that adds to the richness of the setting. The focus is on the human figures, slender and elegantly poised whether in a seated or standing posture, and dressed either in fine translucent fabrics shot with gold thread or in vividly patterned fabrics. Ornamentation is rich and elaborate; in some courts, like Basohli, artists painstakingly cut out beetle wings to simulate emeralds and used raised white paint for pearls. In these paintings and their accompanying verses, inscribed either above the painted border or on the painting's reverse, what is sought to be evoked and conveyed in aesthetic as well as emotional terms is the primacy of the elegant and sensuous human body, and the invariable presence and prominence, in differing situations, of human erotic love.

Three main genres of nonsacred painted manuscripts were produced in these courts. The first, known by the generic term *riti*, sometimes described as "Scholastic-Mannerist,"[3] deals with poetics and the *nayika-bheda* classification of heroines and heroes in love. The three main texts of this type chosen for illustration are the *Rasa-manjari* (*Bouquet of Delights*),[4] the *Rasik-priya* (*Connoisseurs' Delights* or *Poetry for Connoisseurs*), and the *Satsai* (*Seven Hundred* [*Verses*]). The second genre comprises verses and paintings that illustrate the months of the year (*barah-masa* [twelve months]), while the third was devoted to the depiction of musical modes (*raga-mala* [garland of musical modes]). Alongside these texts, painted manuscripts of established texts of sacred import were, of course, commissioned; especially popular were the *Ramayana*, detailing the adventures of Rama; the *Bhagavata-purana*, narrating the legend of Vishnu; and the *Gita-govinda*, describing the passionate love of Krishna and Radha.[5] Successive rulers of the various kingdoms, and the ladies of their courts, too, we assume, commissioned their own copies of these manuscripts for leisure-time viewing, so that numerous illustrated versions of any one text may be found today in the royal libraries of each princely state. Thus the Mewar royal libraries still retain ten illustrated copies of the *Rasik-priya*, ranging in date from 1630 to 1870.

Occupying center stage in the painted manuscripts devoted to nonsacred themes is the archetypal and idealized courtly *nayaka*, often clad in the unique turban and distinctive *jama* tunic associated with each particular state, and his counterpart, the *nayika*, whose costume also reflects local fashion. The artistic formula for beauty also varies from state to state, as will be evident through a comparison of the *nayikas* of painted pages from three different regions. The exceedingly elegant Nurpur/Basohli *nayika* is long-limbed and slender with small, high breasts. She has a wide, almost receding forehead, a sharp nose, a rounded chin, and what has sometimes been described as a "predatory" eye. Dressed in either loose *salwar* pants or a long skirt together with a brief bodice (*choli*), and covered with a transparent overdress and a long scarf, she wears all possible finery. Together with her *nayaka* lover, she dominates the painted page. The distinctive *nayika* from the Kangra region, who appeals most to modern taste, has an exquisite face that features a single, gently curved line that extends all the way from forehead to nose. The slender, elegant, and high-breasted *nayika* wears a long skirt and *choli*, with an *odhni* scarf wrapped elegantly around her richly adorned figure. By contrast, the ideal Mewar *nayika* is compact of body, with a small nose and a rounded chin. Her small, high breasts are enclosed in a brief *choli*, and she wears a long skirt and an *odhni* scarf, with lavish jeweled ornament. While regional stylistic distinctions are evident, the emphasis in these paintings remains, as in preceding centuries, on the elegant, sensuous human form, lavishly adorned.

A scrutiny of these "worldly" painted manuscripts reveals that the courtly *nayaka* is frequently replaced by the god Krishna and, on occasion, by Shiva or Rama. In visual terms, the portrayal of the *nayika* is totally generic; she is not distinguishable as Radha, Parvati, or Sita, although we may be expected to contextually read the figures thus. Only the substitution of the blue god (Krishna, occasionally Rama) or the distinctive Shiva for the archetypal *nayaka* is obvious. It seems clear that neither those who commissioned these paintings nor those who viewed and admired them in the company of the patrons in any way considered the substitution of these divine figures for the courtly hero and heroine as transforming the nature of the manuscript into the category of the sacred. Rather, the consciousness of poets, artists, and patrons was so permeated with the vision of divine lovers that it seemed not only perfectly logical, reasonable, and acceptable, but also both appropriate and proper, for the poet and the painter to insert Krishna and Radha into the courtly world. Were not Krishna and Radha, or indeed Shiva and Parvati, the quintessential lovers, and thereby the prototype for all human lovers? While the insertion of gods into the world of men may seem quite astonishing if taken out of context, we are dealing with a cultural universe that, for the prior fifteen centuries, had routinely blurred the boundaries between sacred and profane.

To place the textual and visual material in its appropriate context, a few prefatory words are necessary on the highly complex subject of Krishna worship in northern India. The prime Vaishnava text, the Sanskrit *Bhagavata-purana*, which may have originated in southern India, was frequently produced as an illustrated manuscript in the various Rajput courts. Its tenth book in particular, which details the exploits of Krishna, was most popular. Equally admired and frequently illustrated was the *Gita-govinda*, a twelfth-century Sanskrit poem that narrates the passionate love of the god Krishna and the cowherdess (*gopi*) Radha. After their initial union, Krishna abandons Radha for other *gopis*, and the poem transforms itself into a delineation of the minutiae of the many and varied sufferings induced by the pangs of separation, expressed to or by Radha's *sakhi* (friend and confidante) and, on occasion, by Krishna to his male companions, until it culminates in the lovers' ecstatic and triumphal reunion. Its composer, Jayadeva, used the vocabulary of earthly passion to convey the "complexities of divine and human love."[6] While artists directly portrayed scenes of erotic passion, erudite commentators down the ages have interpreted the poem as the passionate longing of the human soul for union with the divine, and the despair and anguish of repeated separation that it has to endure before being able to achieve such oneness. In fact, scholars writing on the Hebrew Bible's erotic love poem, Song of Songs, sometimes make use of the *Gita-govinda* in their interpretative strategy.[7] By the sixteenth century, some traditions had elevated the human *gopi* Radha to divine status, making her the queen of Krishna's celestial world of Goloka, where she reigns beside him.[8] It is against such a background that we must evaluate the ready substitution of Krishna for the human hero and "lover" of these various genres of secular texts. It has been suggested that perhaps such a tactic might be an expression of the Indian philosophical belief that "divinity resides within every human being."[9] More patently, however, the easy insertion of the god Krishna as the human *nayaka* may be seen as one further instance of the finer dissolving of boundaries between sacred and profane in the human context.

The world of painted manuscripts is one in which text and image are seen side by side in such a way that the one directly informs the other. Patrons appear to have commissioned illustrated versions of a text soon after its composition. For instance, the popularity achieved by Keshavdas's *riti* text, the *Rasik-priya*, seems to have resulted in an illustrated version of the text being created during the poet's lifetime, perhaps in 1615. The text of this first manuscript is written in the Devanagari script, and the illustrations are painted in the style referred to as "sub-imperial" Mughal. The possibility that this first painted manuscript owes its origins to Keshavdas having spent time in residence at the Mughal court, where he wrote the *Jahangir-jas-chandrika*, extolling the "moonlight of fame" of the Mughal emperor Jahangir, needs further exploration.[10] Whether or not this first illustrated *Rasik-priya* (*Connoisseurs' Delights*) was commissioned by a famous Mughal courtier, the Hindu raja Birbal, as proposed by A. K. Coomaraswamy, although plausible, also remains debatable.[11]

The *Nayika* and the *Nayaka* in the Texts

Riti Texts: Origins

The tradition of a "secular" literature devoted to the theme of love and pleasure has an ancient past in India and dates back to two major literary works. The first is Vatsyayana's *Kama-sutra*, probably belonging to the third century C.E., while the second, dating perhaps a century later, is Bharata's dramaturgical treatise, the *Natya-shastra*. Neither text claims to be the first of its kind; rather, each specifies that its author is merely following a line of exposition initiated by other masters. Neither of these early and influential texts ever seems to have been commissioned in the form of an illustrated manuscript, suggesting that they may have been regarded as scholarly treatises.

Vatsyayana's work, in seven books, commences with the desired qualities that the *nagaraka* (man-about-town) should possess. He lists sixty-four *kalas* (arts) that the *nagaraka*, the accomplished *ganika* courtesan, and women at court should have mastered. Apart from the expected arts of music, dance, and painting, the extraordinary range of accomplishments includes, as we have seen, the art of bodily ornamentation and that of decoration of one's surroundings. In addition, the list covers verbal skills like improvising poetry and solving riddles and puns; a knowledge of gems; mastery of the art of cockfighting, staging plays, and games of dice; and expertise in preparing a variety of delectable drinks.[12] Vatsyayana then devotes two chapters to the art of making love, and the next four to a classification of women as virgins, wives, other men's wives, and courtesans, emphasizing the art of erotic love throughout his classificatory scheme. As one scholar puts it, all phases of experience "are catalogued and categorized, subcategorized and sub-subcategorized compulsively and obsessively," suggesting that "to name is to know."[13]

Equally relevant to our discussion is Bharata's dramaturgical text, which explicates the theory of *rasa* (aesthetic experience) and the related concept of *bhava* (the emotion that gives rise to *rasa*). In chapter 1, we examined the *rasa* theory and pointed out that the erotic *rasa* of *shringara* is considered to be the king of *rasas*. Since this chapter is devoted to painting, it is germane to point out that colors were assigned to the *rasas*. Thus *shringara* was *shyama* (blue-black), the color of the god Krishna; the *hasya* (comic), white; the *karuna* (pathetic), dove-colored; the *raudra* (furious), red; the *virya* (heroic), yellow; the *bhayanaka* (terrible), black; the *bibhatsa* (odious), blue; the *adbhuta* (wondrous), gold; and the *shanta* (quiescent) the color of jasmine and the moon. However, painters do not seem to have taken this scheme as being in any way prescriptive. Of immediate relevance here is the *Natya-shastra*'s twenty-fourth chapter, devoted to *abhinaya* (gestural acting), which contains a list of eight types of *nayikas*, each of whom experiences a different type of love-longing together with its accompanying suffering and pains.[14] Barbara Stoler Miller has pointed out that Radha of the twelfth-century *Gita-govinda* goes through seven phases of the passionate yearnings of separation from the beloved; she suggested that Radha may hence be categorized as belonging, in succession, to seven of these eight early *nayika* types.[15]

Rasa-manjari

The *Rasa-manjari* is a poem of 138 verses written in Sanskrit and devoted to classifications of *nayika* and *nayaka* in a variety of love situations.[16] It was composed by

Maithili Brahmin Bhanudatta around the year 1500, most likely in the Deccani town of Ahmednagar.[17] The *nayika* dominates the text, and Bhanudatta commences with two sets of preliminary classifications of the heroine, which he then sustains throughout. The first is the heroine as one's own wife (*sviya*), another man's wife (*parakiya*), or the prostitute (*samanya*), and the second subdivides each of these three on the basis of love experience into the "naive" (*mugdha*), the "average" (*madhya*), and the "experienced" (*praudha*). Individual chapters then treat a variety of *nayikas*—for instance, one who goes out in search of her lover, one who awaits her lover, one who has been wronged, one who is loyally loved, one who anticipates separation, and one who is estranged by a quarrel. Each type is subdivided according to the twofold preliminary classification so that, for instance, the *nayika* whose lover is away could be one's own wife and "naive," another's wife of "average" experience, or the "experienced" courtesan. These various permutations and combinations of the *nayika* are treated in the work's first ninety-nine verses, some of the most arresting being those on the courtesan.

The basic classification of the *nayaka* is as husband, lover, or libertine, with further subdivisions that result in a total of seventeen types; the stages of yearning, disenchantment, and the like that result in the multiplicity of the *nayika*'s categories do not apply to the hero. The text's remaining verses deal with the heroine's friend and confidante (*sakhi*) and the hero's friend (*sakha*); as with the heroine, it is her female friend, as against the hero's male friend, to whom the larger number of verses is devoted. In eleven of the *Rasa-manjari*'s verses, Bhanudatta portrays Krishna as the *nayaka*, with or without mention of Radha, while three verses are devoted to Shiva and Parvati, and another three to Rama and Sita. Preliminary study suggests that these divine lovers are invoked in verses that seem to be chosen at random from various sections of the poem.[18]

Rasik-priya

In 1591, almost a hundred years after Bhanudatta wrote the *Rasa-manjari*, Keshavdas, court poet to Raja Indrajit of Orchcha, a princely state that owed allegiance to the Mughal emperors, composed the *Rasik-priya* (*Connoisseurs' Delights* or *Handbook for Poetry Connoisseurs*) in Braj, the major northern dialect of literary, precolonial India.[19] This comprehensive work in sixteen chapters, which treats various aspects of poetic theory including *rasa*, focuses on an extensive classification of *nayikas* and *nayakas*, and was to become the most popular and widely illustrated of the *riti* texts. In his introductory chapter, Keshavdas speaks of love as either open or hidden and gives examples of partings and meetings, both open and hidden. This introduction includes an invocation to Ganesha, a set of verses dedicated to Krishna's exploits as illustrative of each of the nine *rasas*, and details of the circumstances of the work's composition. The initial categories of open and hidden are carried throughout the book; for instance, *nayakas* are either openly agreeable or hidden agreeable, openly deceitful or hidden deceitful, and so on. *Nayikas* are classified according to not only physical types, but also the threefold division already used by Bhanudatta into *svakiya* (one's own), *parakiya* (another's), and *samanya* (shared, or the courtesan). The classificatory scheme based on the experience of erotic love as *mugdha* (naive), *madhya* (average), and *pragalba* (experienced) applies only to one's own *nayika*; each is divided into four categories with further subcategories. The *parakiya-nayika* is classified merely as married or unmarried; with the courtesan, the poet quietly elides details.

For Keshavdas, as opposed to Bhanudatta, the hero and heroine are no mere courtly characters; Krishna is the *nayaka* and Radha the *nayika*, which would explain his bypassing the *samanya-nayika* (courtesan) after a quick reference.[20] Allison Busch describes Keshavdas's treatment of a *riti* text as having "a devotional orientation," and she comments on the spheres of *bhakti* and *riti* as having permeable boundaries.[21] She points out that the very title of the work allows for two interpretations, one courtly and the other devotional, since *rasik* can mean either "a connoisseur" or Krishna, and *priya* is "delight" or "a beloved"—in this case, Radha. The corpus of *Rasik-priya* manuscripts reveals that every artist who illustrated the text followed Keshavdas's textual specification, invariably utilizing the image of Krishna for the *nayaka*.

Satsai

Biharilal, perhaps a younger contemporary of Keshavdas, wrote the *Satsai* (*Seven Hundred* [*Verses*]) around 1647 at the court of Jai Singh of Amber (later Jaipur state) in the form of 713 verses in Braj. While his work is classified as a *riti* text, his *dohas* (couplets) stand apart from *riti*'s usual classificatory style. His couplets are to be understood as spoken by the *nayika* to her companion or by the companion to her; by the *nayaka* to his companion or by the companion to him; or by one companion to another. However, as Rupert Snell points out, doubt often remains as to who exactly the speaker is at any given moment.[22] By and large, Biharilal wrote of the aristocratic men and women of the court, although on occasion he spoke, too, of village beauties. Only some eighty of the seven hundred verses refer to Krishna and Radha, and quite often they do so indirectly, without any mention of names, but through a passing reference to the tending of cows or the churning of butter; two couplets speak of Rama. Yet Snell points out that even when Krishna is not specifically mentioned, "the perception of many *Satsai* readers will be that he is very much present by implication."[23] We are in that tricky middle ground that lies between the creator's intention and the reader's interpretive reception, not to mention the blurring of the categories between the sacred and the profane.

Barah-masa Texts

The genre of verses known as *barah-masa* (twelve months) is devoted to a distinctive treatment of the seasons, not as simple climatic variations or changing aspects of the landscape, but as a reflecting index of the relationship between hero and heroine. Aspects of the outer landscape appropriate to each month seem set to capture the inner moods and variations of erotic love. For instance, dry, parched land for summer or dark, lightning-laden skies for the rains, spoken of in the verses, may occupy the background of the painting; but both verbal and visual imagery focuses on the lover and beloved. In Kangra Valley depictions of the months, the scene is often located indoors so that it is the action of the lovers that must reveal the nature of the month; the wintry month of Pausha (December–January) is recognized, for instance, by a portrayal of lovers seated together indoors and wrapped in a quilt. Such a treatment of the months and seasons is in striking contrast to the practice in other parts of the world that produce paintings of this genre. When Chinese and Japanese artists created sets of hanging scrolls to portray the seasons, they frequently used a flowering plant typical of the month as the sole subject of the painting. When sixteenth-century Netherlandish artist Pieter Brueghel the Elder created a set of canvases to portray the seasons, *The Dark Day* represented early spring, *Return of the Herd* suggested autumn, and *Hunters in the Snow* depicted winter. The greater space within his canvases was devoted to a portrayal of the landscape, with tiny figures of men and women carrying out activities appropriate to that season. But in the Indian version of the months of the year, the sensuous and elegant human form, and the accompanying theme of erotic love, takes center stage. The human bodily form, in youth and beauty, in the pangs or the ecstasy of love, is what counts more than the beauty, amicability, or inclemency of nature.

While Kalidasa's Sanskrit *Ritu-samhara* (*Description of the Seasons*) has only tenuous links with the later *barah-masas*, it seems appropriate to make brief mention of it. Divided into six seasons, it commences with summer and moves through the rains, autumn, winter, and the chilly season, concluding with spring. While Kalidasa devotes a range of verses to the beauty of the women who, in season after season, capture the hearts of those who gaze at them, he focuses as much on the natural landscape and the birds and beasts that inhabit it. In his description of summer, he devotes nine verses to the beauty of the women and as many as eighteen to the natural scenery:

> With rounded hips clad in the sheerest silken bands,
> And breasts all decked out in festoons and sandal paste,
> Their flowing hair fresh with a bathing oil perfume—
> The womenfolk soothe their beloved's passion heat.
>
> (verse 4)

The deer are sore pained by the sun's ferocious heat;
Oppressed by great thirst, with their mouths all dry
   and caked;
They dash to far glen, "I see water there," they cry—
But no, like lamp-black, it is just a piece of sky!

(verse 11)

By shining sun's rays as a garland fierce and sharp,
The lake is parched, scorched, and from out its liquid mud
Up jumps a hot frog and he sits beneath the shade—
The parasol-hood of a thirsty cobra-snake.[24]

(verse 18)

The *barah-masa* texts, composed at a much later date and in various northern Indian vernacular languages, seem to have had their origins in folk ballads that were sung across the country.[25] A large proportion of such songs were "separation" *barah-masas* that commenced with the month of Kartik (October–November), which marks the start of the cool, dry season when the man of the house leaves home on his travels, unleashing in women the love-longings experienced in separation. With this focus, the month of Ashadha (May–June), which heralds the rains and hence the return of the beloved, is the longed-for month.

Keshavdas, poet of the *Rasik-priya*, composed a *barah-masa* text that forms the tenth chapter of his *Kavi-priya* (*Poets' Delights*[26] or *Handbook for Poets*), a work on poetics written in 1601.[27] While in the *Rasik-priya*, Keshavdas universally visualized Krishna and Radha as his hero and heroine, he moves away from such a scheme in his *barah-masa*, which contains no mention of Krishna, either directly or by implication. In each month, the *nayika* speaks to her beloved, telling him that this is not the month in which to leave her alone. Painted sets of *barah-masas* have the corresponding verse written along the upper border of the painting or on its reverse. Keshavdas's text, which commences with the month of Chaitra (March–April) and ends with Phalguna (February–March), was extremely popular. Certain other "twelve months" texts are known only from the paintings, and one such is Govinda's "separation" *barah-masa*, often used in paintings produced in the princely state of Bikaner, in which Radha pleads with her *sakhi* month after month to bring Krishna to her.[28] Other *barah-masa* texts do not seem to have inspired illustrated versions.[29]

Raga-mala Texts

The *raga-mala* (garland of musical modes) is the final genre of nonsacred texts and accompanying paintings to be considered here. The earliest extant "album" of such paintings belongs to the mid-sixteenth century and is in the so-called *Chaura-panchashika* style.[30] Such sets were regularly commissioned into the nineteenth century in the various princely courts of Rajasthan, the Pahari hills, and the Deccani sultanates. Only the *ragas* of northern Indian music were visualized and commemorated in these poetic verses and painted pages; southern Indian classical music belongs to an entirely different tradition.

The system of music and the *ragas* themselves provide, as one might expect, the early foundation; the composition of verses to describe the *ragas* followed, and finally came the paintings portraying *ragas*. The *raga* system itself is not as early as one might expect. Of the six chapters of the *Natya-shastra* devoted to music, one discusses instrumental music, three deal with individual varieties of musical instruments, one with songs, and one with *tala* (rhythmic beat).[31] While this reflects a fairly comprehensive system of music, the first occurrence of the term *raga* has been traced to Matanga's *Brihad-deshi* (*An Expanse of Folk Music*), a text dated somewhere between the fifth and seventh centuries.[32] By the twelfth and thirteenth centuries, a range of systematic musical texts are known to have existed.

The earliest extant treatise, however, is the fifteenth-century *Sangita-darpana* (*Mirror on Music*) of Damodara Misra.[33] This text proposes the existence of six male *ragas*, each associated with five female *raginis* visualized as their wives, yielding a system of thirty-six. Verses describe each *raga* (male) and *ragini* (female) to evoke a mood, such as eroticism, heroism, tranquility, devotion, or loneliness. In addition, each *raga* or *ragini* usually also suggests a particular time of day or night, while a few recall a season. As with the *barah-masas*, several *raga-mala* verses are known only from having been written on paintings, rather than from a textual tradition, and represent what has been termed a "painter's system."[34] It is not clear whether the painter's system, also of thirty-six, drew on the text of the *Sangita-darpana*, with which it shares a number of couplets, or whether it was the impetus for the compilation of that text. At any rate, the painter's system of thirty-six is used extensively in the Rajasthan plains and is evident in half of the corpus of four thousand paintings that Klaus Ebeling collated and analyzed in his encyclopedic work on *raga-mala* painting.[35] In the Pahari courts of the Punjab hills, painters followed a different tradition, apparently based on a 1570 text of Mesakarna, a court priest from Rewa.[36] Mesakarna extended the scheme to include eight sons (*raga-putras*) for each *raga*, so his expanded system reached a total of eighty-four. Finally, the existence of a few painted *raga-putris* (daughters of the *ragas*) indicates an even further extension of the system.

Both *raga-mala* verses and paintings focus on the human bodily form, making the expression of human emotion central to the portrayal of a *raga*. Thus the *Sangita-darpana* verse on the *ragini* Asaveri reads as follows:

> On the summit of the sandalwood mount, robed in the peacock's
> plumes, with a splendid necklace strung with pearls and ivory,

the variegated one drawing to herself from the sandalwood tree
the serpent—the proud one wears it as a bracelet (her body),
ablaze with splendour."[37]

Other verses speak of her as having been unsuccessful in love and having retreated to the mountain regions. Artists invariably depicted Asaveri (from the Savara tribe?) as a beautiful young woman, clad in a skirt of peacock feathers, sitting alone on a hilltop or in the wilderness, and playing a snake-charmer's pipe as she captivates the myriad snakes that swarm around her. In this chapter, our specific focus will be the insertion of the figure of Krishna to represent various *ragas*, even in instances where the accompanying verse contains no reference whatsoever to that god.

The Gods as *Nayaka* and as *Raga* in Painted Manuscripts

Illustrated manuscripts and painted albums of these various texts of a nonsacred genre were commissioned by court after court in the Rajasthan plains, the Punjab hills, and the Deccani sultanates; additionally, successive rulers of any one state ordered their own illustrated copy of a text they favored. Thus an immense corpus of painted manuscripts exists, of which no comprehensive listing has yet been produced. I shall focus on a few select versions of each text in order to illustrate their manner of insertion of the gods into the world of mortals. My choice is based sometimes on the stunning visual qualities of a manuscript, at other times on its possession of a colophon providing information on the patron or artist, and on occasion, on its completeness.

Rasa-manjari

Nurpur-Basohli Manuscript of 1660 to 1670: Hindu God Krishna as *Nayaka*

A page from a Pahari *Rasa-manjari* dated to around 1660 to 1670 depicts an elegantly appointed mansion against a deep-yellow background with a sliver of a daytime sky (figure 53). Within, the artist portrays a kneeling Krishna, deep blue in color, wearing an orange dhoti flecked with gold, and a gold scarf slung over his shoulder and bare torso; his lavish adornment includes his signature long garland of wildflowers, a gold and emerald crown topped with lotus buds, rich necklaces, armlets, bangles, and earrings of pearls, gold, and emeralds. This is Krishna, the beautiful Hindu god, par excellence. He bends forward toward the *nayika* with both hands intent on unraveling the knot of her skirt. The richly decked *nayika*, glittering with emeralds and gold and wearing clothes shot with gold threads, sits back demurely against a bolster. Those familiar with Krishna lore, aware of his reputation as a flirt and a trickster, might accept this painting at face

Figure 53. *Shatha-nayaka*, watercolor on paper with applied beetles' wings, Rasa-manjari by Master of the Early Rasa-manjari (Kripal of Nurpur?), Basohli, 1660–1670.

value as just another page from a Krishna manuscript. Even the accompanying verse on the painting's reverse seems to permit such an interpretation:

> He placed a tiara on her hair, painted a dot of musk upon her brow,
>
> Set bangles on her arms, and draped a pearl necklace over her breasts.
>
> Thus gaining her confidence, and pretending to adorn her with a belt,
>
> He untied the skirt of the doe-eyed girl with a very careful hand.[38]

But there is an inscribed label that provides the accurate clue to the painting as depicting the *shatha-nayaka* ("deceptive" hero) of the *Rasa-manjari*, the clever husband who "deceives" his wife into lovemaking. By adorning his *nayika* with jewels, the "deceptive" husband easily undoes her skirt by making her imagine that he is only adorning her further with a hip-belt. Inserting Krishna as the *shatha-nayaka*, even though there is no such suggestion in the text itself, was an easy artistic choice, given the god's reputation as a great lover with a predilection for mischief and deceit.

A second page by this artist, whom we know only as the Master of the Early *Rasa-manjari*, portrays a heroine conversing with her *sakhi* within a mansion set in a yellow background, with trees in the far-left distance and a fragment of a daytime sky above (figure 54).[39] Standing outside, resting one hand on a staff, is the god Krishna, painted deep blue and clad in the identical gold-flecked orange dhoti, gold scarf over his bare

Figure 54. *Vaishika-nayaka*, watercolor on paper with applied beetles' wings, *Rasa-manjari* by Master of the Early *Rasa-manjari* (Kripal of Nurpur?), Basohli, 1660–1670.

torso, and long wildflower garland just seen on the *shatha-nayaka*. The only difference is that, being outdoors, he wears clog-like sandals, while in place of Krishna's
crown, he is now shown with a white turban from which escape long strands of curly
hair. Inside the mansion, the gorgeously adorned *nayika* sits before a bolster cushion, appealing to her elegant *sakhi* confidante not to leave her to suffer at the hero's
hands:

> He feels no shame in his heart, no pity, no trace of fear—
> don't let me fall under his spell again; I'll be crushed like the bud
> of a bakula flower.[40]

Here, again, an inscribed label clues us in that this is not a page from Krishna legend,
but the *Rasa-manjari*'s undesirable hero, the *vaishika-nayaka* (libertine versed in
the ways of courtesans [*veshyas*]). Bhanudatta divides the *vaishika* into the best (*uttama*), average (*madhyama*), and worst (*adhama*) categories. Surprisingly, the artist
of this painting chose to portray even the *adhama-vaishika* (rake versed in the ways
of courtesans) in the guise of Krishna. Only Krishna's crown is lacking here; all other
identification is the same. Perhaps the artist felt a slight hesitation in identifying so
undesirable a "hero" quite so unequivocally with Krishna, and hence made a small
concession by substituting a turban for the god's standard golden crown.

Figure 55. *Madhya-abhisarika-nayika*, watercolor on paper with applied beetles' wings, *Rasa-manjari* by Master of the Early *Rasa-manjari* (Kripal of Nurpur?), Basohli, 1660–1670.

In a third painting, the same master devotes the left half of the page to a night with steady, pouring rain in which a fork-tongued snake slithers through the darkness (figure 55). Bright streaks of golden lightning punctuate the heavy clouds depicted in the sliver of a sky above. The right half of the page depicts the interior of a well-lit, luxurious mansion in which sits deep-blue Krishna, clad in a yellow-and-gold dhoti, a gold scarf over his bare torso, a long wildflower garland, precious ornaments, and a golden crown topped with lotus buds. Before him sits a richly adorned *nayika* who has apparently braved the weather to meet with him. Krishna reaches a hand out toward her breasts as he addresses her:

> What am I to do with you? You're completely unafraid
> Of snakes on the way, but at my very touch you tremble
> Like a leaf. And the rumble of storm clouds leaves you
> Unshaken, but one word from me and your face goes taut.[41]

For those unfamiliar with the text, an inscribed label again provides the correct interpretation of the page as portraying the *madhya-abhisarika-nayika*—the heroine of "average" experience who goes out on a secret rendezvous to meet with her lover, ignoring the dangers on the way.

This early illustrated *Rasa-manjari* carries Bhanudatta's Sanskrit verse in Devanagari on the reverse of each painting. The painted side contains additional notations in the local hill script of Takri: the upper red border has a label that indicates the subject matter of the painting, while the left border carries Takri serial numbers to indicate versification. This vibrant and dynamic creation, in a horizontal page format with deep-red borders, illustrates the style of the region to perfection in its masterly use of deep primary colors, its richly patterned clothes, its unique facial formula with expressive eyes, and its employment of raised white paint for pearls and applied beetles' wings for emeralds. Only 80 or so folios of this series, from an original set of 138, have been located.[42] While the artist followed Bhanudatta's text in portraying Shiva–Parvati and Rama–Sita only in the exact verses specified by the text, he clearly did not feel restricted to portraying Krishna only in the eleven verses prescribed by the text.[43] Instead, he universally converted the *nayaka* into Krishna, making lavish use throughout the pages of the manuscript of the distinctive iconography of Krishna as a Hindu god, with deep-blue skin, yellow dhoti, gold scarf over bare torso, long wildflower garland, and almost always a golden crown adorned with lotus buds or peacock feathers. This is an interesting decision, especially if we consider the fact that Bhanudatta dedicated this *riti* text to Shiva and Parvati, as indicated by its opening verses:

> Lest she feel the least fatigue Hara plants his own foot first on
>   the rocky ground,
> with his own right hand he plucks a flower from the tree, and
>   on the couch
> spread with his rought antelope skin he falls asleep on his
>   right side,
> within his body bearing his beloved fatigued from her deep
>   inner love.

> Glorious Bhanu is publishing
> this sweet Bouquet of Rasas,
> for the acquisition of rasa
> by those bees, the minds of the swarms of learned readers.[44]

What do we know about the milieu and motivation of the unknown master who painted this manuscript, perhaps for the monarch of the small hill state of Basohli, in the decade 1660 to 1670 during the reign of Sangram Pal (r. 1635–ca. 1673)? It has been suggested that the artist was a certain Kripal of Nurpur, a state directly across the Ravi River from Basohli.[45] The state of Nurpur is known for its emphasis on the worship of Krishna,[46] while Basohli apparently witnessed the arrival of "ardent Vaishnavism" during the reign of Sangram Pal, who adopted the vertical Vaishnava *tilaka* mark, as did his half-brother and immediate successor Hindal Pal.[47] Basohli's succeeding rulers went back to the horizontal Shaiva mark, favored also by the earlier rulers. Was it artist or patron who made the decision regarding the insertion of Krishna as the *nayaka* of this early *Rasa-manjari*? It seems probable that the artist of this *Rasa-manjari* was influenced by the pervasive Vaishnava atmosphere of the court; after all, painting workshops depended for their support on the king, whom they attempted to please with their pictures. Perhaps, too, the artist himself was a devotee of the god Krishna.

Nurpur-Basohli Manuscript of 1694/1695: Nobleman as *Nayaka*

A second *Rasa-manjari* dated to the year 1694/1695, painted in the same area, provides a sharp contrast by portraying its *nayaka* as a mere Rajput nobleman rather than as the god Krishna. According to its colophon, this manuscript was painted in the town of Basohli, for Raja Kirpal Pal (r. ca. 1673–1693), by the artist Devidasa of Nurpur, and it has been suggested that Devidasa was the son of the unknown Master of the Early *Rasa-manjari*.[48] Devidasa is a fine artist, but his pages lack the brilliance of color and the stunning emotional impact of those painted by the earlier artist. In his portrayal of the *abhisarika-nayika* of "average" experience, Devidasa opted for a symmetrical composition, placing his well-lit room at the center of the painting with steady, pouring rain on either side; the sky is streaked with lightning, but the slithering snake is gone (figure 56). The *nayika*'s gaze is directed downward, while her *nayaka* lover—portrayed as a fair-skinned Rajput noble clad in a white *chakdar-jama* over *py-jamas*, a white gold-edged scarf, and an orange turban—reaches out and takes her hand as he speaks reassuringly. In a second painting from this set, Devidasa portrays his fair-skinned Rajput nobleman fast asleep on a spacious, well-appointed couch in a well-lit chamber, clad in undershorts and a gold-edged scarf, with his turban still on (figure 57). Reclining beside him, the richly adorned, bare-breasted *nayika*, loosely wrapped in a fine, gold-edged fabric, raises herself on one elbow to gaze lovingly at him. The accompanying verse speaks of her dilemma:

> She thought, If I fall asleep right now I'll lose the chance to see
> My love's face; and if I stay awake, my lover's hands might start
>   to play,
> Over and over she thought it through, that girl with eyes like
>   lotus leaves,
> And finally decided to go to sleep—and to stay awake.[49]

It is intriguing that Devidasa turned away from the Krishna imagery that was so universally used in the first *Rasa-manjari*, painted a mere twenty-five or so years earlier. Perhaps one reason for the altered visualization of the hero was the changed affiliation of the new patron, Basohli raja Kirpal Pal. While a textual source

Figure 56. *Madhya-abhisarika-nayika*, watercolor on paper, *Rasa-manjari* by Devidasa of Nurpur, Basohli, 1694/1695.

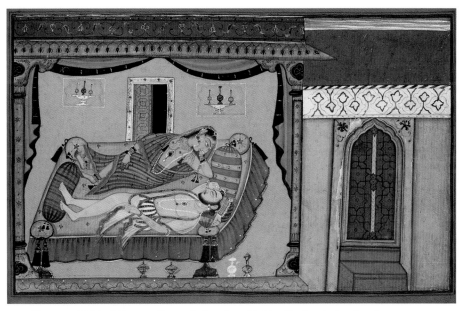

Figure 57. *Ativishrabdha-navodha-nayika* (newly wedded trusting heroine), watercolor on paper, *Rasa-manjari* by Devidasa of Nurpur, Basohli, 1694/1695.

speaks of him as an ardent devotee of Vishnu, his portraits reveal that he abandoned the Vaishnava mark in favor of the horizontal Shiva *tilaka*.[50] Possibly, too, the initiative lay with the artist, who, responding to the changed sectarian atmosphere, may have decided to follow Bhanudatta's text more closely, introducing Krishna only where the text itself so specified. However, since only some sixteen paintings are known from this *Rasa-manjari* painted by Devidasa, this suggestion must remain a mere conjecture.

It is worth noting that a *Rasa-manjari*, composed by Daria Khan and based largely on Bhanudatta's text, seems to have been produced as an illustrated manuscript in the Deccan.[51] The few pages that survive include its colophon, which informs us that it was commissioned by a Mewar *thakur* (subordinate ruler), a certain Sisodiya Shaktavat Mohan Singh, son of Maharaja Jagmalji, and painted in the year 1650 in the town of Aurangabad. The exact relationship of this text to Bhanudatta's celebrated version remains a subject for exploration.

Rasik-priya

Sub-Imperial Mughal Manuscript of 1615: Hindu God Krishna as *Nayaka* and Krishna, Rajput Courtier as *Nayaka*

Since the poet Keshavdas invariably featured Krishna as his *nayaka* in his *riti* text *Rasik-priya*, it will come as no surprise to find that artists followed suit. The very first illustrated manuscript, the Boston *Rasik-priya* of around 1615, is painted in the "sub-imperial Mughal style," a term that one scholar clarifies as being "a catch-all rubric that encompasses the art of many regions and many different hands."[52] The emphasis in the sub-imperial Mughal manuscript is on producing a complete copy of the text; the illustrations (one to every four or five verses of text) are relegated to a strip at the bottom of each page. The artist seems undecided on how exactly to portray Krishna; that some pages depict the *nayaka* as the typical Hindu god and others show him as a Rajput courtier may reflect multiple artists working on the same commission. The manuscript adopts the Mughal vertical-page format, in which two-thirds of each page was reserved for the scribe to write out three or four verses of text, while the painters were given a small horizontal strip at the lower end of the page for the verse chosen for illustration.[53]

On folio 70, the artist focuses on an image of Krishna as a Hindu god, clad in a yellow dhoti and a gold-edged scarf over his bare torso, wearing his wildflower garland and crown with peacock feathers, and seated partly on his knees on a couch in a palace room (figure 58). On the floor before him sits Radha's *sakhi*, who conveys a message to him that is indicated by the gesture of her fingers. The text commences with a verse titled "Radhika's soft laugh" (*manda-hasa*), before proceeding to describe other forms of laughter, and it is this first verse that the artist chose to illustrate:

For the past month or so she smiles
As soon as words of love she hears,
That girl who loves you all the while
Does sit purposely to give ear
To such love-talk; and much delight
I know she finds in love-filled words
Which king Nala's messenger recites
In that love tale so I have heard.
That yearning of your heart's delight
I reckon will now be fulfilled,
It seems to me that now the light
Of your good fortune has been lit.[54]

By contrast, the unknown artist of folio 15 decided to portray the *nayaka* as Krishna in the guise of a Rajput courtier (figure 59). Sitting cross-legged and leaning

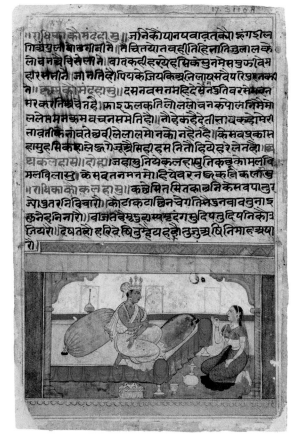

Figure 58. "Radhika's soft laugh," watercolor on paper, *Rasik-priya*, sub-imperial Mughal, ca. 1615.

Figure 59. *Sadara-dhira-nayika*, watercolor on paper, *Rasik-priya*, sub-imperial Mughal, ca. 1615.

against a bolster cushion, blue-skinned Krishna wears a *chakdar-jama* over *py-jamas*, with a golden crown on his head. Krishna reaches out for the wrist of the *nayika* seated before him, holding a fan; beside her is a water vessel, a betel-nut box with condiments, and a dish with prepared betel leaves. Of the set of verses written out on the page, the artist has chosen to illustrate the last, the *sadara-dhira-nayika* (attentive heroine whose love is a formality), and has presented the viewer with the completion of the actions detailed in the verse:[55]

> Seeing the arriving Krishna, she walked to him and gave him
> the seat herself. Bringing a new pot of water, she even washed
> his feet. She prepared the pan herself and placed it in a box
> in front of him. Finally, when she took the fan in her hand,
> Krishna held her wrist, and smiling he said "Have I commit-
> ted such a crime? (that you will not speak to me).[56]

This mature heroine outwardly fulfills all the rituals of welcoming her lord and taking care of his immediate needs, acting in a dignified although distant fashion.

Mewar Manuscript by Sahibdin of 1630: Hindu God Krishna as *Nayaka* and Krishna, Rajput Courtier as *Nayaka*

The earliest *Rasik-priya* from Mewar, painted for Rana Jagat Singh I (r. 1628–1652) by his master artist Sahibdin around 1630, abandons the textual priority of the sub-imperial manuscript.[57] Each page has a single verse of text written at the very top, and its accompanying painting occupies the entire available space.[58] Sahibdin's routine use of the figure of Krishna as the *nayaka* is only natural, since he followed Keshvadas's text closely and exactly in all its details, yet both Sahibdin and the artists of his work-shop portrayed Krishna in two guises.[59] More often, the artists visualized Krishna as a courtly figure, usually with a Mewari turban replacing the crown. Less frequently, they depicted him as the Hindu god, wearing a gold-flecked dhoti and a scarf flung across his bare torso, yet generally sporting a turban rather than his golden crown. Regardless of the guise chosen for Krishna, the artists always painted him a deep Mewari blue. All future Mewari artists followed the example set by Sahibdin, so it is Krishna as Rajput courtier rather than as Hindu god who becomes the standard insertion into Mewari *Rasik-priya* manuscripts.[60]

Sahibdin's interest in having the viewer follow all the action—of which there is not much in the *Rasik-priya* text—is well illustrated by his page on the *sadara-dhira-nayika*, which we have just viewed in its sub-imperial guise. Sahibdin divides his page into four discrete visual spaces, each portraying deep-blue Krishna wearing a translucent *chakdar-jama* over *py-jamas* with a cummerbund *patka*, and a crown topped with pea-cock feathers (figure 60). Moving from left to right and top to bottom, we see the *nayika* greeting Krishna and leading him to a seat, then washing his feet, next presenting him with pan and water to drink, and finally attempting to fan him, at which stage Krishna grasps her wrist. The compressed style of the sub-imperial set was not Sahibdin's mode; rather, he spelled out every portion of Keshavdas's verses for his patron to view and en-joy. That visual enjoyment of a manuscript was the objective of both artist and patron is confirmed by the colophon of the "Battle Book" of the *Ramayana*, which informs us that it was painted by Sahibdin, in Udaipur, for the personal "viewing" (*avalokatartha*) of Jagat Singh.[61]

One of Sahibdin's strategies to add an element of action to a text that centers on "lovers longing for absent beloveds . . . with characters speaking of each other or fantasizing about each other in lieu of being with each other" was to pick up each of the similes and metaphors used in the verbal text and translate them into visual imagery.[62] This technique is unique to Sahibdin, who used it, often with dramatic effect, to create what initially appear to be intriguingly opaque visions until we rec-ognize that the visual is a literal translation of the verbal. Since it is unlikely that Sahibdin or the artists of his workshop understood the original Braj (or, indeed, the Sanskrit Valmiki's *Ramayana*), it is clear that there was close collaboration between the artist and a manuscript supervisor (who is clearly designated as such in the *Ra-mayana* manuscript's colophon).[63] It would appear that the supervisor translated the verses, including all their verbal nuances, into the local Dingal dialect. Quite likely, the supervisor read such a Dingal text out loud to the artist and his workshop as-sistants, with Sahibdin making the decision on the objects to be included in order to animate the page.

Typical of this technique is a page depicting the open separation of the pining *nayika* whose lover has gone away on business (figure 61). The lower half of the page shows a pavilion within which the seated *nayika* is fanned by an attendant, while her remonstrating *sakhi* sits on the floor beside her. Outside, a peacock perches in a glori-ous sprouting mango tree painted in typical Mewari colors, while a small, unattended fire burns beside some tall flowering shrubs. The upper portion of the page contains two vignettes. To the left, blue-skinned Krishna, wearing a gold-flecked dhoti, a gold scarf, and a *pagri* turban, sits within a leafy bower and leans against a cushion; in him, we rightly read the absent lover. To the right, an elegantly attired woman runs after a flying crane in a menacingly dark, storm-laden atmosphere. The entire picture comes to life when we read the gist of two verses from the *Rasik-priya*, both spoken by the *sakhi*, one to the *nayika* and the other to a second *sakhi*, added by the scribe to the painting's reverse. Clearly it is this essence that the artist has absorbed and reproduced for the page's viewers:

Figure 60. *Sadara-dhira-nayika*, watercolor on paper, *Rasik-priya* by Sahibdin, Mewar, ca. 1630.

Figure 61. Pining *nayika*, watercolor on paper, *Rasik-priya* by Sahibdin, Mewar, ca. 1630.

> Who is the woman whose lover does not go abroad?
>
> Who would run after a bird to catch it, tell me?
>
> When a fire is started, does it ever rain immediately
>
> (to put the fire out)?[64]

There is nothing extraneous to the *Rasik-priya* text in Sahibdin's painted pages, but frequently the significance of the imagery eludes modern viewers who do not turn to the text for an explanation.[65] However, the tropes of studied poetry in any Indic language were fairly conventionalized, so it is likely that a picture of a woman running after a bird immediately triggered in the premodern viewer's mind the association with futility. Clearly, too, the aristocratic audience that enjoyed viewing these pages would have either read the accompanying verses or, more likely, had them recited aloud in order to fully appreciate the nuances of the paintings.

Sahibdin provides an unusual and imaginative visual treatment of a verse devoted to the traditional head-to-toe (*nakh-shikh*) description of the *nayika*:

If I compare her beauteous face
To the moon, lip homage I pay;
If her eyes as lotus I declare
The black bees will fly everywhere
Upon her, and annoyed her keep!
If to pomegranates her teeth
Compare I, and her firm round breasts
To quinces; lips to coral red—
Then 'tis not meet, for they are sold
Along with things both new and old
In the open market, and suffer
A million troubles! And if her
Eye, I to ruddy geese compare
And to a snake her braid of hair
Like to an elephant her gait,
And to a lion's her narrow waist,
Voice to a cuckoo's, nose as seems
A parrot's, then all these are deemed
Foul and filthy, for this reason
The nayika's parts are, as I see them,
Unequalled: only with themselves
Can they compared be, with none else![66]

Instead of merely painting a portrait of a lovely woman, Sahibdin decided to provide his viewers with an alternative scheme that challenges their poetic knowledge (they were *rasikas* [connoisseurs], were they not?) and creates a puzzle to be solved (figure 62). Occupying the center of the lower half of the page is Krishna, wearing a translucent *chakdar-jama*, *py-jamas*, and a Mewari turban; sitting in the open air; and being fanned by an attendant. The verse is supposed to be spoken by Krishna to himself, but here it seems that Krishna might be sharing his thoughts with the *sakhi* seated before him or, indeed, that the *sakhi* herself is speaking, to judge from the gesture of her fingers. Either the supervisor did not sufficiently clarify the circumstances of the verse, or Sahibdin just did not think it important enough to follow exactly, perhaps preferring his compositional structure.[67] In a pavilion to the upper left, an attendant fans the *nayika* whose charms are the subject of the verse. The rest of the page is filled with apparently random imagery that becomes meaningful when we read the verse or, alternatively, recall the tropes to realize that each object refers, in one way or another, to the beauty of the *nayika*. To follow the order of the verse, Sahibdin gives us the moon, lotus, black bees, pomegranate, quince, goose, snake, elephant, lion, cuckoo, and parrot. Andrew Topsfield suggests that the inclusion of a jeweler holding tongs and blowing at a fire must be a reference to coral as the color of the *nayika*'s lips.[68] In Topsfield's enthusiastic phraseology, Sahibdin "almost gives the effect of trading image for image with Keshav Das, as in the fast musical exchange of melodic phrases known as *sawal-jawab* ('question-and-answer')."[69]

Figure 62. *Nakh-sikh-nayika*, watercolor on paper, *Rasik-priya* by Sahibdin, Mewar, ca. 1630.

The Mewar *ranas* seem to have divided their attention between the worship of Shiva and that of Vishnu, as evidenced by the two major dynastic shrines of Shiva at Eklingji and Krishna at Nathdvara; these, together with the Amba Mata temple, are featured in the paintings of several later *ranas*. We may assume that the situation was similar during the reign of Jagat Singh, who had not yet commenced the practice of such visual recording of his various activities. The fruitful collaboration between Rana Jagat Singh and his master artist Sahibdin, a Muslim painter, resulted in an outstanding corpus of painted manuscripts. One may assume that the nature of the commissions was the choice of the *rana*, with Sahibdin making the artistic decisions so as to produce paintings that would appeal to Jagat Singh's individual, and apparently knowledgeable, taste.

Satsai

Pahari Manuscript of 1780 to 1790: Hindu God Krishna as *Nayaka*

A visually enchanting page from a manuscript of the *Satsai* of the Pahari hills, painted around 1780 to 1790, focuses on the beautiful figure of the Hindu god Krishna standing within the spacious courtyard of a mansion (figure 63). This gorgeous being of pale-blue hue, with wavy, black hair held in place by a golden crown topped with peacock feathers, wears his characteristic yellow robe and wildflower garland, with a gold scarf over his bare torso. As we closely scrutinize the partly visible house on the left, we distinguish an agitated, love-tormented *nayika*, who runs up and down inside her house to gaze at Krishna and, incidentally, to be the object of his gaze. In the mode of continuous narrative, the *nayika*'s body above the waist is revealed at an upstairs window as she leans her elbow against its ledge to gaze down at Krishna; the rear view of her form is partially visible on the first level as she attempts to gaze at Krishna through the concealing privacy of a grille window; and finally we see her more directly as she stands at ground level in the doorway right in front of Krishna. To the far right, two *sakhis* stand framed in the distant arched entranceway to the compound as they point toward the *nayika* and talk about their infatuated friend. The three verses written on the reverse seem to have been chosen because they speak of the *nayika*'s restless movement up and down the stairs of her house, which reminds her friends of a yo-yo (*charki*):

> Frenzied, ascending and descending the balcony, her
>   body is not the least bit tired,
> Caught in the clever one's love, she is like an acrobat's yo-yo.
>
> (verse 44)

Figure 63. Restlessness of love, watercolor on paper, *Satsai*, Kangra, ca. 1780–1790.

Restless and distressed, between her new love and her
    family's shame,
Pulled both ways, turning and returning, she passes her
    day like a yo-yo.

                                  (verse 50)

From here to there, from there to here, she does not rest
    for a second.
Without resting, like a yo-yo, she comes, and she goes.[70]

                                  (verse 51)

The couplets themselves contain no reference whatsoever to Radha or Krishna, but seem to speak of an ordinary *nayika*'s experience of love-longing. The artist, however, has transformed the hero into the beautiful and beloved figure of god Krishna.

A second painting from the same set also features the god Krishna as its focal point (figure 64). Like most of the other paintings in the set, this one uses an oval frame as the format, with gold scrollwork filling in the corners of the vertical rectangular page. While the *nayika*, seen moving away from the center toward the left, catches our attention at first, if we follow the turn of her head, we see that she is gazing back to look at Krishna, who is seated at a window to the far right. Here again is the beautiful Hindu god, richly ornamented, wearing his yellow dhoti, golden scarf flung across his bare torso, and golden crown topped with peacock feathers. Two pairs of *sakhis*, one positioned along the left curved frame of the picture and the other along the right edge, commune with each other about the *nayika*'s behavior. One *sakhi* of each pair speaks, while the other has a finger raised to her mouth, expressing her astonishment. The lovers' eyes lock, and reference is made to this in the first of the five couplets written on the reverse of the painting, which contains no reference at all to Krishna but merely refers to young lovers:

Speaking, refusing, delighting, angering, meeting, blooming,
    blushing,
In a crowded hall, the eyes do all the talking.[71]

                                  (verse 9)

A degree of ambiguity has been introduced by the artist into the portrayal of Krishna. Annapurna Garimella asks whether we see an actual individual seated at a window with the curtain rolled up or, instead, a painted portrait of the god Krishna with its protective curtain rolled up for worship.[72] One may further query whether the artist has instead portrayed an imagined vision that has taken over the *nayika*'s anguished heart. Molly Aitken's comment

Figure 64. Meeting of the eyes, watercolor on paper, *Satsai*, Kangra, ca. 1780–1790.

about a range of illustrated texts that feature divine figures is noteworthy; they "demanded of painters that they formulate ways clearly to picture more than one moment in time and to distinguish memories, moods, fantasies and visions from the everyday."[73]

The remaining couplets written on the painting's reverse are those in which Biharilal visualizes Radha and Krishna as *nayika* and *nayaka*, and two of these are spoken to a *sakhi* by Radha as she acknowledges her obsession:

> Looking at Krishna's dark body, they have no regard for
> honor or dishonor,
> What can I do? These flirtatious, desirous eyes go
> toward him.

(verse 33)

> I stand filled with his head-to-toe form. Still these eyes
> ask for a smile.
> They will not abandon their covetous nature.[74]

(verse 32)

The verses written on the reverse of these *Satsai* paintings are not necessarily in any strict chronological sequence, but are seemingly chosen from the corpus to best conjure up the image illustrated. It seems likely from a review of these painted pages that the artist first created the painting and then handed it over to the scribes who wrote out those verses that seemed most relevant.

It is a great pity that this exquisite painted *Satsai* set is known today from a mere forty paintings and twenty drawings; one of the drawings contains the notation "drawn by Fattu," a painter known to be the son of Manaku of the state of Guler in the Himalayan foothills.[75] A few definite facts emerge on the religious inclinations of the rulers of Guler and adjoining Kangra. The Kangra royal line traces its descent from Devi, but during the reign of Sansar Chand (r. 1775–1823), the period corresponding to the suggested date of this painted *Satsai*, the worship of Krishna suddenly became prominent. We read that Sansar Chand listened to *Braj-bhasha* songs, made gifts of land out of devotion to Krishna, and, in the year 1790, endowed the Murli-manohar Krishna temple at Sujanpur.[76] It is tempting to entertain the possibility that Sansar Chand may have been the patron of this series; but Fattu, too, may have been a special devotee of Krishna, making the decision to give prominence to the beloved Hindu god throughout his *Satsai* commission. The situation in neighboring Guler is not clear-cut, since both Shiva–Durga devotion and Rama worship played major roles. However, during the eighteenth century the favored mode of Vaishnava worship shifted to Krishna, and Govardhan Chand (r. 1741–1773) was among the rulers who built a Krishna shrine, raising the possibility of his having been the patron of this captivating manuscript.[77]

A complete and extensive *Satsai* manuscript running to 643 pages comes from the state of Mewar and was completed in 1719 by the painter Jagannath for Rana Sangram Singh.[78] It routinely features the blue-skinned, yellow-robed, crowned Hindu god Krishna as its *nayaka*, and the treatment of its pages makes clear that Jagannath followed the visual tradition initiated by Sahibdin some ninety years earlier.[79]

Barah-masa

Bundi-Style Manuscript of 1760 to 1770: Hindu God Krishna as *Nayaka*

Artists painting *barah-masas* in the Rajasthani state of Bundi, and in its various *thikana*s (fiefdoms), invariably insert the Hindu god Krishna into each and every one of the twelve months. While they follow the details of the poet Keshavdas's text, with the appropriate verse written at the top of their painted pages, they totally ignore Keshavdas's invariable use of the worldly *nayaka* in favor of the blue-skinned Hindu god. One among several examples from this region is provided by the twelve paintings of a late-eighteenth-century (ca. 1760–1770) *barah-masa* in the Bundi style, from its *thikana* of Uniara. Artists producing pictorial versions of *barah-masas*, as indeed of *ragas*, seem to have drawn freely on the wide range of visual vocabulary available in their workshops; the result is a number of pictorial conventions held in common with drawings and paintings of the *nayika/nayaka* genre produced for the *riti* commissions.

This *barah-masa* commences with the longed-for rainy month of Ashadha (June–July), which heralds the return home of the menfolk. The artist painted his lovers within a palatial mansion beneath a dramatically dark, cloud-laden sky with serpentine streaks of lightning and wildly fleeing birds (figure 65). Peacocks, suggestive of love-longing, perch in a rich grove of mangoes, plantains, and flowering trees, typical of the style of the Bundi region. On the upper floor of the mansion sit the heroine and her beloved, dark-blue Krishna wearing a yellow dhoti, a gold-edged scarf over his bare torso, a wildflower garland, and a combination headgear of an orange turban topped with a tiara-like crown with a peacock-feather crest. A river flows in the foreground, and on it is a miniature pavilion carrying the reclining Vishnu, whose feet are being massaged by Lakshmi, while in the distance, an ascetic sits in a yogic pose in front of his hut.

Keshavdas's verse is written on the top red border of each painting, and we see that the artist of this set—and of other Bundi-style sets, such as one in the Chatrapati Shivaji (formerly Prince of Wales) Museum, Mumbai—closely followed all the verbal images conjured up by the poet. Keshavdas's verse on Ashadha reads:

Strong winds are blowing all around. In such weather only a man of feeble mind will go out leaving his wife and home. Even the mendicants use only one asana these days, i.e. they avoid going out for begging. What to talk of human beings, even the birds do not leave their nests. Lord Vishnu has taken Shri (Lakshmi) along with him to spend this time in bed (Kshirsagar). Poet Keshavdas says that during the month of Ashadha, he has not heard anybody leaving his home, even in the Vedas and Gathas (ballads).[80]

The Uniara scribe has renumbered Keshavdas's verses, converting Ashadha into the first month, even though it is the fourth month in the poet's scheme. Each inscription, painted in white on the red ground of the border, has the words "it is said" preceding the verse

Figure 65. Month of Ashadha (June–July), watercolor on paper, *barah-masa*, Uniara, ca. 1760–1770.

Figure 66. Month of Pausha (December–January), watercolor on paper, *barah-masa*, Uniara, ca. 1760–1770.

itself. Yet despite the close correspondence between the details of text and image, the artist chose to ignore the fact that Keshavdas never mentions Krishna as his *barah-masa nayaka*.

A glowing morning sky conjures up the winter month of Pausha (December–January), in which the artist has painted the sun as a golden orb in a chariot drawn by seven horses, in the delightful and distinctive mode of the Bundi region (figure 66). The lover is the deep-blue god Krishna, clad in his traditional yellow dhoti, gold-edged scarf over bare torso, wildflower garland, and tiara with peacock feathers atop an orange turban; he sits across from his beloved as they warm their hands over a gold brazier filled with glowing coals. In the kitchen, a maid warms her hands on the fire, above which sits a cooking pot, while in a simple hut in the foreground, a poor man and his wife likewise warm their hands over a fire of twigs. Keshavdas evokes the month with this verse:

> In the month of Pausha nobody likes cold things, whether
> they are water, food, dress, or house. Even the earth and sky
> have become cold. In this season everyone, rich and poor
> alike, like oil (massage of oil), cotton (cotton filled clothes),
> betel, fire (to warm the room), sun-shine and company of
> young women. (During the month) the days are short and
> nights are dark and long. This is not the time to quarrel with
> one's lover (meaning thereby that this is the time of union
> with lover). Keeping all these aspects in mind the Beloved
> asks her lover not to leave her in the month of Pausha.[81]

Once again, the artist has re-created the exact imagery evoked by Keshavdas's verse, but chosen to insert the god Krishna in place of the worldly *nayaka*.

The *barah-masas* commissioned in the various states of the Rajasthan plains, including Bundi and Kotah and their *thikanas*, as well as Jaipur and Alwar, followed the imagery conjured up in Keshavdas's text. However, while Bundi and Kotah routinely replaced the *nayaka* with Krishna as the Hindu god, Jaipur and Alwar fluctuated between the god Krishna and the blue-skinned Rajput courtier. The *barah-masas* from Bikaner tend to focus on the *nayika* and her *sakhis*, largely bypassing the portrayal of the *nayaka* whose absence is the lament of the accompanying verse. In one such set, only three paintings include the *nayaka*, two portraying him as a fair-skinned courtier and only one as the blue-skinned god Krishna.[82] By and large, the *barah-masa* paintings produced in the Pahari schools carry inscribed verses from other sources and portray their hero as a light-skinned, turbaned aristocrat clad in the costume of the local court.[83] Jodhpur artists, too, generally portrayed their *barah-masa nayaka* as a light-complexioned, well-built, bearded courtier.[84]

Raga-malas

Shiva as *Raga–Ragini*

Common to all *raga-mala* systems are the six male *ragas*: Bhairava, Malkos, Hindol, Dipak, Megha, and Shri. Of these, the first, Bhairava (the name itself is one of the many epithets of Shiva), is routinely, although not invariably, depicted as the god Shiva.[85] The renowned Chunar *raga-mala* of around 1591, created in the Mughal dependency of Chunar, whose governor was the Hindu Rao Surjan of Bundi, is among the earliest of this genre, and it sets the example that artists followed thereafter (figure 67). Its striking Bhairava *raga* portrays Shiva seated cross-legged on a set of lotus petals with serpents wrapped around his knees to serve as a yoga band. His matted locks are swept up into a magnificent topknot that features the crescent moon and the face of the goddess Ganga. A tiger skin is wrapped around his limbs, and he wears a garland of severed human heads that glisten on his gray-blue body, as he plays the lute-like *vina*. Two beautiful, richly adorned female attendants flank him within the luxurious interior of an elegant mansion. In the painting traditions of Bundi, Uniara, Kotah, and the Deccan, Shiva is the invariable focus of the Bhairava *raga*.

A verse from the painter's system, which is also part of the *Sangita-darpana*, carries this description of Bhairava *raga*:

> He carries the Ganges, and on his forehead, the digit moon, and three eyes. His body has serpents for orna-ments, and he wears the skin of an elephant. He shines, with a trident in his hand and human skulls (for a gar-land). Victory to Bhairava, the first of all ragas, clad in spotless white.[86]

Another verse of similar visualization comes from a variant painter's system:

> Bhairava was born of the mouth of Shiva, having the notes *dha, ni, sa, ga, ma*. It is to be sung during the morning of an autumn day. . . . The raga is Shiva incarnate. (He wears) the bracelet of serpents and the moon on his forehead. The Ganga is in his matted locks and (human) skulls on his neck.[87]

While none of the verses of the *raga-mala* system sanctions the use of the figure of Shiva for any of the *raginis*, an occasional artist took the liberty of inserting Shiva into

Figure 67. Bhairava *raga*, watercolor on paper, *raga-mala*, Chunar, 1591.

a few other musical modes. The artist of a Kamod *ragini*, perhaps from Bikaner, depicts Shiva seated on a deerskin, while the Ganga from his locks flows across the foreground; a painter of a Madhyamadi *ragini* from Lucknow depicts Shiva and Parvati embracing while sitting on an elephant skin.[88]

In the Rajput courts, the god Shiva is featured largely to introduce a mood of solemnity and grandeur; he is never approached through the mode of erotic love, encountered in chapter 4, which the *nayanmar* saints made a popular alternative in southern India. Yet the ease with which even a divinity as distant and remote as Shiva is introduced into these paintings of musical modes indicates the effortless movement between the worlds of god and men, which one might otherwise have considered to be discrete and unrelated.

Krishna as *Raga–Ragini*

In addition to Shiva's portrayal as Bhairava *raga*, the Hindu god Krishna is frequently portrayed to evoke two other male *ragas*, Hindol and Megha, even though their accompanying verses usually speak of Madana, god of love, rather than Krishna. The remaining three *ragas*—Malkos, Dipak, and Shri—are always portrayed as courtly, turbaned, light-skinned male aristocrats, seated in a palace and surrounded by solicitous attendants. It would appear that artists faced with commissions for a variety of nonsacred texts, including *raga-malas*, inserted Krishna into their pages, naturally and without the slightest sense of impropriety, whenever the subject matter had erotic overtones that suggested joyous union, frolic, or just plain exuberance and merriment in the springtime or in welcoming the rains. We may also note that Krishna is the master player of the flute whose music is compellingly sweet, delicate, and irresistible; for artists, it was both rational and logical to readily personify the *ragas* and *raginis* of music in the form of Krishna.

In just about every known *raga-mala* set, Hindol (literally, "swing") *raga* is depicted as blue-skinned Krishna, seated on a swing and surrounded by adoring women. A late Mughal page from the Delhi-Agra region, painted toward the end of the eighteenth century, is a typical visualization (figure 68). The artist has placed his golden swing, with peacocks perched on it, in a green meadow at the edge of a lotus-filled pond, while dark-blue rain clouds fill the sky. Dark-hued Krishna, clad in a yellow dhoti with a wildflower garland on his bare torso, sits at ease on the swing, wearing a golden crown with peacock feathers that is set off by a gold-edged green halo. Flanking him are rejoicing women, one holding a *mridanga* drum and another a *vina*, as they swing Krishna and applaud the coming rains. However, the verses describing Hindol speak only of a beautiful hero. The painter's system, for instance, contains no reference to the god Krishna, although the attributes of the *raga* could be interpreted as suggesting identification with that great lover:

His complexion is yellow and he is amorous by nature. *Raginis* swing him on a golden swing. The fair and clever women please him. He is petit and extremely handsome.[89]

From an alternative painter's text, and the *Sangita-darpana*, comes this verse, once again with no reference to Krishna:

Figure 68. Hindol *raga*, opaque watercolor and gold on paper, *raga-mala*, Delhi-Agra, late eighteenth century.

> Enjoying frolicsome delight on a swing gently pushed by
> fair-hipped maidens, he is called by the great sages Hindola
> Raga, small, with complexion bright as the pigeon.[90]

Both poets and artists focused on the swing (*hindola*), and who better than handsome Krishna, beloved of the *gopis*, as the swinger on the swing?

To portray Megha (literally, "cloud") *raga*, or Megha-mallara as it is sometimes called, painters chose to portray the beautiful Krishna dancing in the midst of female companions to herald the start of the rainy season. As noted earlier, the rains are the harbinger of all good things and, following the devastating heat of a long summer, are celebrated as an omen of fertility and of human love and desire. An exquisite sub-imperial Mughal painting of early date (ca. 1610) portrays blue-skinned Krishna, wearing a yellow dhoti and scarf and sporting his wildflower garland and golden crown topped with lotus buds (figure 69). The richly adorned Krishna dances with a lute-like *vina* in one hand against a fanciful lavender-pink ground with a central outcrop of craggy rocks reminiscent of the Mughal style. Peacocks dance joyfully, one with tail outspread; a lovely woman to the left plays the cymbals, and one to the right dances while playing a large drum. Curiously, the painting is labeled Megha-mallara *ragini*, not *raga*. The painter's text and the *Sangita-darpana* describe Megha in terms that apply to Krishna, but do not identify him as such:

> With a complexion like the blue lotus and a face like the
> moon, he is dressed in yellow and sought by thirsty cuckoos.
> With bewitching smile, he sits on the throne of the clouds. He
> is one amongst heroes, the youthful melody of the clouds.[91]

A slightly different formula comes from an alternative painter's text, which identifies Megha with Kama, god of love:

> Of blue splendour, attached to the roar of the rain-cloud; of
> tender body and lovely form, proud and playful he—the god
> of love—is said to be Megha Raga.[92]

While there is no mention of Krishna's name in any of the verses, the phraseology allows for easy identification with him, thanks to the mention of a blue complexion and yellow robes in one case, and his description as the great lover in the other.

Another *raga* or *ragini* (there is no unanimity on the gender) frequently portrayed as the beautiful dancing god Krishna surrounded by celebrating women dancers is Vasanta (spring), which readily allows for identification with the popular divine lover. In some textual traditions, Vasanta is a female *ragini* associated with either Dipak *raga*

Figure 69. Megha *raga [ragini]*, watercolor on paper, *raga-mala*, sub-imperial Mughal, ca. 1610.

or Sri *raga*, while in other traditions Vasanta is transformed into a male *raga*. Either way, Vasanta is portrayed as blue-skinned Krishna surrounded by the *gopis*. A painting from Amber, reproduced by Klaus Ebeling, is clearly inscribed, "Vasanta *ragini*, second wife of Dipaka *raga*."[93] Apparently, the painters were not in the least disturbed by the idea of using Krishna to portray a female *ragini*. The painter's text for Vasanta, however, suggests the distinct possibility of Krishna imagery for a male *raga*:

> His topknot, bound with peacock's feathers, is erect; his
> face, because of the burgeoning mango shoot, is as a flower.
> Elephant-like, in the forest joyfully he wanders among the
> gopis, Vasanta Raga.[94]

A Braj–Hindi verse on Vasanta, in contrast, conjures up an image of Madana, god of love, rather than blue-skinned Krishna:

> With crest on head and lute in hand, Madana is resplendent
> and as he dances he enthralls our minds. Mango tendril flow-
> ers on all sides; the cuckoo calls; the peacock cries. Therefore
> a friend, a girl, beats the mridanga drum and describes his
> fair body—Vasanta.[95]

One final instance of Krishna imagery to be introduced here concerns Saranga, described variously as a *raga-putra* or a *ragini*, as portrayed in a striking Mewar painting created in 1628 by Sahibdin in Udaipur for Rana Jagat Singh.[96] Against a deep-red ground, blue-skinned Krishna, clad in a yellow dhoti and scarf, sits beneath a tree with his beloved (Radha?) on his lap, fanned by an attendant as they listen to a sage playing a musical instrument (figure 70). In the *Sangita-darpana*, the male *raga-putra* Saranga is described as "fond of the pleasures of culture, the songs of the Gandhar-vas," and as "a youth of dark complexion"; artists frequently depicted him as Krishna.[97] While Sahibdin's portrayal seems appropriate to the *Sangita-darpana*'s *raga-putra* de-scription, the inscription on its top border clearly indicates that this is Saranga *ragini*: "Saranga, *ragini* of Hindola." A scrutiny of painted *raga-malas* indicates a considerable degree of discrepancy and ambiguity in both the painted and literary visualizations of these musical modes, allowing further leeway for artists so inclined to insert Krishna into their paintings.

In addition to illustrated albums, *raga-malas* were featured in the mural paint-ings that adorned the walls of palaces. One such badly damaged example still remains in the Datia Palace of Bir Singh Dev (r. 1603–1618) as a narrow panel just below ceiling level that runs around a tiny, fourth-floor pleasure terrace. Its positioning literally sug-

Figure 70. Saranga *ragini*, watercolor on paper, *raga-mala* by Sahibdin, Mewar, 1628.

gests that it could be visualized as a "garland" strung above a bed.[98] While there are no inscribed labels attached to these tempera paintings, among the seventeen identifiable panels are two that feature the dancing Krishna, perhaps as Vasanta and Megha.

A few other musical modes occasionally feature Krishna as the focus of their paintings. Such paintings include a Deccani Kanada and Gujari *raginis*, a Jaipur Vibhasa *ragini*, and a Marwar Pancham *raga-putra*, the last portrayed as the four-armed, blue god Krishna.[99]

The Insertion of Gods into a Nonsacred Realm

We have encountered a unique feature of the painted world of the Rajput courts in the insertion of the gods, specially the popular figure of the blue god Krishna, into the worldly realm of nobility and aristocracy. Krishna's dark-hued form, yellow robe, wildflower garland, and crown adorned with peacock feathers make him unmistakable. Without necessary implications of the religious or sacred, Krishna takes the place of a series of "idealized archetypes," the *nayaka* of *riti* texts, the beloved of the *barah-masa*, as also of *raga* or *ragini*.[100] The background of divinity seems only to further enable him to take all forms and stand for all things. Earlier we encountered the blurring of lines between the sacred and the profane in the context of temple and monastery sculpture; in the painted manuscripts considered here, distinctions between the two seem to be abandoned. The easy insertion of the figure of Krishna as the courtly hero, or joyous *raga–ragini*, often in direct contradiction of the very verses inscribed on the painted pages, may be regarded also as an indication of the espousal of devotion to Krishna by the monarch as well as the artist.[101] Apparently neither patrons nor artists found it inappropriate to transfer this beloved deity from the setting of the sacred manuscripts of the *Bhagavata-purana* and *Gita-govinda*—the banks of the Jumna River and its adjoining woods—into the worldly realm of the Rajput elites. The Krishna story in the *Maha-bharata* itself says that he did exactly this, and was a familiar figure in the court of the Kauravas and later of the Pandavas. The repeated production of manuscripts of these nonsacred genres in court after court, featuring this easy insertion of gods into the world of men, and the easy acceptance of such insertion by the patrons, reflects the permeability of the boundaries between the sacred and the worldly. We might even constructively question the value and utility of such terms in the study of the artistic traditions of premodern India.

AFTERWORD
THE BODY REVEALED AND CONCEALED:
ISSUES OF CREATION AND RECEPTION

Readers of this book will have gathered that the beautiful, highly toned human body is the leitmotif of Indian art and that the actual human body, which received prominence in all modes of outer worship in India, is regarded not as an obstacle to be overcome but as a fine-tuned vehicle through which to achieve closeness to the divine. We have encountered the ways in which the idealized body, while modeled on nature, is invariably believed to surpass the beauty of nature. We have demonstrated the crucial role played by ornament with regard to both the female and the male body; ornament is not merely an optional aid to beauty, but something that completes, enhances, and protects the body. In addition, readers will have understood that sacred enclosures and monuments—whether Buddhist, Hindu, or Jain—carry a wide range of imagery that many viewers might see as profane, showing that the boundaries between "sacred" and "secular" spaces are, at best, fluid. The appropriateness of such terms in furthering an understanding of India's cultural history is open to question. Readers will have perceived also the vital role played by the perfect beauty of the body of god in devotional *bhakti*, in the form of three-dimensional sculptures as well as in the word-pictures evoked by the saints and *acharyas* in their sacred songs. Reveling in, and concentrating on, the physical beauty of each part of the deity's body was an accepted mode of approach to the divine. Chapter 5, devoted to painted manuscripts, showed the ease with which gods, regarded as divine, seem to move in the world of men, without in any way transforming that mundane world into a sacred realm. Along the way, readers will also have encountered references to the artist, the patron, the priest, and the devotee; we will now focus on these participant-viewers to evaluate more accurately issues relating to the creation and reception of art.

We may divide the images we have encountered into two distinct categories that are unrelated to the disputed terms, "the sacred" and "the profane." The first category comprises those images created to be inserted into niches on the outer walls of temples, or perhaps sculpted in situ from the stones that are already part of the temple walls. These images are fixed in place on the exterior of a temple or monastery; their beauty of form and line is readily visible in the open, where they may be clearly seen by devotees who perform a ritual circumambulation of the monument. Painted manuscripts, viewed by elite patrons as part of leisure-time interests, and intended to be enjoyed at close quarters, also belong to this category. The second category includes those images enshrined in the sanctum, as well as *utsava-murtis* (portable festival images), which take part in a range of temple rituals. Such images are generally viewed after the *alankara* of *puja*, when they are presented to the devotee lavishly adorned with silks, jewels, and flowers, with their sculpted beauty masked. Before proceeding further in our exploration of issues relating to the creation and reception of these two distinct categories of imagery, it will be helpful to reiterate that the beautiful body of premodern India implies an idealized body, an ornamented body, and a sensuous body.

The experience and attitude of the artist or creator of images of both categories is identical. The mission of the *sthapati* (master artist) was to produce images of bodily perfection, following established iconographic directions. Whether he was creating a stone image to adorn a temple niche or a portable bronze festival icon, he modeled the slender arms of the goddess to resemble pliant vine (in the north) or bamboo (in the south), while her thighs and legs would recall the contours of smooth banana stalks. Aware of the essential element of *alankara*, he carved, or added in wax or paint, abundant embellishment, including drapery and the entire array of jeweled ornament that was a prerequisite to complete the image. If creating a sanctum image, his responsibility was much greater, knowing as he did that the sanctum image for a Shiva temple had to be flawless in order to serve as the vehicle for the deity's temporary occupation during the invocation of *puja*. In creating a Vaishnava image, his responsibility would be equally high, even higher perhaps, knowing that the *archa* image was considered "a little bit of heaven on earth."[1] In either case, the artist gave of his best.

Occasionally, we have evidence that members of an artists' guild, or those from rival guilds, competed with one another to create the finest images. Karnataka is one area where sculptors have left us their personal names and guild affiliations, as well as *birudas* (panegyric titles) proclaiming their reputation. Hoysala temples display such records along the base of the female bracket figures connecting walls to eaves, or pillars to the ceiling, and along the pedestals of the numerous images adorning the exterior walls. We find that the sculptor Malloja described himself as "a pair of large scissors to the necks of titled sculptors"; Malliyanna designated himself as "a thunderbolt to the hill of titled sculptors"; while Chavana from Balligrame gave himself the title Madana Mahesha, indicating that he was to rival sculptors as Shiva was to Kama (a reference to Shiva's third eye burning Kama to ashes).[2] At the Sarasvati temple in the town of Gadag in northern Karnataka, its architect Udega adopted the Madana-Mahesvara *biruda*, and added two others, the first describing himself as one who overpowers his architect opponents as a lion overpowers an elephant, and the second as one who breaks the pride of jealous architects as an expert lover does to a harlot.[3] One may assume that a degree of rivalry must always have existed among artists, even though epigraphic evidence is lacking from other areas. At any rate, it is clear that artists took pride in creating beautiful images, giving them the most elegant and fluid bodily outlines that it was in their ability to create.

In part, the artists' desire and efforts to capture every fine detail of the beauty of bodily form were intended to please the patron who had commissioned the image and from whom they would receive payment. The satisfied patron would consider a beautiful image to be a gift worthy of donation to a monastery or temple; it would be a gift to which he, the patron, was happy to attach his own name. The gift would bring him *punya* (merit) for the future and, in this world, *mariyatai* (Tamil, "temple honors") that would enhance his status. Both artist and patron appear to have rejoiced equally in the creation of a beautiful image. So also did the authorities of the temple or monastery that was the recipient of the gift, whether the image was to be inserted onto the structure or to join its array of portable icons. If it was intended for the sanctum, its perfection was even more vital to the religious authorities entrusted with performing the initial ritual invitation (*arohanam*) invoking the deity to enter and animate the image during *puja*. All these issues, whether of creation or reception, are instances of what I have chosen to term "the body revealed."

When we consider the devotees themselves, we find that their experience of the beauty of sculpted or painted imagery varies radically, depending on whether the image is fixed on the walls of a monument or contained in the pages of a manuscript, on the one hand, or is a sanctum image or a portable festival bronze, on the other. An image created to adorn the walls of a temple or the pages of an illustrated text may be scrutinized in the entirety of its beauty by all who view it. The physical beauty of Durga in the deity-niches on the temple exterior was admired by every devotee at the Ambika-mata temple at Jagat; they viewed her lithe, sensuous form, admired her confident stance, and lauded her valor in dispatching the brutish buffalo-demon. The artist captured magnificently the essence of Durga's wondrous feat so as to astound viewers and to cause them to smile on encountering the adjacent figure of a woman confidently tossing her head as she walks away. Devotees at the Darasuram temple would similarly have marveled at the stone tableau of Shiva as the Enchanting Mendicant. They would have empathized with the lovely women who came to give him alms, only to fall hopelessly in love with his radiant form, and would have delighted in his engaging *gana* attendants. In like fashion, visitors to the Queen's Stepwell in Patan would have stood in admiration before the evocative forms of the avatars of Vishnu, admired the slender flanking women, and marveled at Vishnu's graceful, reclining body carved along the center of the curved well-shaft walls. All these images were out in the open, instances of "the body revealed," and none was intended to be the recipient of the *alankara* of *puja*.[4]

But what of the devotees' experience in the case of the sanctum image or the portable bronze festival images of the deities? The ritual of *puja* involves bathing and anointing the image with a range of liquids, including ghee and milk, and fragrant powders and pastes, such as turmeric and aromatic sandalwood. With the final pouring of holy water, which concludes the rite of *abhisheka* (ritual bathing), the image is elaborately draped in sumptuous silk clothing and adorned with a rich array of gold ornaments that often are studded with rubies, coral, pearls, diamonds, or crystal. Then follows the floral adornment, which is often so abundant and so heavy that it overwhelms, even buries, the image beneath.[5] The prerogative of giving adornment to the sanctum image, or to a festival bronze, often belongs to a temple patron whose sustained donations to the temple have earned him that right as part of *mariyatai*. Temples further make use of *kavachas* (metal coverings for various parts of the body of the image), often made of gold; *kavachas* frequently cover the hands, the feet, and occasionally even the face of the divine image. There is nothing seen of the stone or bronze beneath, but this in no way disturbs the devotee. The temple-goers' reaction to this divine vision is ecstatic; they pat their cheeks with both hands and, in Tamil Nadu, call out the phrase "*Alagu-shottardu!*" (Beauty drips!). To them, this adorned image is the ultimate in beauty.

Inscriptions confirm that such *alankara*, resulting in "the body concealed," is not a modern innovation. Two instances will suffice to make this point. The first comes from the small Chola temple of Koneri-raja-puram, where an inscription dated to the year 976 confirms that the rituals accompanying Tamil festivals have remained much the same over the past thousand years. In laying out details of payments made to an entire range of temple employees, it speaks of the priests who ritually bathed the metal images in milk, curds, ghee, honey, and sugar; carriers of holy water from the Kaveri River for their further bathing; those who prepared sandal-paste for anointing the bronzes; the weaver who supplied cloth for draping them; the dyer of such cloth; and those who held a canopy above the images when they were carried in procession.[6] The second example is from the Tanjavur temple of Rajaraja, where an entire series of inscriptions, dating from 1004 to 1010, provide details of temple jewels given to both the sanctum image and the more than sixty portable bronzes that served the temple's festival needs. We have seen earlier that an image of Uma as consort of the dancing Shiva was given thirty-three gold ornaments, an image of Shiva as Tri-pura-vijaya (Victor of the Three Forts) received twenty-three sets of jewels, while Uma as consort of Tri-pura-vijaya was given seventeen ornaments. That the bronzes are fully adorned in the metal itself, with elaborate clothing and ornament, was clearly irrelevant to the devotees who made further lavish gifts of actual portable jewelry to these images. The priests who handle the images for *puja* are well aware that these glorious images are both clothed and adorned in the bronze itself, but this is irrelevant as far as they are concerned, since ritual temple tradition dating over centuries calls for additional, external *alankara*.[7]

It must be emphasized that the portable bronze icon has a second life of its own, during the extended period of time between festivals when these images rest largely un-noticed, until it is time to reemerge into the spotlight. When these *utsava-vigrahas* are not in active worship, they reside in varying degrees of dress and disarray in the hall enclosing the sanctum, where they may be viewed by any interested party, the art historian included. In temples that today lack the necessary resources, such as the ancient shrine of Kilai-palavur near Tiruchirapalli, an array of bronzes of the Chola period languish for the better part of the year with the remnants of the adornment they acquired

Figure 71. Portable Chola bronzes, between festivals, in the hall enclosing the sanctum, Kilai-palavur temple, Tamil Nadu.

during the annual *brahmotsava* festival (figure 71).[8] At Koneri-raja-puram, the famous bronzes dated by inscription to the year 976, as well as images of later date, may be seen in varying stages of drapery or lack thereof, frequently with dried sandal-paste and faded flower garlands. Any devotee walking past these images may stop and gaze at their bodies, which one might term "partly revealed and partly concealed."

Alternatively, in temples that have more sustained funding, each major festival is followed by a ritual purification of the bronzes, which, having left the temple grounds to be paraded through the town, are perceived as having acquired polluting influences. Before returning the images to their home in the hall enclosing the sanctum, temple priests perform the ceremonial of purification in an outer pavilion within the temple grounds. To restore the metal's coppery sheen, they first scrub the images with tamarind or the olive of the palm tree (*boondi-kottai*), both soaked in water, and follow this up by a rubdown with sacred ash. In these preliminary stages, the bronze is viewed as still in a state of pollution, and priests handle the images as mere hunks of metal, scrubbing the breasts of the goddess, for instance, as if each was a mere *lota* jug (figure 72). When the bronzes are lustrated with holy water, they return to their status as pure and perfected forms that the deity will be called on to enter and inhabit. Both these examples of bronze images beyond the ritual worship circuit may be viewed as instances of the body revealed, although this may be disputed depending on one's perspective. It is revealed, surely, for those who have eyes that wish to see! However, the devout generally walk past them, ignoring them in this unadorned state as being unenlivened and therefore not holy or worship-worthy.

Figure 72. Priest performing a ritual purification, Tiruvenkadu temple, Tamil Nadu.

A direct and explicit instance of bodily beauty revealed is the vision of the divine body presented in the hymns of the saints and the *acharyas* who composed verses in adoration of temple images. Extracts from the twelfth-century *acharya* Vedanta Desika, quoted in chapter 4, convey an ecstatic vision of the body of the image of Vishnu at the Shrirangam temple.[9] Desika's elated contemplation of the temple icon of Vishnu that enthralls and mesmerizes him serves to remind us that the temple devotees' experience of today is perhaps not the sole "authorized" experience of the beauty of images. Many temple devotees will have heard the songs of the saints and *acharyas* and have arrived at a recognition and awareness of the devotion evoked by the bodily beauty of the image of the deity. If they have been sufficiently immersed in these hymns, they might also have become aware of the bodily beauty of the godhead as an unfailing complement of spiritual beauty. Perhaps it is this unapparent inner vision of beauty that is partly responsible for their speaking of "dripping beauty" on viewing the *puja*-adorned image.

I shall conclude with the final instance of the body revealed when a stone image or a Chola bronze is displayed in a museum. One of the clever artifices of the twentieth century is the transformation of objects, never intended to be viewed as "art," into museum-worthy objects. The museum-goer has the opportunity to view at leisure and up close objects that in their original environment would have been glimpsed but fleet-

205

ingly. In Donald Preziosi's sardonic, although totally appropriate, words: "The domain of museology and museography—*art*—is itself one of the most brilliant of European modernist inventions; a notion which has for the past two centuries retroactively re-written the history of the world's peoples."[10] His comment applies as much to medieval European altarpieces and crucifixes as to pre-Columbian pots, Asian Buddha images, or Chola bronzes. This transformation, however, is a fait accompli and is never likely to be reversed. And I, personally, make no apologies for placing these beautiful images on pedestals in quiet spaces, with well-manipulated spot lighting to enhance the sense of wonder and awe at their physical beauty and their innate power.[11]

We encounter, then, a series of settings—all contextually valid, with the possible exception of the modern museum—in which the body stands both revealed and concealed. Festival bronzes, whether of the Chola period or contemporary, are modeled by skilled artists as sensuous, elegant figures. Yet the average temple devotee, whether of a thousand years ago or of today, never views the sensuous body of the images, seeing them instead when totally covered with adornment. By contrast, the priests who have charge of the deities, whether of stone or bronze, view the physical beauty of the body of god on a regular basis, both when performing ritual *puja* and during the intermittent "purification" rites. And, finally, there is the poetic vision of saints and *acharyas* who celebrated the bodily beauty of god, as also the vision of court poets and composers of inscriptional *prashastis* whose subject matter expanded to include the world of royalty and the elite. Their vision of bodily splendor and their detailed exposition of corporeality is seemingly analogous to the museum visitors' experience of the body beautiful—but with the one additional quality that the poetic effusions invariably carry an underlying current of the spiritual significance of beauty in its perfection. While the museum experience is a relatively new phenomenon, the twin facets of what I have termed "the body revealed" and "the body concealed" seem to have been an underlying and deep-rooted part of the original, premodern experience.

Two points may be reiterated in conclusion. The first is the near-identity of visualizations of the body adorned across space, time, and religious faiths, in both the sculptural and poetic corpus. Readers of this book might have been struck by the absence of a rupture in aesthetic sensibilities and priorities over a span of two thousand years. The sensuous, idealized human body remained the leitmotif of art, all the way from Buddhist Bharhut of the second and first centuries B.C.E. right into the nineteenth century C.E., without any sign of a fissure that Islam might have created. While Islam introduced new priorities, it did not provoke a sea change in indigenous artistic sensibilities. Since this book has shown that the artistic and the literary were both created and received in a similar cosmopolitan, elite, urban milieu, it should not surprise the reader to find a comparable continuity in the visualization of the body from early Sanskrit literature to later writings in vernacular languages. It corresponds to the easy linguistic continuities, without ruptures or militancy, that Sheldon Pollock has demonstrated so effectively for the transition from an almost exclusive use of the Sanskrit language to a preference for a range of vernaculars.[12] These vernacular literary expressions were also largely uninterrupted into the nineteenth century.

Returning briefly to the visual material, we may note that with the British endorsement of Raja Ravi Varma's late-nineteenth-century canvases, most of which feature sensuous male and female figures, both mythological and religious, the body continued to be the leitmotif. And the newly emerging nation enthusiastically adopted Ravi Varma's oleographic models for its modern-day, popular "religious pictures" of sensuous gods and goddesses. The resilient and enduring power of the body beautiful, with its spiritual overtones in temple worship, resonates even in the modern art of India, which features the human form to a greater extent than the modern art of many other traditions. It serves to put into context the illogicality and absurdity of current protests over M. F. Husain's portrayal of Hindu goddesses.[13]

The second point relates to the twin facets of the creation and reception of Indian art in general, and of sacred imagery in particular. I would be the first to admit that the urge to relate meanings prescribed in the creative process to those evoked in the reception of art creates a tension evident throughout this book. Working in stone, bronze, clay, wood, or paint, artists created images that exemplified the body adorned, regardless of whether these images would be applauded for beauty of line and form. The sacred image had to be the most beautiful and flawless image possible, down to the finest details of drapery and ornaments; it was equally and totally acceptable that such an image be further adorned with actual silks, flowers, and jewels. In other words, the widespread reception of its beauty as art—admiration for its elegant torso and limbs, and for its flowing sense of movement—was secondary; the primary concern, imperative and essential, was the perfection of bodily form of that same image. A parallel scenario is encountered with the creation and reception of visual narrative, and I will quote just one example that I have cited elsewhere.[14] The artists creating glazed terra-cotta plaques of the entire series of *jataka* stories of the previous lives of the Buddha lavished great care and attention on them, even though they were to be placed above roof level on the Ananda temple in Pagan (Myanmar), with no access stairs, and thus would never be viewed and admired. Yet the patrons of the plaques, the monks who served the temple, and the devotees who came to pay homage to the Buddha all knew that finely modeled images of the Buddha's previous lives adorned the roof levels of the temple. In like manner, devotees of a sacred image in India "knew" it to be a perfect and beautiful image that epitomized the body adorned; they were prepared to recognize it as such, even though they viewed it with its additional masking layer of auspicious *alankara*. By contrast, standing free and unencumbered on the outer walls of the same sacred monuments was its counterpart in bodily beauty, openly displayed for all to admire its perfection of line and form.

NOTES

1. The Body as Leitmotif

1. This phrase is used by the seventh-century child saint Sambandar in the very first of his over three hundred hymns. See Indira Peterson, *Poems to Siva: The Hymns of the Tamil Saints* (Princeton, N.J.: Princeton University Press, 1989), 271.

2. While the Buddhist stupa of Sanchi, discussed in chapter 3, carries numerous donative inscriptions from merchants, traders, monks, and nuns, I assume that its artistic message was directed toward a class of well-placed, if not wealthy, donors rather than workers and laborers.

3. Padma Kaimal highlights Chola temples donated by Chola citizenry rather than royalty; however, citizens able to donate entire stone temples were certainly among the elite of the kingdom and not the average resident.

4. Even today, the villagers of Manakkal, Tiruchirapalli district, pray to the local village goddess, Manakkal Nangai, rather than worship at the regular Shiva temple, which is visited largely by the *agraharam* residents—that is, the brahmins. Even fewer take the bus five miles to the adjoining village of Lalgudi, which boasts a major temple, the Saptarishishvara, dating back to the Chola period.

5. Ronald Inden, *Imagining India* (Cambridge, Mass.: Blackwell, 1990), especially chap. 5, "Reconstructions." For new temples and shifting capitals of successive Chola monarchs, see Vidya Dehejia, *Art of the Imperial Cholas* (New York: Columbia University Press, 1990).

6. For a *prashasti* that switches from Sanskrit to the vernacular to provide the exact boundaries of a gifted village and some adjoining land, see Sheldon Pollock, *The Language of the Gods in the World of Men* (Berkeley: University of California Press, 2006), 121. Pollock's volume, in focusing on the development of Sanskrit and the vernaculars, in many ways sets the scene for my analysis.

7. Sheldon Pollock, "The Cosmopolitan Vernacular," *Journal of Asian Studies* 57, no. 1 (1998): 14.

8. Daud Ali, *Courtly Culture and Political Life in Early Medieval India* (New York: Cambridge University Press, 2004), 79–80. See also Inden, *Imagining India*, 232. Ali's volume, a study of great consequence, makes several important arguments that immensely facilitate the presentation of my own arguments.

9. Richard Salomon, *Indian Epigraphy: A Guide to the Study of Inscriptions in Sanskrit, Prakrit, and the Other Indo-Aryan Languages* (Delhi: Munshiram Manoharlal, 1998), 4–5.

10. N. Karashima, "South Indian Temple Inscriptions: A New Approach to Their Study," *South Asia*, n.s., 19 (1996): 2.

11. Pollock, *Language of the Gods in the World of Men*, 330.

12. Kathleen D. Morrison and Mark T. Lycett, "Inscriptions as Artifacts: Precolonial South India and the Analysis of Texts," *Journal of Archaeological Method and Theory* 4, nos. 3–4 (1997): 215–37.

13. Allison Busch points out that Keshavdas's work on poetics, titled *Kavi-priya*, lists a number of such conventions (*niyamas*) in its fourth chapter, on the subject of the poet's system (*kavi-vyavastha*), in "The Courtly Vernacular: The Transformation of Braj Literary Culture (1590–1690)" (Ph.D. diss., University of Chicago, 2003), 126.

14. A. V. Narasimha Murthy, "A Study of the Label Inscriptions of the Hoysala Sculptors," in *Indian Epigraphy: Its Bearing on the History of Art*, ed. Frederick Asher and M. S. Gai (New Delhi: Oxford University Press and IBH, 1985), 215–20. Some years back, I visited all the Hoysala temples on which Malitamma's signature is known to exist in order to trace the progressive maturity of an artist's work, and to compare the images created by a master artist with those carved by others. The result was a disappointment in the sense that no distinctions were visible. It seems appropriate to use the masses of photographic documentation that I made and write a short paper on the "negative" results of the project, which, quite clearly, has significance in its own way.

15. Lee Siegel, *Fires of Love, Waters of Peace: Passion and Renunciation in Indian Culture* (Honolulu: University of Hawai'i Press, 1983), 3.

16. F. Kielhorn, "Ratnapur Inscription of Prithvideva of the (Vikrama) Year 1247," *Epigraphia Indica* 1 (1892): 51.

17. M. B. Garde, "Mandasor Inscription of Malava Samvat 524," *Epigraphia Indica* 27 (1947–1948): 17. The word "full" (*kshayi*), meaning "may never be exhausted," carries a double meaning here, referring, as it does, to one who indulges in too much sexual pleasure.

18. Ibid., 17–18.

19. D. B. Diskalkar, "The Mandasore Stone Inscription of Kumaragupta and Bandhuvarman," in *Selections from Sanskrit Inscriptions, 2nd cent. to 8th cent. A.D.* (New Delhi: Classical Publishers, 1977), 68.

20. S. R. Phogat, *Inscriptions of Haryana* (Haryana: Vishal, 1978), 47.

21. Richard J. Cohen, "The *Pasanahacariu* of Sridhara: The First Four *Sandhis* of the Apabhramsa Text" (Ph.D. diss., University of Pennsylvania, 1979), 262.

22. Ibid., 239–40.

23. Indira Peterson, *Design and Rhetoric in a Sanskrit*

Court Epic: The Kiratarjuniya of Bharavi (Albany: State University of New York Press, 2003), 111, 19.

24. Ashvaghosa, *The Buddhacarita, or Acts of the Buddha*, trans. E. H. Johnston (Calcutta: Baptist Mission Press, for University of the Panjab, 1936; repr., Delhi: Motilal Banarsidass, 1984), 70.

25. Pollock, *Language of the Gods in the World of Men*, 134.

26. Ibid.

27. Ali cites the instance of the poet Ravikirti, author of Pulakesin II's Aihole inscription, who claimed to have acquired the fame of Kalidasa and Bharavi, in *Courtly Culture and Political Life in Early Medieval India*, 83.

28. See chap. 4, p. 150.

29. F. Kielhorn, "Deopara Stone Inscription of Vijayasena," *Epigraphia Indica* 1 (1892): 315.

30. See chap. 4, p. 149.

31. V. V. Mirashi, "Ratanpur Stone Inscription of the [Kalachuri] Year 915," *Epigraphia Indica* 26 (1941–1942): 267.

32. Pushpa Prasad, *Sanskrit Inscriptions of the Delhi Sultanate, 1191–1526* (Delhi: Oxford University Press, 1990), 75.

33. And, of course, noninscriptional *prashastis* also exist.

34. Pollock, *Language of the Gods in the World of Men*, 134–35.

35. I am grateful to Indira Peterson for pointing out the literary source of this verse.

36. Salomon provides examples of the occasional single verse, Kalidasa's *mangala-shloka* of his *Shakuntala*, *Raghu-vamsha*, and *Vikramorashiya* being quoted in single inscriptions, in *Indian Epigraphy*, 234. He also points to imitations or adaptations of other famous verses.

37. Daniel H. H. Ingalls, "Words for Beauty in Classical Sanskrit Poetry," in *Indological Studies in Honor of W. Norman Brown*, ed. Ernest Bender (New Haven, Conn.: American Oriental Society, 1962), 63.

38. Pollock, *Language of the Gods in the World of Men*, 338–56.

39. In my sample study of this feature in the inscriptions from *Epigraphia Indica*, vols. 1–30, I found forty-two inscriptions that used this formula.

40. *Jayatya vishkritam vishnor varaham kshobitarnavam / Dakshninnata-damshtragra-vishranta-bhuvanam vapuh* (Victorious is the body of Vishnu, manifested in the form of a boar on whose uplifted right tusk rests the world, and who has agitated the ocean). This verse appears on its own from the year 660 into the thirteenth century, largely in the inscriptions of the Chalukyas, Kalyanis, and Rashtrakutas. A series of other repetitive *mangala* verses that exist among the inscriptions of specific dynasties need further study.

41. Bernard Faure, *The Power of Denial: Buddhism, Purity, and Gender* (Princeton, N.J.: Princeton University Press, 2003), 18.

42. Julia Kristeva, *About Chinese Women*, quoted in ibid., 19.

43. Nanette Salomon, "Making a World of Difference: Gender, Asymmetry, and the Greek Nude," in *Naked Truths: Women, Sexuality, and Gender in Classical Art and Archaeology*, ed. Ann Olga Kolowski-Ostrow and Claire L. Lyons (New York: Routledge, 1997), 199.

44. Faure, *Power of Denial*, 12.

45. Richard Davis, *Lives of Indian Images* (Princeton, N.J.: Princeton University Press, 1997), especially chap. 1, "Living Images."

46. John Falconer, "A Passion for Documentation: Architecture and Ethnography," in *India Through the Lens: Photography, 1840–1911*, ed. Vidya Dehejia (Washington, D.C.: Freer Gallery of Art and Arthur M. Sackler Gallery, Smithsonian Institution, 2000), 72. Biggs's reference was specifically to sculptures in the Badami region of the Deccan Plateau.

47. See the various essays in Neil Roughley, ed., *Being Humans: Anthropological Universality and Particularity in Transdisciplinary Perspectives* (New York: Walter de Gruyter, 2000), especially Wilfrede van Damne, "Universality and Cultural Particularity in Visual Aesthetics," 258–84.

48. Irene J. Winter, "Sex, Rhetoric, and the Public Monument: The Alluring Body of Naram-Sin of Agade," in *Sexuality in Ancient Art*, ed. Natalie Boymen Kampen (Cambridge: Cambridge University Press, 1996), 11–26.

49. Ingalls, "Words for Beauty in Classical Sanskrit Poetry."

50. Ali, *Courtly Culture and Political Life in Early Medieval India*, 147.

51. C. Sivaramamurti, *Chitrasutra of the Vishnudharmottara* (New Delhi: Kanak, 1978), 195.

52. John B. Carman, "Conclusion: Axes of Sacred Value in Hindu Society," in *Purity and Auspiciousness in Indian Society*, ed. John B. Carman and Frédérique A. Marglin (Leiden: Brill, 1985), 109–20.

53. John B. Carman and Frédérique A. Marglin, eds., *Purity and Auspiciousness in Indian Society* (Leiden: Brill, 1985).

54. Gloria Goodwin Raheja, *The Poison in the Gift: Ritual, Prestation, and the Dominant Caste in a North Indian Village* (Chicago: University of Chicago Press, 1988).

55. T. N. Madan, "Concerning the Categories *Subha* and *Suddha* in Hindu Culture: An Exploratory Essay," in *Purity and Auspiciousness in Indian Society*, ed. John B. Carman and Frédérique A. Marglin (Leiden: Brill, 1985), 11–29.

56. Ibid., 25.

57. Frédérique A. Marglin, *Wives of the God-King: The Rituals of the Devadasis of Puri* (Delhi: Oxford University Press, 1985), 81.

58. Ronald Inden, "Kings and Omens," in *Purity and Auspiciousness in Indian Society*, ed. John B. Carman and Frédérique A. Marglin (Leiden: Brill, 1985), 30.

59. Martha Ann Selby, *Grow Long, Blessed Night: Love Poems from Classical India* (New York: Oxford University Press, 2000).

60. *Shakuntala* is a major exception of a play, in a forest setting, that contradicts this idea of interior spaces.

61. Selby, *Grow Long, Blessed Night*, 107.

62. *A Bouquet of Rasa (The Rasamanjari of Bhanudatta)*, trans. Sheldon Pollock, Clay Sanskrit Library (New York: New York University Press and JJC Foundation, 2009).

63. A. K. Ramanujan, trans., *The Interior Landscape: Love Poems from a Classical Tamil Anthology* (Bloomington: Indiana University Press, 1967).

64. Selby, *Grow Long, Blessed Night*, 36.

65. Ibid., 35.

66. Mircea Eliade, *The Sacred and the Profane: The Nature of Religion* (New York: Harcourt, Brace, 1959), 14.

67. Ibid., 10 (italics in the original).

68. Ibid., 22.

69. Stella Kramrisch, *The Art of India* (New York: Phaidon, 1954), 10.

70. Alka Patel, *Building Communities in Gujarat: Architecture and Society During the Twelfth Through Fourteenth Centuries* (Leiden: Brill, 2004).

71. I am grateful to Sheldon Pollock for his insights on this issue.

72. Jitendra Mohanty, presentation on the Navya-Nyaya school of Indian logic, given at Columbia University, December 2006.

73. A large number of picture books capitalizing on the sensational character of the erotic sculptures exist. For a serious scholarly treatment of the erotic art of India, see Devangana Desai, *Erotic Sculpture of India: A Socio-cultural Study* (New Delhi: Tata McGraw-Hill, 1975), and *Religious Imagery of Khajuraho* (Mumbai: Franco-Indian Research, 1996).

74. Wendy Doniger O'Flaherty, trans., *The Rig Veda: An Anthology: One Hundred and Eight Hymns* (Harmondsworth: Penguin, 1981), 29–32. This hymn, a late addition to the *Rig-veda*, speaks also of the four *varnas* (castes) and tells us that the Brahmins emerged from Purusha's mouth, *kshatriyas* from his arms, *vaishyas* from his thighs, and *shudras* from his feet.

75. Kramrisch, *Art of India*, 9.

76. Patrick Olivelle, *The Asrama System: The History and Hermeneutics of a Religious Institution* (New York: Oxford University Press, 1993), 27, 30, and in various other places.

77. Ibid., 132. For Kalidasa and inscriptions, see also 203–5.

78. For a fine discussion of the four goals of man, accompanied by quotations from ancient texts, see V. Raghavan and R. N. Dandekar, "Part III: The Hindu Way of Life," in *Sources of Indian Tradition*, vol. 1, *From the Beginning to 1800*, 2nd ed., ed. Ainslie T. Embree (New York: Columbia University Press, 1998), 201–341.

79. *Nayanar* is the singular; *nayanmar* is the plural.

80. Sambandar 3:24.1, *mannil nalla vannam varalam*, in *Tevaram: Hymnes Sivaites du pays Tamoul*, ed. T. V. Gopal Iyer and François Gros (Pondicherry: Institut Français d'Indologie, 1985), 1:303.

81. The contrary view of the body as necessarily decaying and putrefying, while contained in religious texts, only rarely enters the purview of the visual arts. Occasionally, although not often, the poetic corpus,

too, introduces us to this idea. One example is the fourth-century poet Bhartrihari, who wrote a hundred verses titled "Passion" and another hundred titled "Disenchantment." One such verse reads:

> Her breasts, really protuberances of flesh
> Measured against golden jars.
> Her face, just a receptacle of phlegm
> Weighed against the moon.
> Her thigh, wet with flowing urine,
> Rivals the cheek of a majestic elephant.
> But look, her despicable body
> Is made highly prized by distinguished poets.

See Greg Bailey and Richard Gombrich, ed. and trans., *Love Lyrics by Amaru and Bhartrhari, and by Bilhana*, Clay Sanskrit Library (New York: New York University Press and JJC Foundation, 2005), 149.

82. Michael V. Fox, *The Song of Songs and the Ancient Egyptian Love Songs* (Madison: University of Wisconsin Press, 1985), 236.

83. Diana Eck, *Darsan* (Chambersburg, Pa.: Anima Books, 1981).

84. C. J. Fuller, *The Camphor Flame: Popular Hinduism and Society in India* (Princeton, N.J.: Princeton University Press, 1992), especially chap. 3, "Worship."

85. John E. Cort, *Jains in the World: Religious Values and Ideology in India* (New York: Oxford University Press, 2001).

86. See, for instance, Finbarr Barry Flood, "Refiguring Iconoclasm in the Early Indian Mosque," in *Negating the Image: Case Studies in Iconoclasm*, ed. Anne McClanan and Jeff Johnson (Burlington, Vt.: Ashgate, 2005), 15–40, and Patel, *Building Communities in Gujarat*. Patel points out that early "Islamic" architecture in Gujarat is, in fact, an adaptation of the "Hindu" Maru-Gujara style of the region—which, after all, is natural given that the builders were local. She also points to a fifteenth-century architectural text, the *Vrksarnava*, that incorporates the mosque into its architectural categories under the title *rahamana-prasada*, a word that is both "Muslim" (*rahman* [Arabic, "merciful"]) and "Hindu" (*prasada* [Sanskrit, "mansion"]) (10–11).

2. The Idealized Body and Ornament

1. Julian Raby, foreword to *The Sensuous and the Sacred: Chola Bronzes from South India*, by Vidya Dehejia (New York: American Federation of the Arts, 2002), 7.

2. On Kenneth Clark's definition of "the naked" as inferior and "the nude" as superior, and John Berger's seeming inversion of those categories, with "the naked" human as being oneself (that is, natural) and "the nude" as subject to artistic conventions, see Lynda Nead, *The Female Nude: Art, Obscenity, and Sexuality* (New York:

Routledge, 199), 2. There is an element of truth in both distinctions.

3.   Daud Ali, *Courtly Culture and Political Life in Early Medieval India* (New York: Cambridge University Press, 2004), 167. In this work of great significance for an understanding of premodern India's courtly life and values, Ali points out that beauty and refinement include physiology and dress, but also bearing, speech, and the person's environment (143).

4.   A. K. Coomaraswamy, "Ornament," *Art Bulletin* 21 (1939): 375–82, in *Coomaraswamy*, vol. 1, *Selected Papers: Traditional Art and Symbolism*, ed. Roger Lipsey (Princeton, N.J.: Princeton University Press, 1977). Page numbers in the notes refer to this edition.

5.   Ibid., 250.

6.   Jan Gonda, "The Meaning of the Word *Alamkara*," in *Selected Studies*, vol. 2, *Sanskrit Word Studies* (Leiden: Brill, 1975), 257–74. An alternative word for ornamentation, *bhushana*, derives directly from the verb *bhush* (to adorn, to deck, to decorate).

7.   Jan Gonda, "Abharana," in *Selected Studies*, vol. 2, *Sanskrit Word Studies* (Leiden: Brill, 1975), 171–77; Ali, *Courtly Culture and Political Life in Early Medieval India*, 163.

8.   Coomaraswamy, "Ornament," 249.

9.   Kalidasa, *The Recognition of Shakuntala*, trans. Vasudeva Somadeva, Clay Sanskrit Library (New York: New York University Press and JJC Foundation, 2006), 188.

10.   Nanette Salomon, "Making a World of Difference: Gender, Asymmetry, and the Greek Nude," in *Naked Truths: Women, Sexuality, and Gender in Classical Art and Archaeology*, ed. Ann Olga Kolowski-Ostrow and Claire L. Lyons (New York: Routledge, 1997), 197–219.

11.   D. B. Spooner, "The Didarganj Image Now in the Patna Museum," *Journal of the Bihar and Orissa Research Society* 5 (1919): 102–13.

12.   For the elevated position assigned to the *ganika*, see Doris Srinivasan, "Royalty's Courtesans and God's Mortal Wives: Keepers of Culture in Pre-Colonial India," in *The Courtesan's Arts*, ed. Martha Feldman and Bonnie Gordon (Oxford: Oxford University Press, 2006), 161–81. Srinivasan has quite independently come to the same conclusion on the Didarganj figure, in "The Mauryan *Ganika* from Didarganj (Pataliputra)," *East and West* 55 (2005): 345–62.

13.   R. P. Kangle, *The Kautilya Arthasastra* (Bombay: University of Bombay, 1969), bk. 2, chap. 27, "The Superintendent of Courtesans," 81–82 (Sanskrit text), 158–62 (English translation).

14.   Frederick Asher and Walter Spink, "Maurya Figural Sculpture Reconsidered," *Ars Orientalis* 19 (1989): 1–25.

15.   Deven Patel, unpublished translation. See also *Naisadhacarita of Sriharsa*, trans. K. K. Handiqui (Poona: Deccan College, 1965), 90–104.

16.   David Smith, *Ratnakara's Haravijaya: An Introduction to the Sanskrit Court Epic* (Delhi: Oxford University Press, 1985), 179–224.

17.   Indira Peterson, *Kuttralak Kuravanji (The Fortune-teller Play of Kuttralam)* (forthcoming).

18.   V. Ganapati Sthapati, *Indian Sculpture and Iconography: Forms and Measurements* (Pondicherry: Sri Aurobindo Society, 2002), 290.

19.   Of relevance in this context are the results of anthropological field studies of women's waist-to-hip ratio conducted in the United States. Such studies confirm that the hourglass figure was, in fact, the one most admired until very recent times, denoting as it did health and ease in childbearing, both considered to be highly desirable attributes in a woman. The currently admired, more athletic figure continues to be related to health and childbearing, reflecting changing models, shifting health standards, and new norms for ideal and desirable physiques. See Devendra Singh, "Adaptive Significance of Female Physical Attractiveness: Role of Waist-to-Hip Ratio," *Journal of Personality and Social Psychology* 65, no. 2 (1993): 293–307.

20.   Daniel H. H. Ingalls, trans., *Sanskrit Poetry from Vidyakara's Treasury* (Cambridge, Mass.: Harvard University Press, 1965), 135.

21.   Ibid., 140.

22.   I am grateful to Allison Busch for pointing me in the direction of Keshavdas's *Kavi-priya*.

23.   Mark Elvin, quoted in John Hay, "The Body Invisible in Chinese Art?" in *Body, Subject, and Power in China*, ed. Angela Zito and Tani E. Barlow (Chicago: University of Chicago Press, 1994), 46.

24.   Blake Wentworth, "Women's Bodies, Earthly Kingdom: Mapping the Presence of God in the *Tirukayilaya Nana Ula*" (manuscript, Divinity School, University of Chicago, 2003). I am grateful to Wentworth for his generosity in permitting my use of this material, which is yet to be presented in his doctoral dissertation.

25.   Peterson, *Kuttralak Kuravanji*.

26.   Ali, *Courtly Culture and Political Life in Early Medieval India*, 148–62.

27.   Robert A. Hueckstedt, *The Style of Bana: An Introduction to Sanskrit Prose* (Lanham, Md.: University Press of America, 1985), 111.

28.   Peterson, *Kuttralak Kuravanji*.

29.   Edwin Gerow, trans., *Malavika and Agnimitra*, in *Theater of Memory: The Plays of Kalidasa*, ed. Barbara Stoler Miller (New York: Columbia University Press, 1984), 270.

30.   Vidya Dehejia, *Slaves of the Lord: The Path of the Tamil Saints* (Delhi: Munshiram Manoharlal, 1988), 44.

31.   A good example is provided by comparing figs. 206 and 207 with figs. 254 and 255 in J. C. Harle, *The Art and Architecture of the Indian Subcontinent* (Harmondsworth: Penguin, 1986), 19.

32.   Sthapati, *Indian Sculpture and Iconography*, chap. 24, "Talamanam—Rhythmic Measure."

33.   John E. Mosteller, *The Measure of Form: A New Approach for the Study of Indian Sculpture* (New Delhi: Abhinav, 1991).

34. Vidya Dehejia and Daryl Harnisch, "Yoga as a Key to Understanding Indian Art," in *Representing the Body: Gender Issues in Indian Art*, ed. Vidya Dehejia (New Delhi: Kali for Women, 1997).

35. Anne Hollander, *Seeing Through Clothes* (New York: Viking Penguin, 1975), 88.

36. Natalie Kampen, "Epilogue: Gender and Desire," in *Naked Truths: Women, Sexuality, and Gender in Classical Art and Archaeology*, ed. Ann Olga Kolowski-Ostrow and Claire L. Lyons (New York: Routledge, 1997), 267.

37. Andrew Stewart, *Art, Desire, and the Body in Ancient Greece* (Cambridge: Cambridge University Press, 1997), 12. Stewart proceeds to inform us that the ancient Greeks were, in actuality, thickset and sturdy, with relatively short lower limbs, judging from the osteoarchaeological material, which in no way coincides with the idealized representation of the human body in Greek sculpture, or indeed with the idealized form of the literary sources.

38. Ashvaghosa, *The Buddhacarita, or Acts of the Buddha*, trans. E. H. Johnston (Calcutta: Baptist Mission Press, for University of the Panjab, 1936; repr., Delhi: Motilal Banarsidass, 1984), 47.

39. Ibid., 49.

40. Barbara Stoler Miller, trans., *Sakuntala and the Ring of Recognition*, in *Theater of Memory: The Plays of Kalidasa*, ed. Barbara Stoler Miller (New York: Columbia University Press, 1984), 94.

41. Kalidasa, *Malavika and Agnimitra*, trans. Gerow, 304.

42. *The Origin of the Young God: Kalidasa's Kumarasambhava*, trans. Hank Heifetz (Berkeley: University of California Press, 1985), 53.

43. Gail Sutherland, *Disguises of the Demon* (Albany: State University of New York Press, 1991), 152.

44. Wentworth, "Women's Bodies, Earthly Kingdom," 59.

45. Ibid., 62.

46. Ibid., 64.

47. Ibid., 66.

48. *Love Song of the Dark Lord: Jayadeva's Gitagovinda*, trans. Barbara Stoler Miller (New York: Columbia University Press, 1977), 124.

49. Ali, *Courtly Culture and Political Life in Early Medieval India*, 166n.65.

50. Wentworth "Women's Bodies, Earthly Kingdom," 59.

51. Ibid., 60.

52. Ibid., 62.

53. Ibid., 63–64.

54. I am indebted to Allison Busch for this citation. She further points out that this verse is based on an earlier verse of the seventh-century poet Dandin.

55. This was a verse repeatedly used by the Silahara rulers and was clearly a popular poetic trope. For one example, see "The Thana Plates of Mummunirja. Saka 970 [1048 C.E.]," in V. V. Mirashi, *Inscriptions of the Silaharas*, Corpus Inscriptionum Indicarum 6 (New Delhi: Archaeological Survey of India, 1977), 93.

56. Smith, *Ratnakara's Haravijaya*, sarga 18, 212.

57. This manuscript is in the collection of the Rietberg Museum, Zurich.

58. Wentworth, "Women's Bodies, Earthly Kingdom," 65–66.

59. Ibid., 28, 36.

60. When Sonia Gandhi visited southern India in her earlier days as a young wife, with her shoulder-length hair arranged gracefully loose, traditional society maintained that someone should tell her that this was inauspicious. Her hair is always tied back these days.

61. Ali, *Courtly Culture and Political Life in Early Medieval India*, 162–63.

62. David Sanford, "Ramayana Portraits on the Nageshvara Temple at Kumbakonam," in *The Legend of Rama: Artistic Visions*, ed. Vidya Dehejia (Bombay: Marg, 1994), 43–60.

63. Some believe that an image in the Sarabhai collection is of Rajaraja.

64. Vidya Dehejia, "The Very Idea of a Portrait," *Ars Orientalis* 28 (1998): 41–50.

65. *Thirteen Plays of Bhasa*, trans. A. C. Woolner and Lakshman Sarup (London: Published for the University of the Panjab, 1930; repr., Delhi: Motilal Banarsidass, 1985), 172–76.

66. H. Krishna Sastri, "Anmakonda Inscription of Prola, Chalukya-Vikrama Year 42," *Epigraphia Indica* 9 (1907–1908): 266.

67. Sten Konow, "Sarnath Inscription of Kumaradevi," *Epigraphia Indica* 9 (1907–1908): 327.

68. The comparison is used even in modern times, as in M. F. Husain's film *Gaja-gamini* (*She with the Elephant's Gait*), starring his favorite model, Madhuri Dixit.

69. Lionel D. Barnett, "Inscription at Narendra," *Epigraphia Indica* 13 (1915–1916): 312.

70. For instance, Lady Olajale was *ratiyamnalu rupim* in old Kannada: Lionel D. Barnett, "Inscriptions of Huli," *Epigraphia Indica* 18 (1925–1926): 170–218; Mailama is "a *rati* in dalliance": H. Krishna Sastri, "Kuniyur Plates of the Time of Venkata II: Saka Samvat 1556," *Epigraphia Indica* 3 (1894–1895): 236–58.

71. Krishna Deva, *Temples of Khajuraho* (New Delhi: Archaeological Survey of India, 1990), 1:366.

72. Ali, *Courtly Culture and Political Life in Early Medieval India*, 147.

73. Carolyn Woodford Schmidt suggests that these gateway figures represent donors, in "Aristocratic Devotees in Early Buddhist Art from Greater Gandhara: Characteristics, Chronology, and Symbolism," *South Asian Studies* 21 (2005): 25–45.

74. Daud Ali, "Technologies of the Self: Courtly Artifice and Monastic Discipline in Early India," *Journal of the Economic and Social History of the Orient* 41 (1998): 168–69.

75. Bhavabhuti, *Rama's Last Act (The Uttararamacarita)*, trans. Sheldon Pollock, Clay Sanskrit Library (New York: New York University Press and JJC Foundation, 2007).

76. *Raghuvamsam of Kalidasa*, trans. K. N.

Anantapadmanabhan (Madras: Ramayana, 1973), 3.

77. Since Indian portraiture is not veristic, and since names of kings are repeated (more than one Mahendra, and Simhavishnu vs. Narasimhavarman), there has been considerable discussion of the identity of these figures. The current solution rests partly on the notion that the seated figure must be the senior monarch and the standing one his successor.

78. C. Minakshi, *The Historical Sculptures of the Vaikunthaperumal Temple, Kanchi*, Memoirs of the Archaeological Survey of India 63 (Delhi: Manager of Publications, 1941).

79. Ibid.; compare, for instance, pl. IX, 3 (Simhavishnu) with pl. XVI, 2 (Pallavamalla).

80. Frederick Asher, "Historical and Political Allegory in Gupta Art," in *Essays on Gupta Culture*, ed. Bardwell L. Smith (Columbia, Mo.: South Asia Books, 1983), 53–66.

81. Dehejia, *Sensuous and the Sacred*, app. 2, 241.

82. J. F. Fleet, "Chiplun Plates of Pulakesin II," *Epigraphia Indica* 3 (1894–1895): 52.

83. See chap. 4, p. 153.

84. Lionel D. Barnett, "Arthuna Inscription of Paramara Chamundaraja. VS 1136," *Epigraphia Indica* 14 (1917–1918): 305.

85. Ali, *Courtly Culture and Political Life in Early Medieval India*, 144.

86. *The Harsa-Carita of Bana*, trans. E. B. Cowell and F. W. Thomas (London: Royal Asiatic Society, 1897; repr., Delhi: Motilal Banarsidass, 1968), 59–61.

87. T. A. Gopinatha Rao, "Anbil Plates of Sundara Chola: The 4th Year," *Epigraphia Indica* 15 (1919–1920): 69.

88. T. A. Gopinatha Rao, "Kanyakumari Inscription of Vira-Rajendra-Deva," *Epigraphia Indica* 18 (1925–1926): 44.

89. Fleet, "Chiplun Plates of Pulakesin II," 52.

90. F. Kielhorn, "Udayendiram Plates of the Bana King Vikramaditya II," *Epigraphia Indica* 3 (1894–1895): 78.

91. D. R. Bhandarkar, "Two Grants of Indraraja III; Saka Samvat 836," *Epigraphia Indica* 9 (1907–1908): 39.

92. Ibid., 40.

93. R. G. Bhandarkar, "Karhad Plates of Krishna III; Saka-Samvat 880," *Epigraphia Indica* 4 (1896–1897): 289.

94. Barnett, "Inscriptions of Huli," 217.

95. Pushpa Prasad, *Sanskrit Inscriptions of the Delhi Sultanate, 1191–1526* (Delhi: Oxford University Press, 1990), 71.

96. Irene J. Winter, "Sex, Rhetoric, and the Public Monument: The Alluring Body of Naram-Sin of Agade," in *Sexuality in Ancient Art*, ed. Natalie Boymen Kampen (Cambridge: Cambridge University Press, 1996), 11–26, and "Defining 'Aesthetics' for Non-Western Studies: The Case of Ancient Mesopotamia," in *Art History, Aesthetics, and Visual Studies*, ed. Michael Ann Holly and Keith Moxey (Williamstown, Mass.: Clark Art Institute, 2002), 3–28.

97. Ronald Inden, *Imagining India* (Cambridge, Mass.: Blackwell, 1990), sec. "Ceremonial Baths and Luminous Wills," 233–39.

98. Ronald Inden, "Ritual, Authority, and Cyclic Time in Hindu Kingship," in *Kingship and Authority in South Asia*, ed. J. F. Richards (Delhi: Oxford University Press, 1988), 62.

99. Sheldon Pollock refers to it as "an ancient patriarchal trope" (*The Language of the Gods in the World of Men* [Berkeley: University of California Press, 2006], 419).

100. Ronald M. Davidson, *Indian Esoteric Buddhism: A Social History of the Tantric Movement* (New York: Columbia University Press, 2002), 68, 70.

101. In am grateful to Allison Busch for permitting me to use this unpublished material from Keshavdas's *Virsimhdevcarit*, made available to scholars as part of a *nakh-sikh* literary workshop held at Columbia University in the spring of 2006.

102. Bhandarkar, "Two Grants of Indraraja III," 38.

103. *Kalpasutra of Bhadrabahu Svami*, trans. K. C. Lalwani (Delhi: Motilal Banarsidass, 1979), 39–40.

104. Daud Ali, "The *Vikramacholanula*: A Chola Processional Poem," in *Art of the Chola Bronzes* (London: Royal Academy, 2006), app. A, 142–45.

105. David Dean Shulman, *The King and the Clown in South Indian Myth and Poetry* (Princeton, N.J.: Princeton University Press, 1985), 314. Anne Monius made this point in "Being a King the Chola Way: Contested Models of the Dharmic Ruler in Tamil Literary Culture" (paper presented at the Chonadu conference, Berkeley, California, April 22, 2006).

106. Shulman, *King and the Clown in South Indian Myth and Poetry*, 339.

107. Joanne Punzo Waghorne, *The Raja's Magic Clothes: Re-Visioning Kingship and Divinity in England's India* (University Park: Pennsylvania State University Press, 1994), 226.

108. Ibid., 225. The importance that Waghorne assigns to decoration is perhaps best exemplified by her final chapter, "Ornament as Ontology: A Conclusion."

109. See, for instance, the report in the *Telegraph*, Calcutta, India, January 20, 2003, available at http://www.telegraphindia.com.

110. Vidya Dehejia, "Aniconism and the Multivalence of Emblems," *Ars Orientalis* 21 (1992): 45–66. It is interesting to speculate on whether the early need to negate the body was, in fact, triggered by its already high profile in images of *yakshas, yakshis, nagarajas*, and the like. Could this have been an early attempt, later abandoned, at setting the Buddha apart from such semi-divine beings?

111. John H. Strong, *The Legend of King Asoka: A Study and Translation of the Asokavadana* (Princeton, N.J.: Princeton University Press, 1983), 27.

112. Ibid., 246.

113. Ibid., 249.

114. Ashvaghosa, *Buddhacarita, or Acts of the Buddha*, 115–16.

115. Valmiki, *Ramayana: Book Two, Ayodhya*, trans. Sheldon Pollock, Clay Sanskrit Library (New York: New York University Press and JJC Foundation, 2005), 302–43.

116. Indira Peterson, *Design and Rhetoric in a Sanskrit Court Epic: The Kiratarjuniya of Bharavi* (Albany: State University of New York Press, 2003), 59.

117. T. W. Rhys Davids and Caroline A. F. Rhys Davids, trans., *Dialogues of the Buddha*, 3 vols. (London: Oxford University Press, 1899–1921).

118. Kalidasa, *Sakuntala and the Ring of Recognition*, trans. Miller, 165.

119. Frederick Asher, personal communication.

120. Vishakha Desai, "Reflections on the History and Historiography of Male Sexuality in Early Indian Art," in *Representing the Body: Gender Issues in Indian Art*, ed. Vidya Dehejia (New Delhi: Kali for Women, 1997), 42–55.

121. T. W. Rhys Davids and J. Estlin Carpenter, eds., *The Digha-nikaya* (London: Pali Text Society, 1911), 3:143.

122. I am grateful to Gregory Schopen for his note on the levels of meaning of this complicated Pali phrase. Abbreviating his input, we have *kosohita* (confined in a sheath) and *vattha-guhyo* (concealed by clothes). So the compound could be read as "that which should be covered by clothes is enclosed in a sheath" or "that part of the abdomen that should be covered in a sheath." Either way, Schopen writes, it is "an odd way to refer to the penis."

123. Robert L. Brown, "The Feminization of the Sarnath Gupta-Period Buddha Images," *Bulletin of the Asia Institute* 16 (2002): 166–67.

124. Davidson proposes that later Buddhism was hard-pressed to win royal support when Shiva, "represented as a killer deity with a permanent erection," was an alternative (*Indian Esoteric Buddhism*, 90).

125. If the monk and nun patrons had not been satisfied, without rejecting the commission, they could easily have asked the sculptor to cut back the stone and smooth out the protrusion.

126. A. K. Coomaraswamy, "Origin of the Buddha Image," *Art Bulletin* 9 (1927): 300.

127. T. W. Rhys Davids, trans., *Buddhist Birth-Stories: The Commentarial Introduction Entitled Nidana Katha: The Story of the Lineage* (Boston: Houghton Mifflin, 1880; repr., Varanasi: Indological Book House, 1973), 185–86.

128. Brown, "Feminization of the Sarnath Gupta-Period Buddha Images," 165–79.

129. I am grateful to Daud Ali for directing my attention to this text, which so clearly states the linkage between beauty and morality. See Maurice Walshe, trans., *Thus Have I Heard: The Long Discourses of the Buddha* (London: Wisdom, 1995), 441–60.

130. Ibid., 442.

131. Ibid., 447.

132. Ibid., 453.

133. Ibid., 445, 448–50.

134. Gwendolyn Bays, trans., *The Lalitavistara Sutra: The Voice of the Buddha: The Beauty of Compassion* (Berkeley: Dharma, 1983), 182–83.

135. Steven Paul Hopkins, *Singing the Body of God: The Hymns of Vedantadesika in Their South Indian Tradition* (Oxford: Oxford University Press, 2002), 205.

136. Susan L. Huntington, *The Art of Ancient India: Buddhist, Hindu, Jain* (New York: Weatherhill, 1985), pl. 20.58

137. Jack Laughlin suggests that this image may actually have been collected from a site in the vicinity and then brought to Dilwara for safekeeping. This, however, does not affect the thrust of my argument regarding the sensuous presentation of the figures.

138. *Raghuvamsam of Kalidasa*, trans. Anantapadmanabhan, 34.

139. I am grateful to Jack C. Laughlin for his photograph of this piece, which he discusses in *Aradhakamurti/Adhisthayakamurti: Popular Piety, Politics, and the Medieval Jain Temple Portrait* (New York: Peter Lang, 2003), fig 1.

140. S. P. Tewari, "National Museum Inscription of Kelachchadevi, V.S. 1239," *Epigraphia Indica* 41 (1975–1976): 58–60.

141. Laughlin, *Aradhakamurti/Adhisthayakamurti*, 43.

142. Vishakha N. Desai, *Life at Court: Art for India's Rulers, 16th–19th Centuries* (Boston: Museum of Fine Arts, 1985), 93, pl. 74.

143. Lionel D. Barnett, "Inscriptions of Sudi," *Epigraphia Indica* 15 (1919–1920): 103.

144. F. Kielhorn, "Assam Plates of Vallabhadeva: Saka Samvat 1107," *Epigraphia Indica* 5 (1898–1899): 187.

145. Lionel D. Barnett, "Bhubaneswar Inscription in the Royal Asiatic Society," *Epigraphia Indica* 13 (1915–1916): 155.

146. G. Buhler, "The Dewal Prasasti of Lalla, the Chhidda," *Epigraphia Indica* 1 (1892): 75–85.

147. Krishna Sastri, "Kuniyur Plates of the Time of Venkata II," 253.

148. Such a sentiment is not restricted to premodern India. One might refer to the discomfort and disquiet caused some years back among the population of the United States (I do not refer here to the elite) by the revelation that all was not well between President Clinton and the First Lady!

149. Adam Hardy, *Indian Temple Architecture: Form and Transformation: The Karnata Dravida Tradition, 7th to 13th Centuries* (New Delhi: Indira Gandhi National Centre for Arts, 1995).

150. Heinrich Zimmer, *The Art of Indian Asia: Its Mythology and Transformations* (New York: Pantheon Books, 1955), 1:236.

151. Irene J. Winter, "Ornament and the Rhetoric of Abundance in Assyria," *Eretz-Israel: Archaeological, Historical and Geographical Studies* 27 (2003): 252–64.

152. R. S. Gupte and B. D. Mahajan, *Ajanta, Ellora and Aurangabad Caves* (Bombay: Taraporevala, 1962), Cave 16 inscription, 254–56. The word *bhushitam* is not clearly readable, according to Richard S. Cohen, "Appendix: Ajanta's Inscriptions," in *Ajanta: History and Development*, vol. 2, *Arguments About Ajanta*, by Walter M. Spink (Leiden: Brill, 2006), 312–13.

153. Ramachandra Kaulacara, *Silpa Prakasa: Medieval Orissan Sanskrit Text on Temple Architecture*, trans. Alice Boner and Sasasiva Rath Sarma (Leiden: Brill, 1966), 41.

154. Alka Patel, *Building Communities in Gujarat: Architecture and Society During the Twelfth through Fourteenth Centuries* (Leiden: Brill, 2004), 28.

155. Gonda, "Meaning of the Word *Alamkara*," 257.

156. Ibid., 269.

157. Smith, *Ratnakara's Haravijaya*, 132.

158. Pollock, *Language of the Gods in the World of Men*, 109–10.

159. Jan Pieper and George Michell, eds., *The Impulse to Adorn: Studies in Traditional Indian Architecture* (Bombay: Marg, 1982).

160. It is not possible, however, to discover analogies, point by point, between the two.

3. The Sensuous Within Sacred Boundaries

1. Relics could be of three types: bodily (*sariraka*), associated with the Buddha (*paribhogika*), like his alms bowl or robe, or commemorative (*uddesika*) of the site of a major event. Bodily relics were occasionally those of the Buddha's immediate disciples or, later, of other venerated monks.

2. Gregory Schopen, "On Monks, Nuns, and Vulgar Practices: The Introduction of the Image Cult into Indian Buddhism," *Artibus Asiae* 49 (1988–1989): 153–68.

3. Apart from the brick cities of the Indus civilization and brick Vedic altars, excavated foundations of the Mauryan capital at Pataliputra, as well as early shrines such as the temple beside the Heliodorus column, indicate a combined brick-and-wood construction. We assume, too, that the vernacular and city architecture depicted in the bas-reliefs at the Sanchi stupa, none of which has survived, reflects such mixed construction.

4. I use the word "semidivine" to refer to a group of beings of lesser status than the major gods and goddesses, but who are divine. While a *vahana* is always assigned to a deity, it is often, although not invariably, seen with such semidivine beings as *nagas*, *yakshas* and *yakshis*, *gandharvas*, *vidyadharas*, and the like. At Bharhut, it appears that *devatas* (little *devas*) belong to the category of the semidivine.

5. Asvaghosa, *The Saundarananda: or, Nanda the Fair*, trans. E. H. Johnston (London: Humphrey Milford, Oxford University Press, 1932), 20.

6. Ibid., 23–24.

7. Robert DeCaroli, *Haunting the Buddha: Indian Popular Religion and the Formation of Buddhism* (New York: Oxford University Press, 2004), 18, 72–73.

8. It seems likely that this gesture suggests the hierarchical importance of Ajakalaka in the *yaksha* community

9. DeCaroli, *Haunting the Buddha*, 17, 73.

10. Its outer face carries a central lotus medallion, with half-medallions above and below.

11. The outer face of the pillar has been sliced off.

12. A large consignment consisting of the railings and gateways of the Bharhut stupa were on their way to London in 1885 when the Peninsular and Oriental liner *Indus* sank in the waters off the coast of northern Sri Lanka, where they still languish. See a brief reference to this event in C. E. Godakumbura, "Education, Science and Art (G)," part 4 of *Report of the Arcaheological Survey of Ceylon for the Financial Year 1960–61* (Colombo: Government Press, 1962), G78. I am grateful to Robert DeCaroli for this reference.

13. Vidya Dehejia, *Discourse in Early Buddhist Art: Visual Narratives of India* (New Delhi: Munshiram Manoharlal, 1997), 83–84.

14. DeCaroli, *Haunting the Buddha*, 74.

15. A quick glimpse of these narratives may be obtained in Vidya Dehejia, ed., *Unseen Presence: The Buddha and Sanchi* (Bombay: Marg, 1996).

16. Ashvaghosa, *The Buddhacarita, or Acts of the Buddha*, trans. E. H. Johnston (Calcutta: Calcutta: Baptist Mission Press, for University of the Panjab, 1936; repr., Delhi: Motilal Banarsidass, 1984), 71.

17. *Vinaya* 4.289, cited in A. K. Coomaraswamy, "One Hundred References to Indian Painting," *Artibus Asiae* 4 (1930–1932): 42.

18. A. C. Soper, "Early Buddhist Attitudes Toward the Art of Painting," *Art Bulletin* 32 (1950): 147.

19. *Ayaramga Sutta*, bk. 2, lecture 12, cited in Coomaraswamy, "One Hundred References to Indian Painting," 43.

20. For a summary of the oral transmission of the Pali canon, of which the *Theri-gatha* is a part, see Dehejia, *Discourse in Early Buddhist Art*, 60–65. For a detailed study, see K. R. Norman, *Pali Literature* (Wiesbaden: Harrassowitz, 1983).

21. Susan Murcott, *The First Buddhist Women: Translations and Commentary on the Therigatha* (Berkeley: Parallax Press, 1991), 131–34, verses 1, 13, 14.

22. It is true that the monks might have considered Ambapali's poem as an indictment of beauty; however, since I do not believe that the monks were the targeted audience for the sculptures, I wonder if it is relevant that they would have regarded the beautiful images with hermeneutic suspicion. I am skeptical of the idea that the Bharhut or Sanchi *yakshi* figures were there to make a point to monks about dangers to be avoided. Nor can they be seen as poised the way they are out of respect for the mother of the Buddha; we shall see that the first images of Maya and the birth postdate Bharhut and Sanchi, and that the influence seems to have been the other way around.

23. Vidya Dehejia, *Indian Art* (London: Phaidon, 1997), 48, fig. 32.

24. Daud Ali, *Courtly Culture and Political Life in Early Medieval India* (New York: Cambridge University Press, 2004), 148.

25. Sherry Ortner, "Is Female to Male as Nature Is to Culture?" and "So, Is Female to Male as Nature Is to Culture?" in *Making Gender: The Politics and Erotics of Culture*, ed. Sherry Ortner (Boston: Beacon Press, 1996), 21–42, 173–80.

26. The auspicious nature of such imagery has long been recognized. See, for instance, A. K. Coomaraswamy, *Yaksas: Essays in Water Cosmology*, 2 vols. (Washington, D.C.: Smithsonian Institution, 1928, 1931), and Thomas E. Donaldson, *Hindu Temple Art of Orissa* (Leiden: Brill, 1985), 1:151–52.

27. An amazing resource that brings together a huge amount of pertinent material is Leona M. Anderson, *Vasantotsava: The Spring Festivals of India: Texts and Traditions* (New Delhi: D. K. Printworld, 1993). It is essential reading for those interested in the *dohada* theme.

28. For a discussion of *dohada*, see also Coomaraswamy, *Yaksas*.

29. Edwin Gerow, trans., *Malavika and Agnimitra*, in *Theater of Memory: The Plays of Kalidasa*, ed. Barbara Stoler Miller (New York: Columbia University Press, 1984), 283–84.

30. *The Origin of the Young God: Kalidasa's Kumarasambhava*, trans. Hank Heifetz (Berkeley: University of California Press, 1985), 48, *sarga* 3, verse 26.

31. *Kalidasa: The Dynasty of Raghu*, trans. Robert Antoine (Calcutta: Writers Workshop Books, 1972), 96, canto 8, verses 62–63.

32. *The Transport of Love: The Meghaduta of Kalidasa*, trans. Leonard Nathan (Berkeley: University of California Press, 1976), 65, verse 75.

33. Anderson cites a number of these texts in *Vasantotsava*.

34. *The Ratnavali of Sri Harsha-deva*, ed. and trans. M. R. Kale (Bombay: Booksellers Publishing, 1964), 31, act 1.

35. Subandhu, *Vasavadatta: A Sanskrit Romance*, ed. and trans. Louis H. Gray (Delhi: Motilal Banarsidass, 1962), 84.

36. *The Saundaryalahari or Flood of Beauty, Traditionally Ascribed to Sankaracarya*, ed. and trans. W. Norman Brown (Cambridge, Mass.: Harvard University Press, 1958), 82, verse 85.

37. Sadhana Parashar, *Kavyamimamsa of Rajasekhara* (New Delhi: D. K. Printworld, 2000), 208–9.

38. *The Dhvanyaloka of Anandavardhana with the Locana of Abhinavagupta*, ed. Daniel H. H. Ingalls, trans. Daniel H. H. Ingalls, Jeffrey Moussaieff Masson, and M. V. Patwardhan (Cambridge, Mass.: Harvard University Press, 1990), 498.

39. Anderson, *Vasantotsava*, 51.

40. Pratapaditya Pal, *Hindu Religion and Iconology According to the Tantrasara* (Los Angeles: Vichitra Press, 1981), 19–20.

41. *Vadana-madira* is probably not "ambrosia of her mouth," referring to saliva, but a mouthful of wine.

42. J. Ph. Vogel, "The Woman and Tree of *Salabhanjika* in Indian Literature and Art," *Acta Orientalia* 7 (1929): 201–31.

43. Rajashekhara, *Viddhashalabhanjika-Natika* [in Hindi and Sanskrit], trans. Babulal Shukla Sastri (Varanasi: Chaukhambha Oriental, 1976).

44. Irene J. Winter, "Ornament and the Rhetoric of Abundance in Assyria," *Eretz-Israel: Archaeological, Historical and Geographical Studies* 27 (2003): 252–64.

45. This was the standard practice followed in my family.

46. Donaldson speaks of the propitious and apotropaic nature of erotic figures, in *Hindu Temple Art of Orissa*, 1:151–52.

47. Robert L. Brown, "The Feminization of the Sarnath Gupta-Period Buddha Images," *Bulletin of the Asia Institute* 16 (2002): 175.

48. See chap. 1, p. 11.

49. A couple of large, rectangular stone panels from Mathura, carved in high relief with three or four figures, may perhaps represent specific episodes from dramas. See Donald Stadtner, "'The Little Clay Cart' in Early Mathura," *Orientations* 27 (1996): 39–46.

50. Susan L. Huntington, *The Art of Ancient India: Buddhist, Hindu, Jain* (New York: Weatherhill, 1985), 158.

51. Coomaraswamy, *Yaksas*.

52. Doris Srinivasan proposes that a much-abraded panel on a pillar at Bodh Gaya, carved beneath a clear representation of the sun god Surya, is the first representation of the birth scene, in "Genealogy of the Buddha in Early Indian Art," in *Eastern Approaches: Essays on Asian Art and Archaeology*, ed. T. S. Maxwell (Delhi: Oxford University Press, 1992), 38–44. Her argument that Surya and the birth of the Buddha have an integral con nection is powerful (the *Buddha-charita* verses in the birth sequence speak of him as the sun come down to earth). However, it is not clear that the panels on this Bodh Gaya pillar are sequential; other pillars from the site display a random selection of scenes. In its damaged condition, one can only say that the panel features a woman among other figures.

53. In "Like Worms Falling from a Foul-Smelling Sore: The Buddhist Rhetoric of Childbirth in an Early Mahayana Sutra" (Ph.D. diss., Columbia University, 2007), a study of the Buddhist "Entering the Womb Sutra," which appears to have been composed sometime during the first three centuries of this era, Amy Langenberg suggests that its strong language, emphasizing the painful and disgusting nature of childbirth, is the result of Buddhist monks pushing back against the encroachment they felt from a lay culture that celebrated auspiciousness.

54. It is worth noting, however, that in the early texts it is during the moment before enlightenment that the Buddha reviewed all previous births.

55. M. S. Vats, "Unpublished Votive Inscriptions in the Chaitya Cave at Karle," *Epigraphia Indica* 18 (1925–1926): 325–29, nos. 15, 16.

56. Soper, "Early Buddhist Attitudes Toward the Art of Painting," 147.

57. Margaret Miles, *Image as Insight: Visual Understanding in Western Christianity and Secular Cultures* (Boston: Beacon Press, 1985), 9.

58. As a specific example, I would point to the relief carvings at the Sisireshvar Shiva temple at

Bhubaneshvar and at the Buddhist monastery at the site of Ratnagiri. Anyone viewing details of the decoration at these sites would be hard put to distinguish one from the other, surely indicating that the same workshop was involved at both a Buddhist and a Shaivite monument.

59. For a detailed account of the seven mothers and the other male Shaivite figures within this sanctum, see Donaldson, *Hindu Temple Art of Orissa*, 1:100–101.

60. Ramachandra Kaulacara, *Silpa Prakasa: Medieval Orissan Sanskrit Text on Temple Architecture*, trans. Alice Boner and Sasasiva Rath Sarma (Leiden: Brill, 1966), 46.

61. Ibid.

62. Indira Peterson, *Kuttralak Kuravanji (The Fortune-teller Play of Kuttralam)* (forthcoming).

63. Kaulacara, *Silpa Prakasa*, 103.

64. Interested readers may consult a variety of sources, including Michael Meister, "Juncture and Conjunction: Punning and Temple Architecture," *Artibus Asiae* 41 (1979): 226–28; Vidya Dehejia, "Reading Love Imagery on an Indian Temple," in *Love in Asian Art and Culture* (Washington, D.C.: Arthur M. Sackler Gallery, Smithsonian Institution, 1998), 96–113; and Devangana N. Desai, *Religious Imagery of Khajuraho* (Mumbai: Franco-Indian Research, 1996), chap. 7, "Puns and Enigmatic Language in Sculpture."

65. Kirit Mankodi, *The Queen's Stepwell at Patan* (Bombay: Project for Indian Cultural Studies, 1991). One should note that despite its dedication, the stepwell has several areas of "unfinish."

66. More will be seen on Vishnu Varaha and goddess Earth in chapter 4.

67. John E. Cort, *Jains in the World: Religious Values and Ideology in India* (New York: Oxford University Press, 2001), 41–42.

68. Ibid., especially chap. 3, "Going to the Temple: How to Worship God."

69. Ibid., 74–76.

70. Ibid., 62–63.

71. Ibid., 7, 186.

72. M. A. Dhaky, *Complexities Surrounding the Vimalavasahi Temple at Mount Abu* (Philadelphia: University of Pennsylvania Press, 1980).

73. Phyllis Granoff, "Halayudha's Prism: The Experience of Religion in Medieval Hymns and Stories," in *Gods, Guardians, and Lovers: Temple Sculptures from North India, A.D. 700–1200*, ed. Vishakha N. Desai and Darielle Mason (New York: Asia Society Galleries, 1993), 89–90.

74. Cort, *Jains in the World*, 37.

4. To the Divine Through Beauty

1. By and large, Pallava bronzes measure no more than 9 inches in height, are very few in number, and are exclusively images of standing Vishnu.

2. Jack Hawley, *The Bhakti Movement: Excavations in a Master Narrative* (forthcoming). In chapter 3, especially, Hawley cautions us against the use of the term *andolan* (movement) to describe *bhakti*; he points out that the word is at most a hundred years old and bears the marks of having been developed in a strictly northern Indian context.

3. Different circumstances surround "saint" Mirabai of Rajasthan. Forced to marry a human husband in the form of the *rana* of Mewar, she refused to play the part of a dutiful bride, survived an attempt to poison her, and finally abandoned her husband's home to join the company of Krishna devotees at Brindavan.

4. This brief reference to Nataraja is oversimplified because this is not the appropriate place to enter into a discussion on the varying strands, including the Pine Forest myth, that led to the creation of this vision of the god.

5. Vidya Dehejia, *Art of the Imperial Cholas* (New York: Columbia University Press, 1990), 39.

6. Paul Younger, *The Home of the Dancing Sivan: The Traditions of the Hindu Temple in Citamparam* (New York: Oxford University Press, 1995), 206.

7. Indira Peterson, *Poems to Siva: The Hymns of the Tamil Saints* (Princeton, N.J.: Princeton University Press, 1989), 210.

8. Ibid., 211.

9. Sambandar addressed Shiva and Parvati as child to parent; Appar was the humble servant; Sundarar adopted the familiar mode of the friend.

10. Vidya Dehejia, *Slaves of the Lord: The Path of the Tamil Saints* (Delhi: Munshiram Manoharlal, 1988), 48.

11. Peterson, *Poems to Siva*, 248.

12. P. V. Jagadisa Ayyar records a gift of gold and jewels by a certain Amalan Seyyavayar, who also gave lands for the maintenance of the temple, in *South Indian Shrines* (New Delhi: Asian Educational Services, 1982), 265.

13. Dehejia, *Slaves of the Lord*, 54–56.

14. Dehejia, *Art of the Imperial Cholas*, 110–11.

15. R. Nagaswamy, "Melaperumpallam Bronzes," in *Art and Culture of Tamil Nadu*, ed. R. Nagaswamy (Delhi: Sundeep Prakashan, 1980), 95–100.

16. Dehejia, *Art of the Imperial Cholas*, 115–16.

17. Georg Buhler, "Udepur Prasasti of Kings of Malwa," *Epigraphia Indica* 1 (1892): 236.

18. An inscription in the temple speaks of the gift of jewels to the bronze in the year 1047, indicating its creation before that date.

19. Dehejia, *Art of the Imperial Cholas*, 86.

20. Dehejia, *Slaves of the Lord*, 45.

21. *The Origin of the Young God: Kalidasa's Kumarasambhava*, trans. Hank Heifetz (Berkeley: University of California Press, 1985), 26–28.

22. *Songs of the Harsh Devotee: The Tevaram of Cuntaramurttinayanar*, trans. David Dean Shulman (Philadelphia: Department of South Asia Regional Studies, University of Pennsylvania, 1990), 539–42.

23. J. F. Fleet, *Inscriptions of the Early Gupta Kings and Their Successors*, Corpus Inscriptionum Indicarum 3

(Calcutta: Superintendent of Government Printing, 1888), 227.

24. Thomas B. Coburn, *Encountering the Goddess: A Translation of the Devi-Mahatmya and a Study of Its Interpretation* (Albany: State University of New York Press, 1991), 55–56.

25. Shankara, *Saundaryalahiri*, ed. and trans. V. K. Subramaniam (Delhi: Motilal Banarsidass, 1977).

26. Even though she is the goddess, the text does not start with her feet and move upward, commencing instead with her crown and concluding with her feet.

27. Shankara, *Saundaryalahiri*, 42.

28. Images of the sixth-century woman saint Karaikkal Ammaiyar often resemble those of Kali. See Vidya Dehejia, "Iconographic Transference Between Krishna and Three Saiva Saints," in *Indian Art and Connoisseurship: Essays in Honour of Douglas Barrett*, ed. John Guy (Ahmedabad: Mapin, 1995), 140–49.

29. Coburn, *Encountering the Goddess*, 61.

30. Blake Wentworth, "Women's Bodies, Earthly Kingdom: Mapping the Presence of God in the *Tirukayilaya Nana Ula*" (manuscript, Divinity School, University of Chicago, 2003).

31. While its exact authorship may be debatable, the ninth-century date assigned to its composition is not disputed.

32. Quoted in Vidya Dehejia, *The Sensuous and the Sacred: Chola Bronzes from South India* (New York: American Federation of the Arts, 2002), 223–24, adapted from E. Hultzsch and V. Venkayya, eds., *South Indian Inscriptions* (New Delhi: Archaeological Survey of India, 1916), 2:pt. 1, inscription no. 8:87–88. The following system has been used for the conversion of the ancient measures, which are red and black-and-red seeds: 1 *kalanju* = 5.3 grams; 1 *manjadi* = 1.06 grams; 1 *kunri* = 0.5 gram. The grams-to-pounds conversion is 453.6 grams = 1 pound.

33. Hultzsch and Venkayya, eds., *South Indian Inscriptions*, 2:pt. 1, inscription no. 8:89.

34. Richard Salomon, "Appendix: Selection of Typical Inscriptions," no. 10 (Baroda Copper-Plate Inscription of Rastrakuta Karkkaraja [II]), in *Indian Epigraphy: A Guide to the Study of Inscriptions in Sanskrit, Prakrit, and the Other Indo-Aryan Languages* (Delhi: Munshiram Manoharlal, 1998), 292.

35. Any *puja* manual may be consulted for this list. One such is Swami Ishwarananda Giri, *Samvit-saparya* (Varanasi: Anandakanana Press, 1980).

36. The list of limbs adored, from feet to head, is as follows: feet, legs from ankle to knee, knees, thighs, fingers, *kanthi*, navel, stomach, chest/breasts, hands, neck, face, eyes, ears, forehead, head.

37. Vasudha Narayanan, "Arcavatara: On Earth as He Is in Heaven," in *Gods of Flesh, Gods of Stone: The Embodiment of the Divinity in India*, ed. Joanne Punzo Waghorne and Norman Cutler (Chambersburg, Pa.: Anima, 1985), 54.

38. C. J. Fuller, *The Camphor Flame: Popular Hinduism and Society in India* (Princeton, N.J.: Princeton University Press, 1992), 61.

39. Steven Paul Hopkins, *Singing the Body of God: The Hymns of Vedantadesika in Their South Indian Tradition* (Oxford: Oxford University Press, 2002), 205.

40. Ibid., 141–44.

41. Vidya Dehejia, *Antal and Her Path of Love* (Albany: State University of New York Press, 1990), 105.

42. *The Complete Works of Saint Teresa of Jesus*, vol. 3, *Book of the Foundations, Minor Prose Works, Poems, Documents, Indices*, trans. and ed. E. Allison Peers (1946; repr., New York: Sheed and Ward, 1957), 279–81.

43. Nancy Ann Nayar, *Poetry as Theology: The Srivaisnava Stotra in the Age of Ramanuja* (Wiesbaden: Harrassowitz, 1992), 189.

44. Ibid., 190.

45. Hopkins, *Singing the Body of God*, 7–8.

46. Ibid., 157–60.

47. Ibid., 130.

48. Ibid., 161, verse 12.

49. F. Kielhorn, "Two Chandella Inscriptions from Ajaygadh," *Epigraphia Indica* 1 (1892): 325–38.

50. Kalidasa, *Origin of the Young God*, 117, verse 7.

51. Ibid., 130, verse 83.

52. See, for instance, Sheldon Pollock, review of *Vallabhadeva's Kommentar (Sarada-Version) zum Kumarasambhava des Kalidasa*, by M. S. Narayana Murti and Klaus L. Janert, *Journal of the American Oriental Society* 105, no. 2 (1985): 381–83.

53. There is some discussion among literary scholars as to whether the poem is unfinished or intentionally left thus with the description of the great love of Shiva and Parvati.

54. Shankara, *Saundaryalahiri*, 46, verse 86.

55. J. F. Fleet, "Pattadakal Pillar Inscription of the Time of Kirtivarman II," *Epigraphia Indica* 3 (1894–1895): 1–7.

56. Lionel D. Barnett, "Arthuna Inscription of Paramara Chamundaraja. VS 1136," *Epigraphia Indica* 14 (1917–1918): 303.

57. V. V. Mirashi, "Ratanpur Stone Inscription of the [Kalachuri] Year 915," *Epigraphia Indica* 26 (1941–1942): 264.

58. R. G. Basak, "The Puri Plates of Madhavavarman-Sainyabhita," *Epigraphia Indica* 23 (1935–1936): 130.

59. F. Kielhorn, "Deopara Stone Inscription of Vijayasena," *Epigraphia Indica* 1 (1892): 311.

60. F. Kielhorn, "Ratnapur Inscription of Prithivideva of the (Vikrama) Year 1247," *Epigraphia Indica* 1 (1892): 49.

61. Pushpa Prasad, *Sanskrit Inscriptions of the Delhi Sultanate, 1191–1526* (Delhi: Oxford University Press, 1990), 75.

62. This statement is not in any way intended to deny the existence of sectarian rivalries at certain phases of history, but only to demonstrate the parallel existence of acceptance and respect.

63. R. G. Bhandarkar, "Karhad Plates of Krishna III; Saka-Samvat 880," *Epigraphia Indica* 4 (1896–1897): 286.

64. F. Kielhorn, "Mau Chandella Inscription of Madanavarman," *Epigraphia Indica* 1 (1892): 202.

65. Prasad, *Sanskrit Inscriptions of the Delhi Sultanate*, 66.
66. H. Luders, "Two Pillar Inscriptions of the Time of Krishnaraya of Vijayanagara," *Epigraphia Indica* 6 (1900–1901): 127.
67. For a different interpretation, see Robert L. Brown, "The Feminization of the Sarnath Gupta-Period Buddha Images," *Bulletin of the Asia Institute* 16 (2002): 165–79.
68. Salomon, "Appendix: Selection of Typical Inscriptions," no. 12 (Nalanda Inscription of Vipulasrimitra), in *Indian Epigraphy*, 301.

5. Inserting the Gods into the World of Men

1. Woodman Taylor, "Unscrolling Spring Songs: The *Vasanta Vilasa* in the Freer Gallery of Art," *Orientations* 29 (1998): 55–62. See also W. Norman Brown, ed. and trans., *The Vasanta Vilasa* (New Haven, Conn.: American Oriental Society, 1962).
2. W. G. Archer, *Indian Paintings from the Punjab Hills* (Delhi: Oxford University Press, 1973), 1:16.
3. Andrew Topsfield, "Sahibdin's Illustrations to the *Rasikapriya*," *Orientations* 17, no. 3 (1986): 22.
4. Can one term the Sanskrit *Rasa-manjari* a *riti* text, or should one restrict the use of the term to Braj texts—in this case, the *Rasik-priya* and *Satsai*?
5. The question has been raised as to what makes a painted manuscript of the *Gita-govinda* more sacred than that of the *Rasik-priya*. This is an interesting question. If only the figures of Krishna and Radha survived from both a *Gita-govinda* manuscript and one of the *Rasik-priya*, would it be self-evident which text they illustrated? I suggest that the context of the page would clarify whether the images belonged to the "sacred" or the *riti* text. Certainly, the texts themselves may be classified in these terms, since one portrays part of a sacred biography, while the other is devoted primarily to a classification of *nayikas* and *nayakas*, with Krishna and Radha playing those roles.
6. *Love Song of the Dark Lord: Jayadeva's Gitagovinda*, trans. Barbara Stoler Miller (New York: Columbia University Press, 1977), ix.
7. Marvin H. Pope, "Gita-Govinda, the so-called 'Indian Song of Songs,'" in *Song of Songs*, trans. Marvin H. Pope, The Anchor Bible (New York: Doubleday, 1977), 85–89.
8. Mackenzie Brown, "The Theology of Radha in the Puranas," in *The Divine Consort: Radha and the Goddesses of India*, ed. John Stratton Hawley and Donna Marie Wulff (Berkeley: Graduate Theological Union, 1982), 57–71.
9. Pratapaditya Pal, *Ragamala Paintings in the Museum of Fine Arts, Boston* (Boston: Museum of Fine Arts, 1967), 9.
10. Its closing verses, in which he implores Prince Salim to accept "this poor slave's work," may perhaps be read to indicate his physical presence at the Mughal court. However, Allison Busch points out that the patron of this manuscript may have been the son of his chief patron, Bir Singh Deo of Orchcha, who is prominently mentioned in the introductory verses.
11. This suggestion rests partly on the style of the paintings as Mughalized but not imperial, and partly on the fact that in one of his works, the *Virsinghdev charita*, Keshavdas refers to Birbal as his friend and writes verses in his praise. A. K. Coomaraswamy tells us that Keshavdas visited Akbar's court after the emperor imposed a major fine on his patron, and that he had an audience with Birbal at which he recited a poem that so pleased Birbal that he had the fine reduced, in "The Eight *Nayikas*," *Journal of Indian Art* 17 (1914): 105.
12. Daud Ali gives us an easily readable chart of these sixty-four *kalas* in *Courtly Culture and Political Life in Early Medieval India* (New York: Cambridge University Press, 2004), 76–77.
13. Lee Siegel, *Fires of Love, Waters of Peace: Passion and Renunciation in Indian Culture* (Honolulu: University of Hawai'i Press, 1983), 34.
14. Bharata, *The Natyasastra: English Translation with Critical Notes*, trans. Adya Rangacharya, rev. ed. (Delhi: Munshiram Manoharlal, 1996), 196.
15. Jayadeva, *Love Song of the Dark Lord*, 37.
16. A complete translation of the text's 138 verses that is illustrated with paintings from at least three series of painted *Rasa-manjari* manuscripts can be found in M. S. Randhawa and S. D. Bhambri, *Basohli Paintings of the Rasamanjari* (New Delhi: Abhinav, 1982). B. N. Goswamy and Eberhard Fischer prefer to translate the title as *Blossom-Cluster of Delight*, in *Pahari Masters*, Artibus Asiae Supplementum 38 (Zurich: Museum Reitberg, 1992), 30. A new translation of the text, used in this chapter, is *A Bouquet of Rasas (The Rasamanjari of Bhanudatta)*, trans. Sheldon Pollock, Clay Sanskrit Library (New York: New York University Press and JJC Foundation, 2009).
17. Bhanudatta, *Bouquet of Rasas*.
18. The verses mentioning Krishna and Radha are 29, 41, 61, 86, 94, 96, 99, 102, 119, 125, and 136. No specific intentional pattern emerges, and we find, for instance, that Krishna is evoked with three different types of experienced heroines, once when a *sakhi* speaks to Radha and once to Krishna, once when a *sakha* unites the lovers, once to describe a hero equally devoted to all his wives, and so on.
19. Vishakha N. Desai translates the title as *Connoisseur's Delights*, in "Connoisseur's Delights: Early 'Rasikapriya' Paintings in India" (Ph.D. diss., University of Michigan, 1984), while *Handbook for Poetry Connoisseurs* is the preferred translation of Allison Busch, "The Anxiety of Innovation: The Practice of Literary Science in the Hindi/*Riti* Tradition," *Comparative Studies of South Asia, Africa and the Middle East* 24, no. 2 (2004): 45.
20. Busch suggests that the reason for the omission of the courtesan is Keshavdas's "*bhakti*-oriented textual

universe: how could Radha, the primary *nayika* of the *Rasik-priya*, ever be cast in the questionable role of the courtesan?" ("Anxiety of Innovation," 51).

21. Ibid.

22. Rupert Snell, "*Bhakti* versus *Riti*? The *Satsai* of Biharilal," *Journal of Vaisnava Studies* 3, no. 1 (1994): 164.

23. Ibid., 168.

24. *The Seasons: Kalidasa's Ritusamhara*, trans. John T. Roberts (Tempe: Center for Asian Studies, Arizona State University, 1990).

25. Charlotte Vaudeville, *Barahmasa in Indian Literatures: Songs of the Twelve Months in Indo-Aryan Literatures* (Delhi: Motilal Banarsidass, 1986).

26. This is the title used by Desai, "Connoisseur's Delights."

27. Busch, "Anxiety of Innovation," 48.

28. V. P. Dwivedi, *Barahmasa: The Song of Seasons in Literature and Art* (Delhi: Agam Kala Prakashan, 1980).

29. I am indebted to Allison Busch for this information.

30. Milo Beach, *Mughal and Rajput Painting* (Cambridge: Cambridge University Press, 1992), 47, fig. 28.

31. Bharata, *Natyasastra*, 218–98.

32. Klaus Ebeling, *Ragamala Painting* (New Delhi: Ravi Kumar, 1973), 28.

33. This text was composed sometime after 1460 and definitely before 1647, according to ibid., 112.

34. Ibid., 18. This system, so titled by Ebeling, is one that appears in about half the four thousand paintings he studied. He explains that the system does not seem to have a specific literary source but was clearly popular, judging from its extensive use.

35. Ibid., 18.

36. Ibid., 140.

37. Ibid., 126.

38. Bhanudatta, *Bouquet of Rasas*. See also A. K. Coomaraswamy, *Catalogue of the Indian Collections in the Museum of Fine Arts, Boston* (Boston: Museum of Fine Arts, 1923), 5:171.

39. Goswamy and Fischer, *Pahari Masters*, 29.

40. Bhanudatta, *Bouquet of Rasas*. See also Coomaraswamy, *Catalogue of the Indian Collections in the Museum of Fine Arts*, 5:172.

41. Bhanudatta, *Bouquet of Rasas*. See also Randhawa and Bhambhri, *Basohli Paintings of the Rasamanjari*, 91.

42. Sixty are in the Dogra Art Gallery in Jammu; seven in the Museum of Fine Arts, Boston; and twelve in the Victoria and Albert Museum in London.

43. Shiva and Parvati feature in verses 16, 97, and 100 (apart from the invocation); Rama and/or Sita, in verses 95, 101, and 126.

44. Bhanudatta, *Bouquet of Rasas*.

45. Goswamy and Fischer, *Pahari Masters*, 29–57. In my opinion, it is not incorrect to term the style "Basohli," especially in view of the next *Rasa-manjari*—painted, according to its colophon, by Devidasa of Nurpur but in the town of Basohli (59–73).

46. Archer, *Indian Paintings from the Punjab Hills*, 1:382.

47. Ibid., 1:16–17.

48. *Sushrata*, a treatise on medicine written for Raja Kirpal in 1688, cited in ibid., 1:17.

49. Bhanudatta, *Bouquet of Rasas*. See also Goswamy and Fischer, *Pahari Masters*, 17.

50. Archer, *Indian Paintings from the Punjab Hills*, 1:16–17.

51. Saryu Doshi, "An Illustrated Manuscript from Aurangabad Dated 1650 A.D." *Lalit Kala* 15 (n.d.): 19–28.

52. Molly Emma Aitken, *The Intelligence of Tradition: Form and Meaning in Mewar Painting* (New Haven, Conn.: Yale University Press, 2009).

53. Of the sixty or so known pages of this manuscript, only twelve are intact; the rest are known as illustrations only, having been subjected, tragically, to the text being cut away and discarded. Such was the fate of many a manuscript in which early, inexperienced dealers used faulty judgment on what would sell and what would not!

54. *The Rasikapriya of Keshavadasa*, trans. K. P. Bahadur (Delhi: Motilal Banarsidass, 1972), 220–21. Coomaraswamy suggests that the verse illustrated is that of the *sakhi* speaking to the heroine, in *Catalogue of the Indian Collections in the Museum of Fine Arts*, 6:24:

> Who can tell how, when she gave him fresh
> betel to eat, her fingers first touched her
> own fresh mouth?
> Did you mark in what fashion she drew Lala's
> glance?
> And spoke with a smile of enchantment? I
> heard and I understood that her words
> were soaked with love,
> And I know that her darling's heart's desires
> were all fulfilled.

However, the visual image suggests that the *sakhi* is speaking to Krishna, which is the context of the first verse inscribed on the page.

55. The text commences with the *nayika* who esteems her husband's friends, and then goes on to the classification of the *praudha-nayika* (mature heroine).

56. Vishakha N. Desai, "From Illustrations to Icons: The Changing Context of the Rasikapriya Paintings in Mewar," in *Indian Painting: Essays in Honour of Karl J. Khandalavala*, ed. B. N. Goswamy (New Delhi: Lalit Kala Akademi, 1995), 106.

57. Topsfield clarifies that there appear to be two known copies of this text by Sahibdin's workshop, both created around 1630 to 1635, in "Sahibdin's Illustrations to the *Rasikapriya*," 22. Possibly one was for Jagat Singh himself and the other for either a member of the royal family or a highly placed courtier.

58. Desai specifies that the scribe omits the preliminary defining verse (*lakshan*), which precedes each example (*udaharan*), and writes out only the example verse, which is then illustrated by the painter, in "From Illustrations to Icons," 102.

59. It is interesting to note that in both *Rasik-priya* manuscripts, Sahibdin retains the vertical page format of the Mughal court; it is somewhat later in his career, with the *Bhagavata-purana* project of the 1640s, that he turns to the horizontal format, typical of the pre-Mughal style, which was to become standard in Rajasthan.

60. See images reproduced in Desai, "From Illustrations to Icons."

61. Vidya Dehejia, "Narrative Structure in Jagat Singh's *Ramayana*: A Preliminary Study," *Artibus Asiae* 54 (1996): 303–4.

62. Aitken, *Intelligence of Tradition*.

63. Dehejia, "Narrative Structure in Jagat Singh's *Ramayana*," 303–24.

64. Topsfield, "Sahibdin's Illustrations to the *Rasikapriya*," 27–28.

65. This is a technique that Sahibdin used throughout his career. I have shown that he uses a similar mode of textual reference in his *Ramayana* paintings, which belong to the very end of his career, in "Narrative Structure in Jagat Singh's *Ramayana*," 323.

66. *Rasikapriya of Keshavadasa*, trans. Bahadur, 139–40.

67. The verse deals with the third of ten stages of love, which consists of detailing the merits, physical and otherwise, of the beloved; it is treated as a hidden telling by the *nayaka* because he is speaking to himself, listing the merits of the *nayika*.

68. Topsfield, "Sahibdin's Illustrations to the *Rasikapriya*," 31.

69. Ibid.

70. Annapurna Garimella, "A Handmaid's Tale: *Sakhis*, Love, Devotion, and Poetry in Rajput Painting," in *Love in Asian Art and Culture* (Washington, D.C.: Arthur M. Sackler Gallery, Smithsonian Institution, 1998), 86.

71. Ibid., 89.

72. Ibid. In the context of the artist's possible allusion to the sacred, one might note a second inscribed verse: "Facing everyone for a moment, her glance shifts, turning away from all, / Like a mystic's magic bowl divines the guilty thief, it rests on that side" (verse 8). Garimella points out that since Braj words have complex etymologies and double meanings, the same verse can also be read as follows: "Facing everyone for a moment, her glance shifts, turning away from all, / It rests on that side, like the faithful's compass finds Mecca." Was this couplet inserted to highlight the artist's intentional ambiguity?

73. Aitken, *Intelligence of Tradition*.

74. Garimella, "Handmaid's Tale," 90.

75. The set was discovered by N. C. Mehta in the collection of Maharaj Narendra Shah of Tehri Garhwal, which also contained the *Gita-govinda* manuscript with a colophon informing us that it was painted by Manaku, according to M. S. Randhawa, *Kangra Paintings of the Bihari Sat Sai* (New Delhi: National Museum, 1966), 19. For the Fattu inscription on a drawing in the collection of the National Museum, New Delhi, see Goswamy and

Fischer, *Pahari Masters*, 350.

76. Archer, *Indian Paintings from the Punjab Hills*, 1:245.

77. W. Moorcroft and G. Trebeck, *Travels in the Himalayan Provinces of Hindustaan and the Panjab; in Ladakh and Kashmir; in Peshawar, Kabul, Kunduz and Bokhara, from 1819 to 1825*, ed. H. H. Wilson (London, 1841), cited in ibid., 1:125.

78. Andrew Topsfield, *Court Painting at Udaipur: Art Under the Patronage of the Maharanas of Mewar*, *Artibus Asiae* Supplementum 44 (Zurich: Artibus Asiae, 2004), 143–44.

79. B. N. Goswamy, *The Essence of Indian Art* (San Francisco: Asian Art Museum of San Francisco, 1986), 46, cat. no. 14.

80. Dwivedi, *Barahmasa*, app. A, 132.

81. Ibid., 138.

82. Ibid., pls. 46–57.

83. Ibid., pls. 18–39.

84. Ibid., pls. 93–102.

85. Ebeling, *Ragamala Painting*. For instance, both a Malwa Bhairava *raga* (31, pl. C3) and a Jaipur Bhairava (fig. 242) portray royal, king-like figures. This section on *Raga-malas* has drawn heavily on Ebeling's documentation.

86. Ibid., 128. Painter's Text C.

87. Ibid., 138. Hindi verse from an Amber manuscript dated 1709, Text I.

88. Ibid., 209, fig. 87; 215, fig. 97.

89. Ibid., 138. Hindi Text I of 1709.

90. Ibid., 122.

91. Ibid., 128. Painter's Text C.

92. Ibid., 126. Painter's Text B.

93. Ibid., 79, pl. C27.

94. Ibid., 124. Painter's Text B.

95. Ibid., 116. Text A, ca. 1550.

96. Ibid., 127, pl. C51.

97. Ibid., 126–28.

98. Ibid., 163–64.

99. Ibid., 83, pl. C29; 95, pl. C35; 105, pl. C40; 141, pl. C58.

100. Aitken, *Intelligence of Tradition*.

101. The need for caution regarding the importance of the artist's religious affiliation is sounded by the instance of the Mewari Muslim artist Sahibdin, who painted *raga-malas* and *Rasik-priyas* portraying Krishna. Other comparable examples exist, including the Bikaner artist Ruknuddin, whose work includes a magnificent Vishnu and Lakshmi painting (1678; Beach, *Mughal and Rajput Painting*, 166–67, pl. J), and his son Ibrahim, who produced a *Rasik-priya* (1691; Gautam Vajracharya, *Watson Collection of Indian Miniatures at the Elvehjem Museum of Art* [Madison: University of Wisconsin Press, 2002], 75–76). The workshop tradition, with its amassed stock of drawings to serve as models, would have aided in such a process.

Afterword. The Body Revealed and Concealed

1. Vasudha Narayanan, "Arcavatara: On Earth as He Is in Heaven," in *Gods of Flesh, Gods of Stone: The*

Embodiment of the Divinity in India, ed. Joanne Punzo Waghorne and Norman Cutler (Chambersburg, Pa.: Anima, 1985), 54.

2. A. V. Narasimha Murthy, "A Study of the Label Inscriptions of the Hoysala Sculptors," in *Indian Epigraphy: Its Bearing on the History of Art*, ed. Frederick Asher and M. S. Gai (New Delhi: Oxford University Press and IBH, 1985), 215–20.

3. Shrinivas H. Ritti, "Udega, the Chief Architect of the Saraswati Temple at Gadag," in *Indian Epigraphy: Its Bearing on the History of Art*, ed. Frederick Asher and G. S. Gai (New Delhi: Oxford University Press and IBH, 1985), 213–14.

4. Admittedly, the image of Durga on the outer walls of several small Chola temples is today anointed with sandal-paste, adorned with flowers, and often draped with cotton cloth. But such was not the original intention.

5. See the many photographs of images adorned for procession in Joanne Punzo Waghorne, "Dressing the Body of God: South Indian Bronze Sculpture in Its Temple Setting," *Asian Art* 5, no. 3 (1992): 8–33.

6. H. Krishna Sastri, *South Indian Inscriptions* (Madras: Superintendent Government Press, 1920), pt. 3:300–322, nos. 151, 151A.

7. Occasionally, although not often, calling attention to this aspect has enabled me to photograph the images without additional clothing, jewels, and flowers.

8. Waghorne, "Dressing the Body of God."

9. Steven Paul Hopkins, *Singing the Body of God: The Hymns of Vedantadesika in Their South Indian Tradition* (Oxford: Oxford University Press, 2002), 157–60.

10. Donald Preziosi, "Museology and Museography," in "A Range of Critical Perspectives: The Problematics of Collecting and Display, Part I," *Art Bulletin* 77 (1995): 13–15.

11. Vidya Dehejia, "Identity and Visibility: Reflections on Museum Displays of South Asian Art," in *New Cosmopolitanisms: South Asians in the U.S.*, ed. Gita Rajan and Shailja Sharma (Stanford, Calif.: Stanford University Press, 2006), 71–90.

12. Sheldon Pollock emphasizes that the vernaculars are "languages of Place," and not of "ethnicized peoples," in *The Language of the Gods in the World of Men* (Berkeley: University of California Press, 2006), 573.

13. History demonstrates, too, that Muslim artists were often employed by Hindu masters to illustrate sacred texts, including the *Ramayana*, the *Bhagavata-purana*, and the *Gita-govinda*. Sahibdin, master artist of Mewar Rana Jagat Singh, is one example encountered in this book.

14. Vidya Dehejia, *Discourse in Early Buddhist Art: Visual Narratives of India* (New Delhi: Munshiram Manoharlal, 1997), 35.

BIBLIOGRAPHY

Aitken, Molly Emma. *The Intelligence of Tradition: Form and Meaning in Mewar Painting*. New Haven, Conn.: Yale University Press, 2009.

Ali, Daud. *Courtly Culture and Political Life in Early Medieval India*. New York: Cambridge University Press, 2004.

——. "Technologies of the Self: Courtly Artifice and Monastic Discipline in Early India." *Journal of the Economic and Social History of the Orient* 41 (1998): 159–84.

——. "Vikramacholanula: A Chola Processional Poem." In *Art of the Chola Bronzes*, appendix A, 142–45. London: Royal Academy, 2006.

Anandavardhana. *The Dhvanyaloka of Anandavardhana with the Locana of Abhinavagupta*. Edited by Daniel H. H. Ingalls. Translated by Daniel H. H. Ingalls, Jeffrey Moussaieff Masson, and M. V. Patwardhan. Cambridge, Mass.: Harvard University Press, 1990.

Anderson, Leona M. *Vasantotsava: The Spring Festivals of India: Texts and Traditions*. New Delhi: D. K. Printworld, 1993.

Archer, W. G. *Indian Paintings from the Punjab Hills*. 2 vols. Delhi: Oxford University Press, 1973.

Asher, Frederick. "Historical and Political Allegory in Gupta Art." In *Essays on Gupta Culture*, edited by Bardwell L. Smith, 53–66. Columbia, Mo.: South Asia Books, 1983.

Asher, Frederick, and Walter Spink. "Maurya Figural Sculpture Reconsidered." *Ars Orientalis* 19 (1989): 1–25.

Ashvaghosa. *The Buddhacarita, or Acts of the Buddha*. Translated by E. H. Johnston. Calcutta: Baptist Mission Press, for University of the Panjab, 1936. Reprint, Delhi: Motilal Banarsidass, 1984.

——. *The Saundarananda: or, Nanda the Fair*. Translated by E. H. Johnston. London: Humphrey Milford, Oxford University Press, 1932.

Ayyar, Jagadisa P. V. *South Indian Shrines*. Rev. and enl. ed. New Delhi: Asian Educational Services, 1982.

Bahm, Archie J. "Comparative Aesthetics." *Journal of Aesthetics and Art Criticism* 24, no. 1 (1965): 109–19.

Bailey, Greg, and Richard Gombrich, eds. and trans. *Love Lyrics by Amaru and Bhartrhari, and by Bilhana*. Clay Sanskrit Library. New York: New York University Press and JJC Foundation, 2005.

Bana. *The Harsa-Carita of Bana*. Translated by E. B. Cowell and F. W. Thomas. London: Royal Asiatic Society, 1897. Reprint, Delhi: Motilal Banarsidass, 1968.

Barnett, Lionel D. "Arthuna Inscription of Paramara Chamundaraja. VS 1136." *Epigraphia Indica* 14 (1917–1918): 295–310.

——. "Bhubaneswar Inscription in the Royal Asiatic Society." *Epigraphia Indica* 13 (1915–1916): 150–55.

——. "Inscription at Narendra." *Epigraphia Indica* 13 (1915–1916): 298–326.

——. "Inscriptions of Huli." *Epigraphia Indica* 18 (1925–1926): 170–218.

——. "Inscriptions of Sudi." *Epigraphia Indica* 15 (1919–1920): 73–112.

Basak, R. G. "The Puri Plates of Madhavavarman-Sainyabhita." *Epigraphia Indica* 23 (1935–1936): 122–31.

Bays, Gwendolyn, trans. *The Lalitavistara Sutra: The Voice of the Buddha: The Beauty of Compassion*. 2 vols. Berkeley: Dharma, 1983.

Beach, Milo. *Mughal and Rajput Painting*. Cambridge: Cambridge University Press, 1992.

Bhadrabahu Svami. *Kalpasutra of Bhadrabahu Svami*. Translated by K. C. Lalwani. Delhi: Motilal Banarsidass, 1979.

Bhandarkar, D. R. "Two Grants of Indraraja III; Saka Samvat 836." *Epigraphia Indica* 9 (1907–1908): 24–41.

Bhandarkar, R. G. "Karhad Plates of Krishna III; Saka-Samvat 880." *Epigraphia Indica* 4 (1896–1897): 278–90.

Bhanudatta. *A Bouquet of Rasas (The Rasamanajari of Bhanudatta)*. Translated by Sheldon Pollock. Clay Sanskrit Library. New York: New York University Press and JJC Foundation, 2009.

Bharata. *The Natyasastra: English Translation with Critical Notes*. Translated by Adya Rangacharya. Rev. ed. Delhi: Munshiram Manoharlal, 1996.

Bhasa. *Thirteen Plays of Bhasa*. Translated by A. C. Woolner and Lakshman Sarup. London: Published for the University of the Panjab, 1930. Reprint, Delhi: Motilal Banarsidass, 1985.

Bhavabhuti. *Rama's Last Act (The Uttararamacarita)*. Translated by Sheldon Pollock. Clay Sanskrit Library. New York: New York University Press and JJC Foundation, 2007.

Bihari. *The Satasai*. Translated by K. P. Bahadur. Harmondsworth: Penguin, 1990.

Brown, Mackenzie. "The Theology of Radha in the Puranas." In *The Divine Consort: Radha and the Goddesses of India*, edited by John Stratton Hawley and Donna Marie Wulff, 57–71. Berkeley: Graduate Theological Union, 1982.

Brown, Robert L. "The Feminization of the Sarnath Gupta-Period Buddha Images." *Bulletin of the Asia Institute* 16 (2002), 165–79.

Brown, W. Norman, ed. and trans. *The Vasanta Vilasa*. New Haven, Conn.: American Oriental Society, 1962.

Buhler, Georg. "The Dewal Prasasti of Lalla, the Chhidda." *Epigraphia Indica* 1 (1892): 75–85.

———. "Udepur Prasasti of Kings of Malwa." *Epigraphia Indica* 1 (1892): 222–38.

Busch, Allison. "The Anxiety of Innovation: The Practice of Literary Science in the Hindi/*Riti* Tradition." *Comparative Studies of South Asia, Africa and the Middle East* 24, no. 2 (2004): 45–59.

———. "The Courtly Vernacular: The Transformation of Braj Literary Culture (1590–1690)." Ph.D. diss., University of Chicago, 2003.

Carman, John B. "Conclusion: Axes of Sacred Value in Hindu Society." In *Purity and Auspiciousness in Indian Society*, edited by John B. Carman and Frédérique A. Marglin, 109–20. Leiden: Brill, 1985.

Carman, John B., and Frédérique A. Marglin, eds. *Purity and Auspiciousness in Indian Society*. Leiden: Brill, 1985.

Carroll, Noël. "Art and the Domain of the Aesthetic." *British Journal of Aesthetics* 40, no. 2 (2000): 191–208.

Cattanar. *Manimekhalai (The Dancer with the Magic Bowl)*. Translated by Alain Daniélou. New York: New Directions, 1989.

Coburn, Thomas B. *Encountering the Goddess: A Translation of the Devi-Mahatmya and a Study of Its Interpretation*. Albany: State University of New York Press, 1991.

Cohen, Richard J. "The *Pasanahacariu* of Sridhara: The First Four *Sandhis* of the Apabhramsa Text." Ph.D. diss., University of Pennsylvania, 1979.

Cohen, Richard S. "Appendix: Ajanta's Inscriptions." In *Ajanta: History and Development*. Vol. 2, *Arguments About Ajanta*, 273–339, by Walter M. Spink. Leiden: Brill, 2006.

Coomaraswamy, A. K. *Catalogue of the Indian Collections in the Museum of Fine Arts, Boston*. 5 vols. Boston: Museum of Fine Arts, 1923.

———. *Coomaraswamy*. Vol. 1, *Selected Papers: Traditional Art and Symbolism*. Edited by Roger Lipsey. Princeton, N.J.: Princeton University Press, 1977.

———. "The Eight *Nayikas*." *Journal of Indian Art* 17 (1914): 99–116.

———. "One Hundred References to Indian Painting." *Artibus Asiae* 4 (1930–1932): 41–57.

———. "Origin of the Buddha Image." *Art Bulletin* 9 (1927): 287–329.

———. "Ornament." *Art Bulletin* 21 (1939): 375–82.

———. *Yaksas: Essays in Water Cosmology*. 2 vols. Washington, D.C.: Smithsonian Institution, 1928, 1931.

Cort, John E. *Jains in the World: Religious Values and Ideology in India*. New York: Oxford University Press, 2001.

Cuntarar. *Songs of the Harsh Devotee: The Tevaram of Cuntaramurttinayanar*. Translated by David Dean Shulman. Philadelphia: Department of South Asia Regional Studies, University of Pennsylvania, 1990.

Davids, T. W. Rhys, trans. *Buddhist Birth-Stories: The Commentarial Introduction Entitled Nidana Katha: The Story of the Lineage*. Boston: Houghton Mifflin, 1880. Reprint, Varanasi: Indological Book House, 1973.

Davids, T. W. Rhys, and Caroline A. F. Rhys Davids, trans. *Dialogues of the Buddha*. 3 vols. London: Oxford University Press, 1899–1921.

Davids, T. W. Rhys, and J. Estlin Carpenter, eds. *The Digha-nikaya*. 3 vols. London: Pali Text Society, 1890–1911.

Davidson, Ronald M. *Indian Esoteric Buddhism: A Social History of the Tantric Movement*. New York: Columbia University Press, 2002.

Davies, Stephen. "Non-Western Art and Art's Definition." In *Theories of Art Today*, edited by Noël Carroll, 199–216. Madison: University of Wisconsin Press, 2000.

Davis, Richard. *Lives of Indian Images*. Princeton, N.J.: Princeton University Press, 1997.

———. *Ritual in an Oscillating Universe: Worshiping Siva in Medieval India*. Princeton, N.J.: Princeton University Press, 1991.

DeCaroli, Robert. *Haunting the Buddha: Indian Popular Religion and the Formation of Buddhism*. New York: Oxford University Press, 2004.

Dehejia, Vidya. "Aniconism and the Multivalence of Emblems." *Ars Orientalis* 21 (1992): 45–66.

———. *Antal and Her Path of Love*. Albany: State University of New York Press, 1990.

———. *Art of the Imperial Cholas*. New York: Columbia University Press, 1990.

———. *Discourse in Early Buddhist Art: Visual Narratives of India*. New Delhi: Munshiram Manoharlal, 1997.

———. "Iconographic Transference Between Krishna and Three Saiva Saints." In *Indian Art and Connoisseurship: Essays in Honour of Douglas Barrett*, edited by John Guy, 140–49. Ahmedabad: Mapin, 1995.

———. "Identity and Visibility: Museum Displays of South Asian Art." In *New Cosmopolitanisms: South Asian Art in the U.S.*, edited by Gita Rajan and Shailja Sharma, 71–90. Stanford, Calif.: Stanford University Press, 2006.

———. *Indian Art*. London: Phaidon, 1997.

———. "Narrative Structure in Jagat Singh's *Ramayana*: A Preliminary Study." *Artibus Asiae* 54 (1996): 303–24.

———. "Reading Love Imagery on an Indian Temple." In *Love in Asian Art and Culture*, 96–113.

Washington, D.C.: Arthur M. Sackler Gallery, Smithsonian Institution, 1998.

——. *The Sensuous and the Sacred: Chola Bronzes from South India*. New York: American Federation of the Arts, 2002.

——. *Slaves of the Lord: The Path of the Tamil Saints*. Delhi: Munshiram Manoharlal, 1988.

——. "The Very Idea of a Portrait." *Ars Orientalis* 28 (1998): 41–50.

——, ed. *Representing the Body: Gender Issues in Indian Art*. New Delhi: Kali for Women, 1997.

——, ed. *Unseen Presence: The Buddha and Sanchi*. Bombay: Marg, 1996.

Dehejia, Vidya, and Daryl Harnisch. "Yoga as a Key to Understanding Indian Art." In *Representing the Body: Gender Issues in Indian Art*, edited by Vidya Dehejia, 68–81. New Delhi: Kali for Women, 1997.

Desai, Devangana. *Erotic Sculpture of India: A Socio-cultural Study*. New Delhi: Tata McGraw-Hill, 1975.

——. *Religious Imagery of Khajuraho*. Mumbai: Franco-Indian Research, 1996.

Desai, Vishakha N. "Connoisseur's Delights: Early 'Rasikapriya' Paintings in India." Ph.D. diss., University of Michigan, 1984.

——. "From Illustrations to Icons: The Changing Context of the Rasikapriya Paintings in Mewar." In *Indian Painting: Essays in Honour of Karl J. Khandalavala*, edited by B. N. Goswamy, 97–127. New Delhi: Lalit Kala Akademi, 1995.

——. *Life at Court: Art for India's Rulers, 16th–19th Centuries*. Boston: Museum of Fine Arts, 1985.

——. "Reflections on the History and Historiography of Male Sexuality in Early Indian Art." In *Representing the Body: Gender Issues in Indian Art*, edited by Vidya Dehejia, 42–55. New Delhi: Kali for Women: 1997.

Dhaky, M. A. *Complexities Surrounding the Vimalavasahi Temple at Mount Abu*. Philadelphia: University of Pennsylvania Press, 1980.

Diskalkar, D. B. "The Mandasore Stone Inscription of Kumaragupta and Bandhuvarman." In *Selections from Sanskrit Inscriptions*, 61–75. New Delhi: Classical Publishers, 1977.

Donaldson, Thomas E. *Hindu Temple Art of Orissa*. 2 vols. Leiden: Brill, 1985, 1987.

Doniger O'Flaherty, Wendy, trans. *The Rig Veda: An Anthology: One Hundred and Eight Hymns*. Harmondsworth: Penguin, 1981.

Doshi, Saryu. "An Illustrated Manuscript from Aurangabad Dated 1650 A.D." *Lalit Kala* 15 (n.d.): 19–28.

Dutton, Dennis. "'But They Don't Have Our Concept of Art.'" In *Theories of Art Today*, edited by Noël Carroll, 217–38. Madison: University of Wisconsin Press, 2000.

Dwivedi, V. P. *Barahmasa: The Song of Seasons in Literature and Art*. Delhi: Agam Kala Prakashan, 1980.

Ebeling, Klaus. *Ragamala Painting*. New Delhi: Ravi Kumar, 1973.

Eck, Diana. *Darsan*. Chambersburg, Pa.: Anima Books, 1981.

Eliade, Mircea. *The Sacred and the Profane: The Nature of Religion*. New York: Harcourt, Brace, 1959.

Falconer, John. "A Passion for Documentation: Architecture and Ethnography." In *India Through the Lens: Photography, 1840–1911*, edited by Vidya Dehejia, 69–118. Washington, D.C.: Freer Gallery of Art and Arthur M. Sackler Gallery, Smithsonian Institution, 2000.

Faure, Bernard. *The Power of Denial: Buddhism, Purity, and Gender*. Princeton, N.J.: Princeton University Press, 2003.

Fleet, J. F. "Chiplun Plates of Pulakesin II." *Epigraphia Indica* 3 (1894–1895): 50–53.

——. *Inscriptions of the Early Gupta Kings and Their Successors*. Corpus Inscriptionum Indicarum 3. Calcutta: Superintendent of Government Printing, 1888.

——. "Pattadakal Pillar Inscription of the Time of Kirtivarman II." *Epigraphia Indica* 3 (1894–1895): 1–7.

Flood, Finbarr Barry. Refiguring Iconoclasm in the Early Indian Mosque." In *Negating the Image: Case Studies in Iconoclasm*, edited by Anne McClanan and Jeff Johnson, 15–40. Burlington, Vt.: Ashgate, 2005.

Fox, Michael V. *The Song of Songs and the Ancient Egyptian Love Songs*. Madison: University of Wisconsin Press, 1985.

Fuller, C. J. *The Camphor Flame: Popular Hinduism and Society in India*. Princeton, N.J.: Princeton University Press, 1992.

Garde, M. B. "Mandasor Inscription of Malava Samvat 524." *Epigraphia Indica* 27 (1947–1948): 12–18.

Garimella, Annapurna. "A Handmaid's Tale: *Sakhis*, Love, Devotion, and Poetry in Rajput Painting." In *Love in Asian Art and Culture*, 70–95. Washington, D.C.: Arthur M. Sackler Gallery, Smithsonian Institution, 1998.

Gonda, Jan. "Abharana." In *Selected Studies*. Vol. 2, *Sanskrit Word Studies*, 171–77. Leiden: Brill, 1975.

——. "The Meaning of the Word *Alamkara*." In *Selected Studies*. Vol. 2, *Sanskrit Word Studies*, 257–74. Leiden: Brill, 1975.

Gopal Iyer, T. V., and François Gros, eds. *Tevaram: Hymnes Sivaites du pays Tamoul*. 2 vols. Pondicherry: Institut Français d'Indologie, 1985.

Gopinatha Rao, T. A. "Anbil Plates of Sundara Chola: The 4th Year." *Epigraphia Indica* 15 (1919–1920): 44–72.

———. "Kanyakumari Inscription of Vira-Rajendra-Deva." *Epigraphia Indica* 18 (1925–1926): 21–55.

Goswamy, B. N. *The Essence of Indian Art*. San Francisco: Asian Art Museum of San Francisco, 1986. Originally published as *Rasa, les neuf visages de l'art indien* (Paris: Galeries Nationales du Grand Palais, 1986).

Goswamy, B. N., and Eberhard Fischer. *Pahari Masters*. Artibus Asiae Supplementum 38. Zurich: Museum Reitberg, 1992.

Granoff, Phyllis. "Halayudha's Prism: The Experience of Religion in Medieval Hymns and Stories." In *Gods, Guardians, and Lovers: Temple Sculptures from North India, A.D. 700–1200*, edited by Vishakha N. Desai and Darielle Mason, 66–93. New York: Asia Society Galleries, 1993.

Gupte, R. S., and B. D. Mahajan. *Ajanta, Ellora and Aurangabad Caves*. Bombay: Taraporevala, 1962.

Hardy, Adam. *Indian Temple Architecture: Form and Transformation: The Karnata Dravida Tradition, 7th to 13th Centuries*. New Delhi: Indira Gandhi National Centre for Arts, 1995.

Harle, J. C. *The Art and Architecture of the Indian Subcontinent*. Harmondsworth: Penguin, 1986.

Harsha. *The Ratnavali of Sri Harsha-deva*. Edited and translated by M. R. Kale. Bombay: Booksellers Publishing, 1964.

Hart, George, III. *The Poems of Ancient Tamil, Their Milieu and Their Sanskrit Counterparts*. Berkeley: University of California Press, 1975.

Hawley, Jack. *The Bhakti Movement: Excavations in a Master Narrative*. Forthcoming.

Hay, John. "The Body Invisible in Chinese Art?" In *Body, Subject, and Power in China*, edited by Angela Zito and Tani E. Barlow, 42–77. Chicago: University of Chicago Press, 1994.

Hertel, Johannes, ed. *The Panchatantra: A Collection of Ancient Hindu Tales* [in Sanskrit]. Cambridge, Mass.: Harvard University, 1908.

Hiltebeitel, Alf. "Purity and Auspiciousness in the Sanskrit Epics." In *Purity and Auspiciousness in Indian Society*, edited by John B Carman and Frédérique A. Marglin, 41–54. Leiden: Brill, 1985.

Hollander, Anne. *Seeing Through Clothes*. New York: Viking Penguin, 1975.

Hopkins, Steven Paul. *Singing the Body of God: The Hymns of Vedantadesika in Their South Indian Tradition*. Oxford: Oxford University Press, 2002.

Hueckstedt, Robert A. *The Style of Bana: An Introduction to Sanskrit Prose*. Lanham, Md.: University Press of America, 1985.

Hultzsch, E., and V. Venkayya, eds. *South Indian Inscriptions*. Vol. 2. New Delhi: Archaeological Survey of India, 1916.

Huntington, Susan L. *The Art of Ancient India: Buddhist, Hindu, Jain*. New York: Weatherhill, 1985.

Ilanko Atikal. *The Tale of an Anklet: An Epic of South India: The Cilappatikaram of Ilanko Atikal*. Translated by R. Parthasarathy. New York: Columbia University Press, 1993.

Inden, Ronald. *Imagining India*. Cambridge, Mass.: Blackwell, 1990.

———. "Kings and Omens." In *Purity and Auspiciousness in Indian Society*, ed. John B. Carman and Frédérique A. Marglin, 30–40. Leiden: Brill, 1985.

———. "Ritual, Authority, and Cyclic Time in Hindu Kingship." In *Kingship and Authority in South Asia*, edited by J. F. Richards, 41–91. Delhi: Oxford University Press, 1988.

Ingalls, Daniel H. H. "Words for Beauty in Classical Sanskrit Poetry." In *Indological Studies in Honor of W. Norman Brown*, edited by Ernest Bender, 87–107. New Haven, Conn.: American Oriental Society, 1962.

———, trans. *Sanskrit Poetry from Vidyakara's Treasury*. Cambridge, Mass.: Harvard University Press, 1965.

Ingold, Tim, ed. *Key Debates in Anthropology*. New York: Routledge, 1996.

Ishwarananda Giri, Swami. *Samvit-saparya*. Varanasi: Anandakanana Press, 1980.

Jayadeva. *Love Song of the Dark Lord: Jayadeva's Gitagovinda*. Translated by Barbara Stoler Miller. New York: Columbia University Press, 1977.

Kalidasa. *Kalidasa: The Dynasty of Raghu*. Translated by Robert Antoine. Calcutta: Writers Workshop Books, 1972.

———. *Malavika and Agnimitra*, translated by Edwin Gerow. In *Theater of Memory: The Plays of Kalidasa*, edited by Barbara Stoler Miller, 253–314. New York: Columbia University Press, 1984.

———. *The Origin of the Young God: Kalidasa's Kumarasambhava*. Translated by Hank Heifetz. Berkeley: University of California Press, 1985.

———. *Raghuvamsam of Kalidasa*. Translated by K. N. Anantapadmanabhan. Madras: Ramayana, 1973.

———. *The Recognition of Shakuntala*. Translated by Somadeva Vasudeva. Clay Sanskrit Library. New York: New York University Press and JJC Foundation, 2006.

———. *Sakuntala and the Ring of Recognition*, translated by Barbara Stoler Miller. In *Theater of Memory: The Plays of Kalidasa*, edited by Barbara Stoler Miller, 85–176. New York: Columbia University Press, 1984.

———. *The Seasons: Kalidasa's Ritusamhara*. Translated by John T. Roberts. Tempe: Center for Asian Studies, Arizona State University, 1990.

——. *Theater of Memory: The Plays of Kalidasa*. Edited by Barbara Stoler Miller. New York: Columbia University Press, 1984.

——. *The Transport of Love: The Meghaduta of Kalidasa*. Translated by Leonard Nathan. Berkeley: University of California Press, 1976.

Kampen, Natalie. "Epilogue: Gender and Desire." In *Naked Truths: Women, Sexuality, and Gender in Classical Art and Archaeology*, edited by Ann Olga Kolowski-Ostrow and Claire L. Lyons, 267–78. New York: Routledge, 1997.

——, ed. *Sexuality in Ancient Art*. New York: Cambridge University Press, 1996.

Kangle, R. P. *The Kautilya Arthasastra*. Bombay: University of Bombay, 1969.

Karashima, N. "South Indian Temple Inscriptions: A New Approach to Their Study." *South Asia*, n.s., 19 (1996): 1–12.

Kaulacara, Ramachandra. *Silpa Prakasa: Medieval Orissan Sanskrit Text on Temple Architecture by Ramachandra Kaulacara*. Translated by Alice Boner and Sadasiva Rath Sarma. Leiden: Brill, 1966.

Kersenboom-Story, Saskia C. *Nityasumangali: Devadasi Tradition in South India*. Delhi: Motilal Banarsidass, 1987.

Keshavdas. *The Rasikapriya of Keshavadasa*. Translated by K. P. Bahadur. Delhi: Motilal Banarsidass, 1972.

Kielhorn, F. "Assam Plates of Vallabhadeva: Saka Samvat 1107." *Epigraphia Indica* 5 (1898–1899): 181–88.

——. "Deopara Stone Inscription of Vijayasena." *Epigraphia Indica* 1 (1892): 305–15.

——. "Mau Chandella Inscription of Madanavarman." *Epigraphia Indica* 1 (1892): 195–214.

——. "Ratnapur Inscription of Prithvideva of the (Vikrama) Year 1247." *Epigraphia Indica* 1 (1892): 45–52.

——. "Two Chandella Inscriptions from Ajaygadh." *Epigraphia Indica* 1 (1892): 325–38.

——. "Udayendiram Plates of the Bana King Vikramaditya II." *Epigraphia Indica* 3 (1894–1895): 74–79.

Konow, Sten. "Sarnath Inscription of Kumaradevi." *Epigraphia Indica* 9 (1907–1908): 319–28.

Kramrisch, Stella. *The Art of India*. New York: Phaidon, 1954.

Krishna Deva. *Temples of Khajuraho*. 2 vols. New Delhi: Archaeological Survey of India, 1990.

Krishna Sastri, H. "Anmakonda Inscription of Prola, Chalukya-Vikrama Year 42." *Epigraphia Indica* 9 (1907–1908): 256–67.

——. "Kuniyur Plates of the Time of Venkata II: Saka Samvat 1556." *Epigraphia Indica* 3 (1894–1895): 236–58.

——, ed. *South Indian Inscriptions*. Vol. 3. Madras: Superintendent Government Press, 1920.

Langenberg, Amy. "Like Worms Falling from a Foul-Smelling Sore: The Buddhist Rhetoric of Childbirth in an Early Mahayana Sutra." Ph.D. diss., Columbia University, 2007.

Laughlin, Jack C. *Aradhakamurti/Adhisthayakamurti: Popular Piety, Politics, and the Medieval Jain Temple Portrait*. New York: Peter Lang, 2003.

Luders, H. "Two Pillar Inscriptions of the Time of Krishnaraya of Vijayanagara." *Epigraphia Indica* 6 (1900–1901): 108–33.

Madan, T. N. "Concerning the Categories *Subha* and *Suddha* in Hindu Culture: An Exploratory Essay." In *Purity and Auspiciousness in Indian Society*, edited by John B. Carman and Frédérique A. Marglin, 11–29. Leiden: Brill, 1985.

Mankodi, Kirit. *The Queen's Stepwell at Patan*. Bombay: Project for Indian Cultural Studies, 1991.

Marglin, Frédérique A. "Types of Oppositions in Hindu Culture." In *Purity and Auspiciousness in Indian Society*, edited by John B. Carman and Frédérique A. Marglin, 65–83. Leiden: Brill, 1985.

——. *Wives of the God-King: The Rituals of the Devadasis of Puri*. Delhi: Oxford University Press, 1985.

Meister, Michael. "Juncture and Conjunction: Punning and Temple Architecture." *Artibus Asiae* 41 (1979): 226–28.

Miles, Margaret. *Image as Insight: Visual Understanding in Western Christianity and Secular Cultures*. Boston: Beacon Press, 1985.

Minakshi, C. *The Historical Sculptures of the Vaikunthaperumal Temple, Kanchi*. Memoirs of the Archaeological Survey of India 63. Delhi: Manager of Publications, 1941.

Mirashi, V. V. *Inscriptions of the Silaharas*. Corpus Inscriptionum Indicarum 6. New Delhi: Archaeological Survey of India, 1977.

——. "Ratanpur Stone Inscription of the [Kalachuri] Year 915." *Epigraphia Indica* 26 (1941–1942): 255–67.

Morrison, Kathleen D., and Mark T. Lycett. "Inscriptions as Artifacts: Precolonial South India and the Analysis of Texts." *Journal of Archaeological Method and Theory* 4, nos. 3–4 (1997): 215–37.

Mosteller, John E. *The Measure of Form: A New Approach for the Study of Indian Sculpture*. New Delhi: Abhinav, 1991.

Murcott, Susan. *The First Buddhist Women: Translations and Commentary on the Therigatha*. Berkeley: Parallax Press, 1991.

Nagaswamy, R. "Melaperumpallam Bronzes." In *Art and Culture of Tamil Nadu*, edited by R. Nagaswamy, 95–100. Delhi: Sundeep Prakashan, 1980.

Narasimha Murthy, A. V. "A Study of the Label Inscriptions of the Hoysala Sculptors." In *Indian Epigraphy: Its Bearing on the History of Art*, edited by Frederick Asher and M. S. Gai, 215–20. New Delhi: Oxford University Press and IBH, 1985.

Narayanan, Vasudha. "Arcavatara: On Earth as He Is in Heaven." In *Gods of Flesh, Gods of Stone: The Embodiment of the Divinity in India*, edited by Joanne Punzo Waghorne and Norman Cutler, 52–67. Chambersburg, Pa.: Anima, 1985.

——. *The Vernacular Veda: Revelation, Recitation, and Ritual*. Columbia: University of South Carolina Press, 1994.

——. *The Way and the Goal: Expressions of Devotion in the Early Srivaisnava Tradition*. Washington, D.C.: Institute for Vaishnava Studies Press, 1987.

Nayar, Nancy Ann. *Poetry as Theology: The Srivaisnava Stotra in the Age of Ramanuja*. Wiesbaden: Harrassowitz, 1992.

Nead, Lynda. *The Female Nude: Art, Obscenity, and Sexuality*. New York: Routledge, 1992.

Norman, K. R. *Pali Literature*. Wiesbaden: Harrassowitz, 1983.

Olivelle, Patrick. *The Asrama System: The History and Hermeneutics of a Religious Institution*. New York: Oxford University Press, 1993.

Orr, Leslie. *Donors, Devotees, and Daughters of God: Temple Women in Medieval Tamilnadu*. Oxford: Oxford University Press, 2000.

Ortner, Sherry. "Is Female to Male as Nature Is to Culture?" In *Making Gender: The Politics and Erotics of Culture*, edited by Sherry Ortner, 21–42. Boston: Beacon Press, 1996.

——. "So, Is Female to Male as Nature Is to Culture?" In *Making Gender: The Politics and Erotics of Culture*, edited by Sherry Ortner, 173–80. Boston: Beacon Press, 1996.

Pal, Pratapaditya. *Hindu Religion and Iconology According to the Tantrasara*. Los Angeles: Vichitra Press, 1981.

——. *Ragamala Paintings in the Museum of Fine Arts, Boston*. Boston: Museum of Fine Arts, 1967.

Parashar, Sadhana. *Kavyamimamsa of Rajasekhara*. New Delhi: D. K. Printworld, 2000.

Patel, Alka. *Building Communities in Gujarat: Architecture and Society During the Twelfth Through Fourteenth Centuries*. Leiden: Brill, 2004.

Paul, Diana Y. *Women in Buddhism: Images of the Feminine in the Mahayana Tradition*. Berkeley: Asian Humanities Press, 1979.

Perniola, Mario. "Between Clothing and Nudity." In *Fragments for a History of the Human Body*, edited by Michel Feher. Cambridge, Mass.: MIT Press, 1989.

Peterson, Indira. *Design and Rhetoric in a Sanskrit Court Epic: The Kiratarjuniya of Bharavi*. Albany: State University of New York Press, 2003.

——. *Kuttralak Kuravanji (The Fortune-teller Play of Kuttralam)*. Forthcoming.

——. *Poems to Siva: The Hymns of the Tamil Saints*. Princeton, N.J.: Princeton University Press, 1989.

Phogat, S. R., ed. *Inscriptions of Haryana*. Haryana: Vishal, 2006.

Pieper, Jan, and George Michell, eds. *The Impulse to Adorn: Studies in Traditional Indian Architecture*. Bombay: Marg, 1982.

Pollock, Sheldon. "The Cosmopolitan Vernacular." *Journal of Asian Studies* 57, no. 1 (1998): 6–37.

——. "The Death of Sanskrit." *Comparative Studies in Society and History* 43, no. 2 (2001): 392–426.

——. *The Language of the Gods in the World of Men*. Berkeley: University of California Press, 2006.

——. Review of *Vallabhadeva's Kommentar (Sarada-Version) zum Kumarasambhava des Kalidasa*, by M. S. Narayana Murti and Klaus L. Janert. *Journal of the American Oriental Society* 105, no. 2 (1985): 381–83.

——. "Sanskrit Literary Cultures from the Inside Out." In *Literary Cultures in History: Reconstructions from South Asia*, edited by Sheldon Pollock, 39–130. Berkeley: University of California Press, 2003.

Pope, Marvin H., trans. *Song of Songs*. The Anchor Bible. New York: Doubleday, 1977.

Prasad, Pushpa. *Sanskrit Inscriptions of the Delhi Sultanate, 1191–1526*. Delhi: Oxford University Press, 1990.

Prettijohn, Elizabeth. *Beauty and Art, 1750–2000*. Oxford: Oxford University Press, 2005.

Preziosi, Donald. "Museology and Museography." In "A Range of Critical Perspectives: The Problematics of Collecting and Display, Part I." *Art Bulletin* 77 (1995): 13–15.

Raghavan, V., and R. N. Dandekar. "Part III: The Hindu Way of Life." In *Sources of Indian Tradition*. Vol. 1, *From the Beginning to 1800*, 2nd ed., edited by Ainslie T. Embree, 201–341. New York: Columbia University Press, 1998.

Raheja, Gloria Goodwin. *The Poison in the Gift: Ritual, Prestation, and the Dominant Caste in a North Indian Village*. Chicago: University of Chicago Press, 1988.

Rajashekhara. *Viddhashalabhanjika-Natika* [in Sanskrit and Hindi]. Translated by Babulal Shukla Sastri. Varanasi: Chaukhambha Oriental, 1976.

Ramanujan, A. K., trans. *The Interior Landscape: Love Poems from a Classical Tamil Anthology*. Bloomington: Indiana University Press, 1967.

Ramanujan, A. K., V. Narayana Rao, and David Shulman, eds. and trans. *When God Is a Customer: Telegu Courtesan Songs by Ksetrayya and Others*. Berkeley: University of California Press, 1994.

Randhawa, M. S. *Kangra Paintings of the Bihari Sat Sai*. New Delhi: National Museum, 1966.

Randhawa, M. S., and S. D. Bhambri. *Basohli Paintings of the Rasamanjari*. New Delhi: Abhinav, 1982.

Ritti, Shrinivas H. "Udega, the Chief Architect of the Saraswati Temple at Gadag." In *Indian Epigraphy: Its Bearing on the History of Art*, edited by Frederick Asher and G. S. Gai, 213–14. New Delhi: Oxford University Press and IBH, 1985.

Roodbergen, J. A. F. *Mallinatha's Ghantapatha on the Kiratarjuniya, I–VI*. Leiden: Brill, 1984.

Roughley, Neil, ed. *Being Humans: Anthropological Universality and Particularity in Transdisciplinary Perspectives*. New York: Walter de Gruyter, 2000.

Ryder, Arthur W., trans. *The Panchatantra*. 1925. Reprint, Chicago: University of Chicago Press, 1964.

Salomon, Nanette. "Making a World of Difference: Gender, Asymmetry, and the Greek Nude." In *Naked Truths: Women, Sexuality, and Gender in Classical Art and Archaeology*, edited by Ann Olga Kolowski-Ostrow and Claire L. Lyons, 197–219. New York: Routledge, 1997.

Salomon, Richard. *Indian Epigraphy: A Guide to the Study of Inscriptions in Sanskrit, Prakrit, and the Other Indo-Aryan Languages*. Delhi: Munshiram Manoharlal, 1998.

Sanford, David. "Ramayana Portraits on the Nageshvara Temple at Kumbakonam." In *The Legend of Rama: Artistic Visions*, edited by Vidya Dehejia, 43–60. Bombay: Marg, 1994.

Schmidt, Carolyn Woodford. "Aristocratic Devotees in Early Buddhist Art from Greater Gandhara: Characteristics, Chronology, and Symbolism." *South Asian Studies* 21 (2005): 25–45.

Schopen, Gregory. *Bones, Stones, and Buddhist Monks*. Honolulu: University of Hawai'i Press, 1997.

——. *Buddhist Monks and Business Matters*. Honolulu: University of Hawai'i Press, 2004.

——. *Figments and Fragments of Mahayana Buddhism in India*. Honolulu: University of Hawai'i Press, 2005.

——. "On Monks, Nuns, and Vulgar Practices: The Introduction of the Image Cult into Indian Buddhism." *Artibus Asiae* 49 (1988–1989): 153–68.

Schweig, Graham M., trans. *Dance of Divine Love: The Raaz Lila of Krishna from the Bhagavata Purana, India's Classic Sacred Love Story*. Princeton, N.J.: Princeton University Press, 2005.

Selby, Martha Ann. *Grow Long, Blessed Night: Love Poems from Classical India*. New York: Oxford University Press, 2000.

Shankara. *Saundaryalahiri*. Edited and translated by V. K. Subramaniam. Delhi: Motilal Banarsidass, 1977.

——. *The Saundaryalahari or Flood of Beauty, Traditionally Ascribed to Sankaracarya*. Edited and translated by W. Norman Brown. Cambridge, Mass.: Harvard University Press, 1958.

Shulman, David Dean. *The King and the Clown in South Indian Myth and Poetry*. Princeton, N.J.: Princeton University Press, 1985.

Siegel, Lee. *Fires of Love, Waters of Peace: Passion and Renunciation in Indian Culture*. Honolulu: University of Hawai'i Press, 1983.

Singh, Devendra. "Adaptive Significance of Female Physical Attractiveness: Role of Waist-to-Hip Ratio." *Journal of Personality and Social Psychology* 65, no. 2 (1993): 293–307.

Sivaramamurti, C. *Chitrasutra of the Vishnudharmottara*. New Delhi: Kanak, 1978.

Smith, David. *Dance of Siva: Religion, Art, and Poetry in South India*. Cambridge: Cambridge University Press, 2002.

——. *Ratnakara's Haravijaya: An Introduction to the Sanskrit Court Epic*. Delhi: Oxford University Press, 1985.

Snell, Rupert. "*Bhakti* versus *Riti*? The *Satsai* of Biharilal." *Journal of Vaisnava Studies* 3, no. 1 (1994): 153–70.

Soper, A. C. "Early Buddhist Attitudes Toward the Art of Painting." *Art Bulletin* 32 (1950): 147–51.

Spooner, D. B. "The Didarganj Image Now in the Patna Museum." *Journal of the Bihar and Orissa Research Society* 5 (1919): 102–13.

Sriharsa. *Naisadhacarita of Sriharsa*. Translated by K. K. Handiqui. Poona: Deccan College, 1965.

Srinivasan, Doris. "Genealogy of the Buddha in Early Indian Art." In *Eastern Approaches: Essays on Asian Art and Archaeology*, edited by T. S. Maxwell, 38–44. Delhi: Oxford University Press, 1992.

——. "The Mauryan *Ganika* from Didarganj (Pataliputra)." *East and West* 55 (2005): 345–62.

——. "Royalty's Courtesans and God's Mortal Wives: Keepers of Culture in Pre-Colonial India." In *The Courtesan's Arts*, edited by Martha Feldman and Bonnie Gordon, 161–81. Oxford: Oxford University Press, 2006.

Stadtner, Donald. "'The Little Clay Cart' in Early Mathura." *Orientations* 27 (1996): 39–46.

Stewart, Andrew. *Art, Desire, and the Body in Ancient Greece*. Cambridge: Cambridge University Press, 1997.

Sthapati, V. Ganapati. *Indian Sculpture and Iconography: Forms and Measurements*. Pondicherry: Sri Aurobindo Society, 2002.

Strong, John. *The Legend of King Asoka: A Study and Translation of the Asokavadana*. Princeton, N.J.: Princeton University Press, 1983.

Subandhu. *Vasavadatta: A Sanskrit Romance.* Edited and translated by Louis H. Gray. Delhi: Motilal Banarsidass, 1962.

Sutherland, Gail. *Disguises of the Demon.* Albany: State University of New York Press, 1991.

Symons, Donald. "Beauty Is in the Adaptations of the Beholder: The Evolutionary Psychology of Human Female Sexual Attractiveness." In *Sexual Nature, Sexual Culture*, edited by Paul Abramson and Steven Pinkerton, 80–118. Chicago: University of Chicago Press, 1995.

Talbot, Cynthia. *Precolonial India in Practice: Society, Religion, and Identity in Medieval Andhra.* New York: Oxford University Press, 2001.

Taylor, Woodman. "Unscrolling Spring Songs: The *Vasanta Vilasa* in the Freer Gallery of Art." *Orientations* 29 (1998): 55–62.

Teresa of Ávila. *The Complete Works of Saint Teresa of Jesus.* Vol. 3, *Book of the Foundations, Minor Prose Works, Poems, Documents, Indices.* Translated and edited by E. Allison Peers. 1946. Reprint, New York: Sheed and Ward, 1957.

Tewari, S. P. "National Museum Inscription of Kelachchadevi, V.S. 1239." *Epigraphia Indica* 41 (1975–1976): 58–60.

Topsfield, Andrew. *Court Painting at Udaipur: Art Under the Patronage of the Maharanas of Mewar.* *Artibus Asiae* Supplementum 44. Zurich: Artibus Asiae, 2004.

——. "Sahibdin's Illustrations to the *Rasikapriya.*" *Orientations* 17 (1986): 18–31.

Tubb, Gary. "Heroine as Hero: Parvati in the *Kumarasambhava* and the *Parvatiparinaya.*" *Journal of the American Oriental Society* 104, no. 2 (1984): 219–36.

Vajracharya, Gautam V. *Watson Collection of Indian Miniatures at the Elvehjem Museum of Art.* Madison: University of Wisconsin Press, 2002.

Van Damne, Wilfrede. "Universality and Cultural Particularity in Visual Aesthetics." In *Being Humans: Anthropological Universality and Particularity in Transdisciplinary Perspectives*, edited by Neil Roughley, 258–84. New York: Walter de Gruyter, 2000.

Vats, M. S. "Unpublished Votive Inscriptions in the Chaitya Cave at Karle." *Epigraphia Indica* 18 (1925–1926): 325–29.

Vaudeville, Charlotte. *Barahmasa in Indian Literatures: Songs of the Twelve Months in Indo-Aryan Literatures.* Delhi: Motilal Banarsidass, 1986.

Vogel, J. Ph. "The Woman and Tree of *Salabhanjika* in Indian Literature and Art." *Acta Orientalia* 7 (1929): 201–31.

Waghorne, Joanne Punzo. *Diaspora of the Gods: Modern Hindu Temples in an Urban Middle-Class World.* New York: Oxford University Press, 2004.

——. "Dressing the Body of God: South Indian Bronze Sculpture in Its Temple Setting." *Asian Art* 5, no. 3 (1992): 8–33.

——. *The Raja's Magic Clothes: Re-Visioning Kingship and Divinity in England's India.* University Park: Pennsylvania State University Press, 1994.

Walshe, Maurice, trans. *Thus Have I Heard: The Long Discourses of the Buddha.* London: Wisdom Publications, 1995.

Wentworth, Blake. "Women's Bodies, Earthly Kingdom: Mapping the Presence of God in the *Tirukayilaya Nana Ula.*" Manuscript, Divinity School, University of Chicago, 2003.

Winter, Irene J. "Defining 'Aesthetics' for Non-Western Studies: The Case of Ancient Mesopotamia." In *Art History, Aesthetics, and Visual Studies*, edited by Michael Ann Holly and Keith Moxey, 3–28. Williamstown, Mass.: Sterling and Francine Clark Art Institute, 2002.

——. "Ornament and the Rhetoric of Abundance in Assyria." *Eretz-Israel: Archaeological, Historical and Geographical Studies* 27 (2003): 252–64.

——. "Sex, Rhetoric, and the Public Monument: The Alluring Body of Naram-Sin of Agade." In *Sexuality in Ancient Art*, edited by Natalie Boymen Kampen, 11–26. Cambridge: Cambridge University Press, 1996.

Younger, Paul. *The Home of the Dancing Sivan: The Traditions of the Hindu Temple in Citamparam.* New York: Oxford University Press, 1995.

——. *Playing Host to Deity: Festival Religion in the South Indian Tradition.* New York: Oxford University Press, 2002.

Zimmer, Heinrich. *The Art of Indian Asia: Its Mythology and Transformations.* 2 vols. New York: Pantheon Books, 1955.

Zito, Angela, and Tani E. Barlow, eds. *Body, Subject, and Power in China.* Chicago: University of Chicago Press, 1994.

FIGURE CREDITS

1. Tanjavur Art Gallery. Photograph courtesy of Job Thomas

2. The Metropolitan Museum of Art, Promised Gift of Florence and Herbert Irving, 1993 (L.1993.88.2). Image © 1994 The Metropolitan Museum of Art

3. Patna Museum. Photograph courtesy of the American Institute of Indian Studies, Gurgaon

4. Patna Museum. Photograph courtesy of the American Institute of Indian Studies, Gurgaon

5. Photograph courtesy of the author

6. Indian Museum, Calcutta. Photograph courtesy of the American Institute of Indian Studies, Gurgaon

7. Photograph courtesy of the author

8. Photograph courtesy of the author

9. The Metropolitan Museum of Art, Purchase, Bequests of Mary Clarke Thompson, Fanny Shapiro, Susan Dwight Bliss, Isaac D. Fletcher, William Gedney Beatty, John L. Cadwalader and Kate Read Blacque, Gifts of Mrs. Samuel T. Peters, Ida H. Ogilvie, Samuel T. Peters and H. R. Bishop, F. C. Bishop and O. M. Bishop, Rogers, Seymour and Fletcher Funds, and other gifts, funds and bequests from various donors, by exchange, 1982 (1982.220.2). Image © 1982 The Metropolitan Museum of Art

10. Photograph courtesy of the American Institute of Indian Studies, Gurgaon

11. Photograph courtesy of the author

12. Ex-Skanda Collection. © AAAUM Photograph courtesy of the American Council of Southern Asian Art

13. National Museum, New Delhi. Photograph courtesy of the American Institute of Indian Studies, Gurgaon

14. National Museum, New Delhi. Photograph courtesy of the American Institute of Indian Studies, Gurgaon

15. National Museum, New Delhi. Photograph courtesy of the author

16. Photograph courtesy of the author

17. National Museum, New Delhi. Photograph courtesy of the author

18. Photograph courtesy of the American Institute of Indian Studies, Gurgaon

19. Photograph courtesy of the author

20. Indian Museum, Calcutta. Photograph courtesy of the American Institute of Indian Studies, Gurgaon

21. Indian Museum, Calcutta. Photograph courtesy of the American Institute of Indian Studies, Gurgaon

22. Indian Museum, Calcutta. Photograph courtesy of the American Institute of Indian Studies, Gurgaon

23. Indian Museum, Calcutta. Photograph courtesy of the American Institute of Indian Studies, Gurgaon

24. Indian Museum, Calcutta. Photograph courtesy of the American Institute of Indian Studies, Gurgaon

25. Photograph courtesy of the American Institute of Indian Studies, Gurgaon

26. National Archaeological Museum of Naples. Reproduced by permission of the Soprintendenza Archeologica per le Province de Napoli e Caserta

27. Mathura Museum. Photograph courtesy of the American Institute of Indian Studies, Gurgaon

28. © Copyright the Trustees of The British Museum

29. Photograph courtesy of the American Institute of Indian Studies, Gurgaon

30. Nagarjunakonda Museum, Hyderabad. Photograph courtesy of the author

31. Photograph courtesy of the author

32. Photograph courtesy of the author

33. Photograph courtesy of the American Institute of Indian Studies, Gurgaon

34. Photograph courtesy of the author

35. Photograph courtesy of the American Institute of Indian Studies, Gurgaon

36. Freer Gallery of Art, Smithsonian Institution, Washington, D.C., Purchase–Margaret and George Haldeman, and Museum Funds, F2003.2

37. © The Cleveland Museum of Art, 2002. John L. Severance Fund 1961.94

38. Tanjavur Art Gallery. Photograph courtesy of the American Institute of Indian Studies, Gurgaon

39. Photograph courtesy of the author

40. Tanjavur Art Gallery. Photograph courtesy of the author

41. Madras Government Museum, Chennai. Photograph courtesy of the author

42. Asia Society, New York. Photograph courtesy of the author

43. Photograph courtesy of the American Institute of Indian Studies, Gurgaon

44. Photograph courtesy of Thomas Donaldson, Cleveland State University

45. Photograph courtesy of the American Institute of Indian Studies, Gurgaon

46. Photograph courtesy of the Los Angeles County Museum of Art

47. Photograph courtesy of the author

48. © Copyright the Trustees of The British Museum

49. Tanjavur Art Gallery. Photograph courtesy of the author

50. Photograph courtesy of the author

51. Photograph courtesy of the author

52. Photograph courtesy of the American Institute of Indian Studies, Gurgaon

53. The Basohli Master. *Krishna Loosens His Beloved's Belt*. Indian, Pahrai about 1660–70. Basohli, Punjab Hills, Northern India. Opaque watercolor, silver, gold, and beetle wing on paper. Overall: 23.3 × 33 cm

(9³⁄₁₆ × 13 in.). Without borders: 17.9 × 27 cm (7¹⁄₁₆ × 10⅝ in.). Photograph © 2006 Museum of Fine Arts, Boston. Ross-Coomaraswamy Collection 17.2780

54. *Adhama Vaishika Nayaka* (*The Depraved Hero*). Indian, Pahari, 1660–70. Basohli, Punjab Hills, Northern India. Opaque watercolor, silver, gold, and beetle wing on paper. Overall: 22.6 × 32.3 cm (8⅞ × 12¹¹⁄₁₆ in.). Image only: 26.2 × 17.3 cm (10⁵⁄₁₆ × 6¹³⁄₁₆ in.). Photograph © 2006 Museum of Fine Arts, Boston. Ross-Coomaraswamy Collection 17.2782

55. Dogra Art Gallery, Jammu

56. Dogra Art Gallery, Jammu

57. Dogra Art Gallery, Jammu

58. *Radha's Smile*. Indian, Subimperial Mughal, late 16th or early 17th century. Northern India. Opaque watercolor on paper. 11.7 × 15 cm (4⅝ × 5⅞ in.). Photograph © 2006 Museum of Fine Arts, Boston. Ross-Coomaraswamy Collection 17.3110

59. *The Romantic Flurried Heroine*. India. Opaque watercolor and gold on paper. 142 × .228 cm. Photograph © 2006 Museum of Fine Arts, Boston. Ross-Coomaraswamy Collection 17.3108

60. Government Oriental Museum, Udaipur. Photograph courtesy of Andrew Topsfield

61. Government Oriental Museum, Udaipur. Photograph courtesy of Andrew Topsfield

62. Government Oriental Museum, Udaipur. Photograph courtesy of Andrew Topsfield

63. Courtesy of Cynthia Hazen Polsky

64. Collection of Gursharan and Elvira Sidhu

65. Photograph courtesy of Rietberg Museum, Zurich

66. Photograph courtesy of Rietberg Museum, Zurich

67. V&A Images / Victoria & Albert Museum, London

68. Photograph courtesy of Art of the Past, New York

69. Bharat Kala Bhavan, Varanasi. © AAAUM. Photograph courtesy of the American Council of Southern Asian Art

70. Bharat Kala Bhavan, Varanasi. © AAAUM. Photograph courtesy of the American Council of Southern Asian Art

71. Photograph courtesy of the author

72. Photograph courtesy of the author

INDEX